RETAIL PRODUCT MANAGEMENT

Retail Product Management represents a specialist text resource for students of retail management or marketing courses and modules. It provides the reader with the opportunity to acquire a deeper knowledge of a key area of retailing management – managing the product range – which more generalist retail textbooks are unable to offer. Designed to be challenging, yet approachable to students, this book links established academic theory to the buying and merchandising functions within retail organisations, and current operational practice. Covering all retail operations which revolve around the procurement of products, from stock level management, through allocation of outlet space for products, to the placement of products within the retail environment, this text is essential reading for anyone studying retail product management or buying and merchandising as part of their degree course. *Retail Product Management* also offers the following additional features:

- chapter introductions and summaries
- review and discussion questions
- boxed features and illustrative figures
- multi-sector mini-cases and three major case studies
- coverage of international aspects of retail product management

Rosemary Varley has worked extensively in retail product management. She is currently a senior lecturer within the Marketing Department of Huddersfield University Business School, where she teaches a wide range of retail marketing modules.

RETAIL PRODUCT MANAGEMENT

BUYING AND MERCHANDISING

Rosemary Varley

Artwork by
David Gillooley

LONDON & NEW YORK

First published 2001
by Routledge
11 New Fetter Lane, London EC4P 4EE

Simultaneously published in the USA and Canada
by Routledge
29 West 35th Street, New York, NY 10001

Routledge is an imprint of the Taylor & Francis Group

Typeset in Plantin and Rockwell by Keystroke, Jacaranda Lodge, Wolverhampton
Printed and bound in Great Britain by TJ International Ltd, Padstow, Cornwall

British Library Cataloguing in Publication Data
A catalogue record for this book is available from the British Library

Library of Congress Cataloging in Publication Data
Varley, Rosemary
    Retail product management : buying and merchandising / Rosemary Varley.
        p. cm.
    Includes bibliographical references and index.
    1. Retail trade–Management. 2. Product management. I. Title.

    HF5429 .V35 2000
    381′.1′0685–dc21   00–062575

    ISBN 0–415–21605–2 (hbk)
    ISBN 0–415–21606–0 (pbk)

Contents

Figures

Mini case studies

Boxes

Tables

Preface

Since an early age retailing activity has fascinated me, and before I reached double figures I had become something of a shopaholic. My parents tolerated this addiction through my teenage years, breathing a sigh of relief when I was old enough to earn the funds to feed my habit. Living in the country, opportunities to experience retailing on a large or sophisticated scale were restricted to occasional visits to nearby cities, and it was a visit to the Biba store in Kensington, London in the 1970s that confirmed my destiny. Founded by designer Barbara Hulanicki, this huge emporium of the most delightful products, packaged and displayed as works of art, in an environment that was more luxurious and exciting that any house, museum or even dance venue I had encountered, showed me the heights to which the 'shopping experience' could be taken.

My own college training and subsequent career was geared towards finding out how the retail process worked; and in particular the relationship between the product, the selling environment and the consumer has been the focus of my attention. Time spent in commercial product management in the 1980s took me through buying offices, stores and design rooms, and gradually the fascination with retailing that I had always fostered became the preserve of the masses. The service economy boomed, people talked about shops, newspapers featured serious articles on retail companies, a career in retailing became an admirable choice, and, most importantly for my own personal development, universities began to expand the subject of retailing from the fourth 'P' of the marketing mix to a specialist subject area, and then to dedicated courses.

In the transformation from practitioner to educator, my enthusiasm for retailing has not waned. Retailing is a subject that moves fast; it is interesting and fun to teach. It is an accessible subject which most students engage well with and then find challenging in its complexity. This book is a contribution to the process of enthusing and educating retailers of the future.

Rosemary Varley

Acknowledgements

I would like to acknowledge a number of valuable contributions to this project. I thank Stuart Hay for his enthusiasm and encouragement in the initial stages, followed by the patience and guidance of Michelle Gallagher, Allison Bell and the rest of the editorial and production team at Routledge.

I thank Dr Norman Marr, Professor of Marketing at the Huddersfield University Business School, who has given me time and space to work on the project. Also thanks go to my department colleagues who have been supportive in a variety of ways. In particular I am grateful to Glynis Jones for her input on international retail activities.

I am indebted to Lluís Martínez-Ribes and María Dolores De Juan Vigaray for the contribution of the Olympic Museum Shop case. I would also like to thank James and Laraine Davis, Gennaro Cuomo, Alberto Pastore, Richard Fawdry and Lorraine Crosby for their contributions to mini case studies. I am also grateful to Debenhams for the permission to use company literature in chapter two. I would like to extend my thanks to the following publishers who have given permission for material to be used in this book: Blackwell Publishers, Kogan Page Publishers and Macmillan Press Ltd. I am also grateful to Christopher Moore and Dr Elizabeth Howard for their extremely helpful reviews. I should also like to thank David Gillooley for his fine illustrations in chapters ten and eleven.

Finally, I wish to acknowledge my students, in particular the 'class of 97', as the inspiration for this work. However, I would not have completed the project without huge amounts of support at home, and I dedicate the end result to my family: Pete, Sam and Sophie.

Introduction

Product management has always been at the centre of a healthy retail business. In the past, traders and merchants who thrived did so because they gave their customers a better product offer than their contemporaries; intuitively knowing what the consumer market will judge to be a superior product offer is the prowess of the retail entrepreneur. In the retail environment of modern developed economies, opportunities to exploit really new products are rare, yet talented retailers manage to create the illusion of newness and freshness in their product ranges by selecting and developing innovative product variations.

The aim of this book is to combine two managerial viewpoints. It blends product marketing with retail management, exploring an often hidden and overlooked part of the retail strategy. Products are the roots from which all other retail activity stems and as such they provide an appropriate focus for the text. However, recent retail history has highlighted the dangers of taking a one-sided view of product management. Products are managed for consumers; they are managed in order to create and respond to customer demand, to satisfy existing customers and attract potential new ones. In a crowded retail market, it is perilous to forget the close and complex relationship between products, consumers and the arena in which product exchange takes place.

In response to the physical product needs of consumers, retailers provide products where, when and however a window of shopping opportunity is created in busy lifestyles. Consumers combine these physical needs with personal aspirations and desires, and so the retailer has also to be seen as the right place to shop, to be in tune with its customers and to have desirable values. Consumers take a multi-level approach to their shopping activities, and so retailers have to take a multi-level approach to the running of their businesses. Retailers have to ensure that operations are set up to provide a smooth flow of goods to the places and at the times the buying public wants. However, operational efficiency has to be overlaid with the strategic management of retail brands to ensure that the retail arena in which products are acquired retain their own desirability. The retail brand management process involves the creation and reinforcement of the 'branded shopping experience', being separate to but integrated with the brands attached to the product ranges within. Branding an experience requires a skilful and integrated marketing approach, blending a communication, service and location strategy to complement the product offer. This text acknowledges the contribution of these interrelated components of a retail strategy, focusing on the product range and exploring the linkage between operational and strategic product management.

Even in retail markets where consumers have seemingly endless choice, the product range retains its role as a means by which one competitor can differentiate itself from another. A retailer's product differentiation may be great, as in the case of a specialist retailer where no other outlet matches the depth of choice within a particular category of merchandise. On the other hand, the product differentiation may be slight, for example in a supermarket, with the difference between one competitor and another being largely a perceived one, and may rely on the contribution of a handful of key items to make the difference. Alternatively, the product range may provide the link into other means by which retailers can position themselves away from competitors, for example by using price or service differentiation.

The relationship between the product range and the position that a retailer carves out, not only in the market place but also in the mind of the customer, is a recurring theme in this book. Considered by many academics and practitioners to be the most important aspect of a retailer's strategy, a retailer's positioning remains intangible and difficult to measure. However, the operational support mechanisms *are* tangible and measurable, and in order to fill a resource gap this book concentrates on these. As such, this retail textbook brings together subjects from a number of different academic subject areas in order to reflect the multi-faceted role that retail product management plays. Logistic principles, accounting principles and design principles are all part of the product management process, yet the overriding principles are marketing ones, concerning consumer knowledge and understanding.

The sub-title of this book, 'Buying and Merchandising', reflects its operational focus. Buyers and merchandisers carry out the managerial roles within retail organisations that have traditionally had a significant involvement in the product management process. Buyers and merchandisers normally manage the interface between product and consumer, and organise the supply chain support to maximise opportunities given by that interface. However, using these managerial terms as a subtitle acknowledges that retail product management has a wider remit and is fully integrated into an overall retail strategy. The product range and the way it is managed directly relate to the on-going levels of income and profitability, which will determine the long-term survival and strategic development of the business.

This book has been designed to provide accessibility to a previously overlooked area of retail study. It takes a general rather than a sector specific viewpoint in order to cover as many aspects of product management as possible, but it is acknowledged within the text that retail sector differences will impact strongly on the way products are managed. The book contains a wide selection of examples and boxed features, along with case studies of various lengths in order to build awareness of the variety of challenges that product managers face in different retail contexts, and to explore solutions to retail product management problems. The text also provides review questions in order to assess understanding and discussion questions to broaden the area of knowledge; and although this subject area is sparsely researched, each chapter provides suggestions for further reading for students to pursue.

Every retail academic, student and practitioner is painfully aware of the rate of change within the industry, and whilst this text is relevant to the current situation in retailing, some features will become inevitably become dated over a period of time. In general the book concentrates on the principles of retail product management, which will remain broadly applicable in spite of advances in technology and changes in practice. The book begins by exploring the role and scope of product management in the retail business, followed by a review of the product management organisational structures and processes in chapters two and three. The following three chapters are concerned with the main stages in the traditional buying process, starting in chapter four with the need for retailers to track consumer-purchasing trends and then select appropriate products accordingly. Chapter five reviews the different supply sources, the effect of different types of relationships between retailer and supplier and the impact this has on the product management process, whilst chapter six looks at the operations behind the scenes that determine product availability and service to the customer. Efficient retailing in terms of managing ranges, product profitability and space are considered in chapters seven to nine, whilst the relationship between the product and the selling arena is considered in chapter ten on store design and chapter eleven on visual merchandising. The final two chapters explore some specific product management challenges, in the form of non-store retailing in chapter twelve and international dimensions in chapter thirteen.

Product management is an essential ingredient of successful retailing irrespective of the size and the geographical location of the business, and so a broad range of retail businesses are used as examples and case studies, from the independent retailer to the international multi-channel conglomerate.

chapter
<u>*one*</u>

PRODUCT MANAGEMENT IN A RETAIL BUSINESS

INTRODUCTION

Products are central to most organisations whether they are in the form of tangible goods or of services. Traditionally, manufacturers have been concerned with the design and production of products, whilst retailers have had the task of gathering together a relevant and inspiring selection of goods and making them available to consumers at convenient locations and times. These boundaries are becoming blurred, as we shall see throughout the book; some business organisations engage in retailing, even though the majority of their activity is concerned with some other enterprise, such as production or entertainment, and some retailers do have their own factories. However, if a business is to be classed as a retailer, its core activity, which accounts for over half of its total revenue has to come from selling finished products or providing personal services to the final consumer. Most retailers do not engage in any other primary business activity, and so the collection of products that they offer to their customers determines the nature of the business and influences all other aspects of their business strategy.

A PRODUCT DEFINED

A marketers definition of a product is 'a physical good, service, idea, person or place that is capable of officering tangible and intangible attributes that individuals or organisations regard as so necessary, worthwhile or satisfying that they are prepared to exchange money, patronage or some other unit of value in order to acquire it' (Brassington and Pettitt 2000: 262). Most of the topics included in this text will be concerned with physical goods, although retailers have also to concern themselves with the service they offer alongside their 'goods' offer, its place, or location, and the idea or position that it occupies in a customer's mind, relative to competitors in its market sector. The relationship between the tangible product and the less tangible retail service elements is a reoccurring theme throughout this book. Tangible products, whether they are durable, high involvement purchases such as household furnishings or non-durable, convenience orientated products such as food and toiletries, require a very different set of managerial approaches compared with service products such as hairdressing and travel. These service products have a very high proportion of intangibility and the product is not 'distributed' in the same way. The quality of a service product depends extensively on how the exchange is actually delivered with the 'product' experience being immediate and perishable. These additional challenges are beyond the scope of this text and have received the specialist attention that they deserve elsewhere (for example, Baron and Harris 1995; Christopher *et al.* 1994; Grönroos 1990).

RETAIL PRODUCT SECTORS

The retail industry is broken down into a number of sectors. For the purpose of industry reporting, the type of product sold determines the sector into which an individual business falls. In many cases it is perfectly clear which sector a particular retailer would fit into. For example, Dixons is classed as an electrical retailer, Burtons is classed as a clothing retailer and Waterstones is classed as a book retailer.

Some retailers, on the other hand, sell a very wide range of products, where no one type of product dominates sales. In UK there is a 'non-specialist retailer' sector into which some of the largest retail businesses are placed. Marks & Spencer, BhS, Woolworth's and Boots are all classified as non-specialist or 'mixed' retailers, as are the large 'grocery' supergroups, such as Tesco, J. Sainsbury and Asda. Table 1.1 shows how the UK retail market is broken down into product sectors. The domination of the 'non-specialist' category shows how the sector distinctions used by government to categorise retailers do not adequately reflect modern retail activity, yet it does provide evidence of the success gained by retailers who offer an all-encompassing, one-stop approach to their product assortments, at the expense of the specialist retailer.

As in the UK, a large share of retail activity in most economically developed markets is dominated by large retail organisations, although structural

Table 1.1 **The UK retail industry by sector**

Business type	Total retail turnover (£m)	%
Food specialist	5,451	2.82
Alcohol and tobacco	7,713	3.99
Pharmaceutical, medical, cosmetics and toiletries	7,375	3.82
Clothing/textiles	25,245	13.06
Footwear	3,783	1.96
Furniture/household	6,764	3.50
Electrical	8,280	4.28
Hardware/paint/glass	6,345	3.28
Books/newspaper/stationery	4,542	2.35
Floor coverings	1,463	0.76
Photographic/optical	3,047	1.58
Second-hand goods	1,511	0.78
Non-specialist (food/drink/tobacco)	71,968	37.24
Non-specialist (other)	17,687	9.15
Repair	438	0.23
Non-store sales	9,204	4.76
Others	12,419	6.43
Total	193,236	100.00

Source: Adapted from figures produced by the Office for National Statistics in Neilson 2000

differences can vary from country to country and impact upon the product sector characteristics in different ways. For example, the domination of the department store in countries like the US, Japan and Germany initially slowed the progress of speciality retailers (Alexander 1997). In less developed economies, a greater percentage of per capita expenditure would be allocated to food and medical supplies with lower percentages in sectors such as electrical goods and clothing. In addition, these types of economies are likely to have a more fragmented retail structure, with fewer international players.

THE ROLE OF PRODUCT MANAGEMENT IN RETAILING

Traditionally, the retailer's role within the distribution channel was to provide suitable selections of products in small quantities through outlets located close to viable groups of consumers. In fact, a dictionary definition of the verb to retail is 'the sale of goods in relatively small quantities to the public' (*Concise Oxford English Dictionary* 1996).

The most fundamental role that a retailer plays then is to 'break bulk'. Until about half way through the twentieth century retailers were typically seen as 'stockists' of a particular range of a manufacturer's products.

However, the role of the retailer has changed significantly from being a passive distributor to an active intermediary who controls the product range offering by carefully selecting products from manufacturers.

An historical overview

In the UK it was the abolition of resale price maintenance legislation in 1964 that accelerated the changes within the retail distribution industry: retailers were allowed to determine their own pricing strategy for their product ranges, rather than having to adhere to prices set by the manufacturers. The transfer of power allowed retailers to discount prices in order to increase volumes, and thereby profits, and to reinvest the profits in more outlets, resulting in greater buying power. Manufacturers had little choice but to co-operate with the growing multiple retailers, who then wielded their power in many other areas of their business, such as developing their own brands and improving store formats. The more recent advances in information technology have given the retailers even more power as a result of the sales analysis afforded by EPOS (electronic point of sale) systems and the database information that can be generated by customer-loyalty and other direct communication schemes. The result is a high level of retail concentration: an industry that is dominated by a relatively small number of extremely powerful, marketing orientated organisations (Davies 1993; McGoldrick 1990)

The retailer's role has always been geared towards customer convenience. Their role in the distribution channel (see Figure 1.1) is to provide outlets that are accessible to consumers, to store a sufficient quantity of a product so that consumers can buy products as and when they need them and revisit the outlet when the need arises again. For this service to the customer the retailer adds a profit margin. The profit that a retailer makes contributes towards the costs of running the outlet(s), such as the costs of staffing, paying rent, rates and other maintenance costs and the costs of financing the stock. It also has to cover the costs incurred by the support activities of the retail organisation, such as sourcing, marketing, distribution and systems. Any profit left can then be distributed to the owners or shareholders of the business (see Figure 1.2).

THE STRATEGIC ROLE OF PRODUCT MANAGEMENT

In order to carry out their traditional role in the distribution channel effectively, retailers need to offer a range of goods that satisfy the requirements of the customers who visit their outlet at the time they enter. Retailers are in the best position to know what their customers require because they have direct contact with them in the store. Whether knowledge is gained informally, for example in the case of a small independent owner/manager retail concern, or whether there is a highly sophisticated and complex information system based on EPOS data generation, retailers may need to

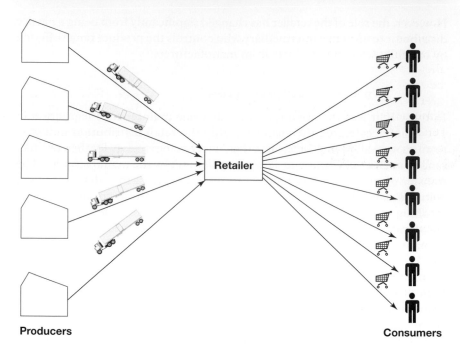

Figure 1.1 **The traditional role of the retailer in the distribution channel**

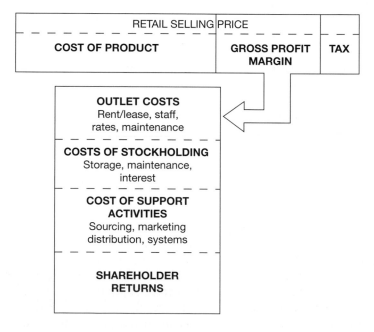

Figure 1.2 **Retail selling price structure**

adapt part or all of their product range in line with their customers' changing requirements. Retailers, therefore, need to have a good level of understanding of who their customers are, what their product preferences are and how their consumer needs and desires change over time. The time period may be through the day, within the week or according to season throughout the year. Retailers also need to adapt to long term changes in customer shopping habits. The mini case at the end of this chapter compares how two small retail businesses have adapted their product ranges to meet the needs of consumers in two different localities.

Retailing, in its contribution to the marketing management process, offers a great opportunity to add value to the tangible product, discussed earlier in the chapter. Marketing-led organisations should not only give customers what they need, but should also identify and anticipate customer requirements. The product assortment that a retailer offers and the environment in which it is presented gives the retailer a powerful advantage over the producers of those goods, who now rely on the retailers as masters of this craft. Nevertheless, most successful retailers work in collaboration with their producers and suppliers, pooling resources to make a better job of the identification and anticipation of needs and wants, and then formulating a response to them.

Figure 1.3 illustrates how retailers have provided added value to consumers as they have grown to their positions of power. It is retailers who have seized the opportunity to establish close relationships with customers and gain a deep understanding of their purchasing habits, manifesting their authority in the development of strong retail brand identities. The internet and other forms of direct marketing offer opportunities for producers to fight back, by establishing a channel to take products directly from the producer to the consumer; but it is the retailers who have the greater opportunity to build on their existing knowledge and experience of consumers and use new marketing channels to their advantage (Tat Key and Park 1998).

THE STRATEGIC ROLE OF THE PRODUCT RANGE

Retailers capture their customers' interest by the nature of their product range. It communicates to the customer what kind of retailer they are entering and therefore helps them in the search stage of their individual buying process. The nature of a retailer's business may be obvious with specialist retailers such as jewellers, but it may be less obvious in a mixed retailer, for example. The product range helps to position a retailer against its competitors within a market sector. The range may be limited but extremely specialist; it may be geared towards high quality products, or those with a strong fashion element; or alternatively the product selection may be wide, offering value for money to a wide section of the consumer market. In a concentrated and relatively saturated retail market, such as the UK, the position that a retailer etches out in the consumer mind is a vital element of its strategy. Customers must be given a good reason to shop with one retailer rather than another.

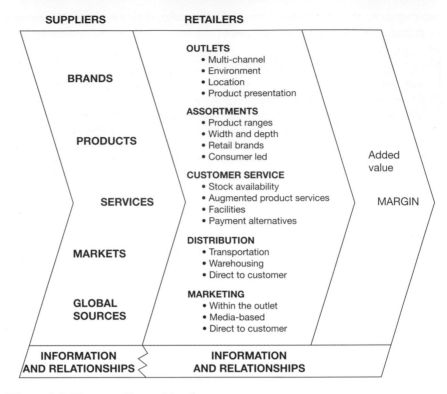

Figure 1.3 **How retailers add value**

If they are paying a premium price then they must feel that the product and the shopping experience has been worthwhile, or, if price is the main motivator in the purchase, the product range must represent the best value around. The complexity of the consumer is reflected in the diverse positioning of retailers in the industry, although in the UK there is an increasing polarisation towards low, best-value prices for everyday goods and an opportunity to charge premiums for aspirational and time-buying products

Some retailers have a diverse range of different products. Whether it is a small convenient store or a large superstore, the offering may include food products, household goods, entertainment products, alcoholic drinks, greeting cards and fresh flowers. These generalist retailers have a wide variety of products in the attempt to cover a wide number of basic consumer needs. Other retailers have a narrow product range, where a small number of product categories are offered in substantial depth so that the more specific consumer needs can be met in the majority of cases. These specialist retailers can be large, for example Toys 'R' Us, or they may be small, such as Tie Rack or Dappledown (see Box 1.1), but the key difference is the approach to the width and depth of the product assortment. Table 1.2 describes different retail formats and their likely approach to product assortment, in terms of variety and depth.

BOX 1.1   DAPPLEDOWN

The Trafford Centre, located on the outskirts of Manchester, is one of the largest regional shopping centres in the UK. Within the centre there are 280 outlets, housed within four themed areas. Regent Crescent features a mix of fashion retailers and department stores, while Peel Avenue encompasses a selection of familiar variety stores and multiple retailers in a number of traditional product sectors. The Orient, an entertainment destination in its own right, provides a range of food outlets spread around a massive food court, and the fourth area, Festival Village, houses over fifty small, specialist shops. Some of the Festival Village retailers are major national chains, such as Sock Shop and Vodafone, but many of the stores are small independents, offering every option imaginable of one product type. There is The Stencil Store, The Stationery Box, The Nut Co. and The Flower Pot, all of which need no further introduction, but a favourite store for many customers is Dappledown, which offers a wide range of traditional confectionery. All those sweet products remembered from childhood, like liquorice whirls, sherbet fountains and jelly babies in jars, can be found here as well as a self-select range of chocolates and fudges. The jars, tins and see-through packages tied with ribbon make a vibrant and colourful display, whilst the aroma of toffee and chocolate combine to break the resolve any shopper who tries to resist!

Table 1.2 **Retail format and typical product assortments**

Retail format	Example	Depth of assortment	Width of assortment
Department store	Harrods Debenhams	Deep	Wide
Variety store	Marks & Spencer BhS	Shallow	Wide
Category killer (category specialist)	Toys 'R' Us Carpetwise	Deep	Narrow
Speciality store	Body Shop The Link	Deep	Narrow
Convenience store	7-Eleven Alldays	Shallow	Medium
Discount supermarket	Aldi Netto	Shallow	Wide
Superstore	Wal-Mart J. Sainsbury	Medium	Wide
Mail order catalogue	La Redoute Great Universal Stores	Shallow	Wide
Specialist catalogue	Land's End Innovations	Deep	Narrow

It is not always possible to classify retailers in the way that Table 1.2 describes. Some retailers specialise in part of their product range, and then have a generalist approach to another part. Boots, for example, began as a company which specialised in pharmacy and healthcare products but over the years they have extended their range substantially (see Box 1.2). They still specialise in healthcare, pharmaceutical and beauty products, which draw customers into the store on a regular basis. However, the additional products offer the customer the chance to purchase a much wider range of products once they are in the store. As a retailer extends its product ranges, there is a danger that the initial specialism, or the core range, will get lost in the proliferation of additional products. This tendency is called 'product scram-

---

BOX 1.2   BOOTS THE CHEMIST

Boots the Chemist is a highly successful retail company. In 1997 it generated a sales turnover of just over £3,300 million from its 1,258 outlets. Originally a specialist retailer in the pharmacy sector, trading in healthcare products, pharmaceuticals, toiletries and cosmetics, Boots now has an extensive product range which includes gifts, music, photographic supplies and processing, and electrical appliances. The range is so diverse that the company is now classified as a variety store operating in the mixed retail sector.

Boots is a centralised retailer. Its company headquarters in Nottingham, UK, houses all the operational areas: store development, information systems, finance, logistics, and merchandise and marketing. The merchandise and marketing section of the company is then split into divisions according to product area:

- Healthcare, dispensing baby consumables and dietary food;
- Beauty (including toiletries);
- Leisure (includes gifts, children's clothing, photographic processing/supplies, and food).

It is within the merchandise and marketing section of the company that most of the product management functions are carried out.

Boots has a wide range of own-label products which is constantly being updated and developed in response to market opportunities. Over the years they have developed a number of own-branded product ranges; many of these are leading brands in their respective product markets, such as Soltan (suncream products), Shapers (slimming foods) and No. 7 (cosmetics). Boots can be found on the main high street of most towns and regional shopping centres in the UK where they benefit from a high customer flow (it is estimated that one in three people in the UK visit a Boots store every week). They have also been opening stores in airport terminals, motorway service stations and hospital sites, where the product range is tailored to the specific needs of customers in those locations.

(Extracted from 'A Case Study of Buying Operations at Boots the Chemist' – see Appendix One)

bling' and can result in a retailer's offer becoming less meaningful to customers. Woolworth's is perhaps the best known retailer who 'unscrambled' their merchandise range, which at one time included food, DIY products and clothing for all the family, to concentrate on the product categories in which they had the greatest market share: home entertainment, toys, children's clothing, stationery and confectionery (Kingfisher Group, *Annual Report* 1999).

Product ranges offered by retailers have to be managed within the context of an ever-changing business environment. Consumers' product preferences change according to their life-stage, lifestyle and personal wealth. One retailer's product offer is subject to scrutiny by consumers alongside those offered by many other retailers, which also are likely to change over time; therefore product management is part of an on-going strategic management process which ultimately bears on the ability of a business to meet its long term objectives.

THE SCOPE OF RETAIL PRODUCT MANAGEMENT

Retail product management is not just about making sure that the best product range is available in the store. Equally important to the customer is how products are presented to them. The way products are displayed, whether it is on a shelf in a store or on a website, the logic of the layout, the relationship between one product group and another and the atmosphere created around the products, are all-important aspects of the retail product management process.

In a small retail organisation product management may be incorporated into the general running of the store. In a quiet moment an owner/manager may phone through an order to a supplier or stock up a depleted shelf display; but in large retail organisations product management is an extensive task, involving many different layers of management and dedicated teams of experts in massive central buying offices. Figure 1.4 illustrates the scope of product management in a large multiple retailer, where many areas of product management decision-making are centralised within a head office.

Product management is a strategic process, supported, in the case of a large retailer, by a complex array of operational practices and organisational structures. Strategic product management shapes the direction of growth taken by a retailer in response to changing consumer requirements, whilst carving out a market position to appeal to identified consumer market groups. Its strategic contribution is augmented by the role that product management takes in keeping operational costs as low as possible whilst generating sales volumes to maximise profitability. It is also about managing risks, identifying and pursuing product/market opportunities, whilst making realistic assessments about the resources available to do so. Introducing new products is a very good way of achieving differentiation and enhancing a retail identity in an over-subscribed retail market, but without corporate support new products may fail or go unnoticed.

STRATEGIC PRODUCT MANAGEMENT
Product opportunities and objectives
Market opportunities and objectives
Sales and profit objectives
Resource deployment
Business environment auditing
Integrated information systems planning
Range planning
Category management
OPERATIONAL PRODUCT MANAGEMENT
Product development and selection
Sourcing
Sales forecasting
Supply chain management
Pricing
Space allocation
Store profiling
Visual merchandising
Promotions
PRODUCT MANAGEMENT WITHIN THE OUTLET
Allocate space to merchandise
Display merchandise
Receive and prepare stock
Implement promotions
Sell merchandise

Figure 1.4 **The scope of product management**

RETAIL PRODUCT MANAGEMENT: AN EVOLVING DISCIPLINE

Product management in retail organisations encompasses a wide range of functions and, as social organisational structures, many retailers have unique approaches to this area of their business. In most centrally managed retail organisations, product management, or buying and merchandising as it frequently termed, is seen as a key functional area alongside financial, human resource and systems management. The extent to which marketing and logistics are integrated into the product management area varies from one retailer to another. To a certain extent it is possible to trace the evolutionary path along which product management has moved as the retail industry itself has changed over the years in developed economies. This is shown in Figure 1.5.

At one time buyers were considered to be kings and queens within the retail business. In some retail institutions such as department stores, buyers frequently worked their way up through the organisation, from the sales floor,

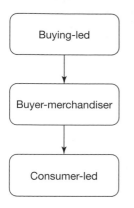

Figure 1.5 **The evolution of product management**

through department management, then buyer's clerk, finally to make it to the ivory tower and be able to use the esteemed title of buyer, coupled with benefits such as the 'buyer's cloakroom'! In more modern retail companies, such as the multiple chains, buying experience is still valued highly, and although these days buyers are likely to be graduates, they still have to spend time in a kind of apprenticeship, gaining product and supply knowledge and generally becoming familiar with the retailer's strategic and operational aims.

In the late 1970s and through the 1980s, the centralised multiple emerged as a strong force, and with it a new approach to buying which essentially split the buying role into qualitative considerations (product selection) and quantitative considerations (merchandising). This offered the benefit of allowing the buyer to concentrate on getting the product detail right and selecting suppliers who could meet the required price and service standard in terms of delivery, technical skill, capacity and so on. In the meantime, the merchandiser concentrated on sales forecasting, stock planning and managing product sell through.

Through the 1990s a new approach emerged, broadly termed 'consumer-led' product management. This is geared to responding to consumers rather than forecasting what they will buy. It is a more marketing orientated approach and relies on multi-functional teams focused on the performance of narrow bands of products. In many respects, it is an adaptation of the brand management organisation found in many fast moving consumer goods producers, where teams manage the sales and distribution of an individual or interrelated product group as a strategic business unit. This management approach has led to the adoption of the category management role, which is a broader role than buying or merchandising, encompassing elements of both and adding a strong marketing emphasis (Wills 1999).

SUMMARY

Product management is central to retailing essentially because it is the product range that most effectively communicates to the consumer what the focus of the business is. The product range may be generalist, offering a wide variety of merchandise, or it may have a narrower assortment, giving the consumer the chance to find specialist products. The product range contributes significantly to the strategic success of retail businesses. It is through the product range that retailers implement their pricing strategies and profitability levels, and it is through the product range that retailers maintain a consumer's interest and adapt to their changing shopping requirements.

Product management in retailing has become wider in scope as the customer orientation of retailing has grown. The product management process involves procurement, logistics and implementation of range formulation at store level, and as such a new organisational structure in retailers is emerging in which products are managed from conception to sale on a product category basis. The following chapters explore the organisational structures within which the product management process takes place. First, the traditional buying organisation is outlined in chapter two, followed by a discussion of the category management approach in chapter three.

MINI CASE STUDY 1   HOLMBRIDGE AND LOCKFIELD POST OFFICES

Holmbridge is a village in West Yorkshire, in the North of England, UK, with a population of approximately 1,400 residents. The village features a church, a public house, a combined Post Office and general store and, of course, a cricket ground. A main road passes through the village, linking West Yorkshire to the next county, Derbyshire, via the Pennine Hills. The Post Office provides local residents with the usual postal and state payment services, and a carefully selected range of essential grocery and convenience goods. James and Laraine Davis run the Post Office with the part-time help of Susan, who lives nearby.

Once a week James visits a cash and carry wholesaler 15 miles away where he buys well known branded products such as Heinz canned products, Kellogg's cereals and essential 'Better-buy' wholesaler branded items, such as cleaning fluid and kitchen paper. The total selling space is around 180 square metres, yet over 1,200 product items are offered, including a good range of fresh fruit, vegetables and delicatessen produce. On the traditional oak wood counter where customers wait to pay are strategically placed seasonal items, such as wrapping paper at X-mas, Parkin in November,[1] Rhubarb in the early days of spring[2] and small boxes of chocolates in March for Mother's Day. Nearby on the counter are tempting fresh cream cakes, supplied daily along with a range of bread products from a local bakery. The Post Office supplies a limited range of stationery products, to complement the Post Office activities, which are displayed alongside an extensive and attractive range of cards for every occasion. Fresh flowers are always available and small bedding plants are offered during the warmer months of the year.

Ten miles away, in a suburb of Huddersfield, a large industrial town in the North of England, is another Post Office and store, run by Rajeev Patel. Here at Lockfield, the same postal and state payment services are provided, yet the product range is completely different. In this store the vegetable selection includes five varieties of chilli peppers, bhindi (okra) and fresh coriander in massive bundles. The dry-goods section offers an extensive variety of rice and lentils and spices. At the payment counter there is a colourful selection of milk-based Asian sweet products such as barfi, as well as the freshly cooked samosas and bhajis for a tempting tasty snack. These emit an exotic spicy aroma, which blends with the heavy sweet smell of the incense which is stacked in an array of colourful boxes on a shelf nearby. Customers are invited to join the video rental club, which includes a number of titles in the language of Urdu, alongside the popular mainstream films and programmes. It also offers a photocopying and a fax service.

Notes

1 Parkin is a rich and sticky gingerbread, traditionally eaten in the North of England around 5 November, when many people celebrate 'Bonfire Night'.
2 Yorkshire is renowned for 'forced' rhubarb, grown under earthenware pots to encourage growth through the later winter months.

REVIEW QUESTIONS

1 Consider the traditional role of the retailer as breaker of bulk supplies, and explain how the retailer's role has evolved since the 1980s.
2 Review the scope of product management in retailing, using a chosen retailer to illustrate your discussion.
3 Explain why product management has to be part of a retailer's strategic development, upon which long term success is dependent.
4 Referring to the case study at the end of the chapter, explain how the product ranges at Holmbridge and Lockfield Post Offices reflect the needs of their respective customers.
5 Referring to Box 1.1, explain how small specialist retailers can prosper in a large planned regional shopping centre such as the Trafford Centre, Meadowhall, Lakeside or the Metro Centre.

DISCUSSION QUESTIONS

1 Explain the reasons for the domination of the non-specialist retailer in the UK retail industry (as shown in Table 1.1).
2 Choose one sector of the retail industry and, using Table 1.2, conduct an analysis of the sector according to retail format, companies operating within the sector, and their product assortments.
3 Boots the Chemist is a retailer that began as a specialist, but over the years has broadened its product assortment. Explain why you think Boots the Chemist has evolved in this way.
4 Discuss the contribution that product ranges make to the positioning of retailers within their product sector, using retailers of your choice to illustrate your discussion.

REFERENCES AND FURTHER READING

Alexander, N. (1997) *International Retailing*, Blackwell, Oxford.
Baron, S. and Harris, K. (1995) *Services Marketing: Text and Cases*, Macmillan, Basingstoke, Hants.
Brassington, F. and Pettitt, S. (2000) *Principles of Marketing*, Pearson Education, Harlow, Essex.
Christopher, M., Payne, A. and Ballntyne, D. (1994) *Relationship Marketing: Bringing Quality, Customer Service and Marketing Together*, 2nd edn, Butterworth-Heinemann, Oxford.
Davies, G. (1992a) 'The two ways in which retailers can be brands', *International Journal of Retail and Distribution Management* 20 (2): 24–34.

Davies, G. (1992b) 'Positioning, image and the marketing of multiple retailers', *International Review of Retail Distribution and Consumer Research* **2** (1): 13–33.

Davies, G. (1993) *Trade Marketing Strategy*, Paul Chapman, London.

Davies, G.J. and Brooks, J.M. (1989) *Positioning Strategy in Retailing*, Paul Chapman, London.

Grönroos, C. (1990) *Service Management and Marketing*, Free Press/Lexington Books, Lexington, MA.

Howe, W.S. (1998) 'Vertical market relations in the grocery trade: analysis and government policy', *International Journal of Retail and Distribution Management* **26** (6): 212–24.

McGoldrick, P.J. (1990) *Retail Marketing*, McGraw-Hill, Maidenhead, Berks.

Nielsen, A.C. (2000) *The Retail Pocket Book*, A.C. Nielsen with NTC Publications, Henley-on-Thames, Oxon.

Samli, A. Coskun (1998) *Strategic Marketing for Success in Retailing*, Quorum Books, Westport, CT.

Tat Key, H. and Park S.Y. (1998) 'An expanded perspective on power in distribution channels: strategies and implications', *International Review of Retail, Distribution and Consumer Research* **8** (1): 101–15.

Wills, J. (1999) *Merchandising and Buying Strategies: New Roles for a Global Operation*, Financial Times Retail and Consumer, London.

chapter two

THE DECISION-MAKERS IN RETAIL PRODUCT MANAGEMENT

INTRODUCTION

Being such an important part of the retail business, considerable attention must be paid to the organisation of the sections of the retailer that carry out the functions which are included within product management. A buying organisation could be defined as the entity within a retail organisation that carries out the essential task of bringing goods into the retail business from the supply base to be sold on to retail customers. In the following two chapters the structure of buying organisations will be reviewed within the context of the overall approach to product management. This chapter will concentrate on the buying and merchandising-led approach (see Figure 1.5), which is still commonly used throughout the UK. Chapter three will then move on to consider a 'new' organisation structure that consumer-led buying organisations have adopted.

Although it is the most directly concerned with the product offer, the buying organisation is not the only 'department' or section within a retail business that is involved in product management. Logistics and visual merchandising, for example, have a deep involvement with products, but their role is one of support rather than control. The people who essentially 'control' the product offer are referred to, either in title or as a collective team, as retail buyers. In later chapters other sections or departments that are involved in product management will be considered; for example, the logistical aspects of product management are discussed in chapter five, and later, in chapter eleven, the role of the visual merchandising team is considered. In this chapter we shall examine the role of those people who have the most direct control over product management.

CENTRALISED RETAIL BUYING ORGANISATIONS

Product management in most sizeable retail organisations is a centralised operation, and buying offices are usually housed at or near the company headquarters. In employment terms, buying personnel usually account for the greatest number of people in any centralised retail operational area. Debenhams for example employ close to 2,000 people in their central buying office, of which 750 are buying and merchandising personnel (see Box 2.1).

Although it is difficult to make generalisations about the 'typical' levels of authority within retail businesses, the structure in Figure 2.2 provides an outline that seems to bear a resemblance to many retail buying office structures. Wills (1999) suggests that within the more generic structure outlined in Figure 2.2 buying office structures show sectoral differences. In clothing, the structure incorporates the technologist's role; in the electrical sector there is more emphasis on 'trading' because of the dominance of manufacturers' brands and the emphasis on product/price promotions; whilst in food, the buyers concentrate on new product development, a trader acts like a merchandiser, and a logistics manager becomes a key part of the buying team because of the leading role it takes in food retailing and distribution.

Centralised decision-making offers a retail organisation many advantages. McGoldrick (1990: 190) provides a summary of these, which includes the following key points:

- Increased buying power allows buyers to negotiate better terms with suppliers.
- Specialist buyers can devote more time to product / market analysis.
- Sales data can be aggregated to improve forecasting.
- Economies of scale are achieved as sourcing and selection costs are lower; buyers' salaries are comparatively high within a retail business.
- The quality level of the product offer is better controlled, for example by having a team of technologists and quality controllers who work centrally alongside buyers.
- A more consistent product assortment is presented in order to reinforce the retail brand identity and support national promotions.
- The quality of buying and stock control decisions is consistent across outlets.
- Store personnel are freed from buying responsibilities, allowing them to concentrate on creating a high quality shopping experience for customers in the retail outlet.

BOX 2.1 DEBENHAMS (RETAIL) PLC

Debenhams is the UK's largest department store retailer. Founded in 1778, Debenhams now operates almost 100 stores with a geographical spread from Exeter to Inverness. In the period 1985–98, Debenhams was owned by the Burton Group, but the department store chain was de-merged from the specialist clothing retailers (now trading under the name of the Arcadia Group) to enable it to develop its own strategic direction. The company entered the home shopping sector in 1998 with Debenhams Direct, and is expanding internationally by working with local franchise partners.

The central buying office for the stores is located behind their flagship store on Oxford Street in central London. The diversity and the volume of products sold in Debenhams makes it one of the largest buying offices in the UK, employing around 750 people.

Most of the buying departments conform to the structure shown in Figure 2.1, which outlines typical career development paths within the Buying, Merchandising and Distribution section.

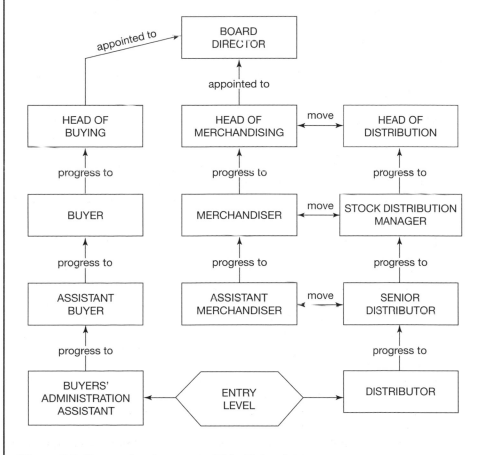

Figure 2.1 **Career development within Debenhams**

continued

The role of the buying team is to develop profitable product ranges that reflect current trends and offer the Debenhams customer product choice at all times. The role involves supplier sourcing, negotiating costs, quality and quantities, and monitoring delivery schedules. The merchandise teams decide how many units of every single stock-keeping unit will be sold throughout the store network, and work closely with the buyers to ensure that need is satisfied by the supply base. The distribution team has the responsibility of ensuring that each store has the goods to satisfy the expected demand and to generate profit. Success in a highly pressurised environment, where new challenges emerge on a daily basis, relies on departmental teamwork.

(Source: Adapted from Debenhams' careers literature, 1998)

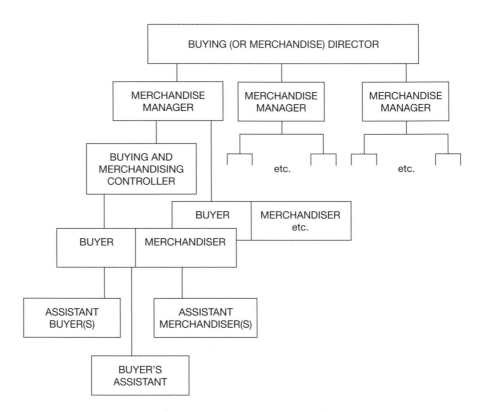

Figure 2.2 **A typical buying organisation for a multiple retailer**

One of the problems encountered in a centralised retail organisation is the split between head office and stores. Although they are working for the same company and have the same goals, conflict between store personnel and head office personnel is common in many retail businesses. This conflict frequently arises when store personnel feel that the wrong products have been 'sent by head office' for them to sell. In the case of seasonal goods, products have to be 'pushed' into stores so that they are ready in sufficient quantities for the seasonal uplift in sales. Likewise, fashion trends may seem extreme, until the rest of the high street is offering similar skirt lengths, trouser widths or colour combinations, so the initial reaction to new styles may be negative.

An open channel of communication between the central buying organisation and branch stores is key to the product management process. Feedback from customers via store personnel, store management and retail operations area management on the more and less successful aspects of the product range is vital if steps are going to be taken to rectify mistakes or prevent the repetition of errors. Sales information from the most sophisticated electronic point of sale system may only tell product managers what has sold and who has bought it: these systems do not give information on why something has not sold, so some mechanism for capturing qualitative data on the product range should be part of the product management process.

DECENTRALISED BUYING

Retailers who have a product range that is dominated by products with a relatively stable demand have more opportunity to allow the retail outlets to have an element of control over the buying for their stores. Store or even department managers may place orders, according to the sales pattern occurring within their outlet, within the parameters of a centrally determined product range assortment. This allows the outlets to respond to local variations in demand whilst maintaining a consistent corporate product offer. In some cases, however, the product itself requires a decentralised approach. Highly regional products, such as local newspapers or heritage gifts, must be sourced locally. Additionally, fresh produce such as meat is often bought on a local or regional basis because of the (relatively) fragmented supply market and the need to minimise transportation and storage times.

Allowing the retail outlet to respond effectively and efficiently to local product preference is a way of improving customer service and the productivity of the outlet. In this respect, store retailers have an advantage over non-store retailers such as mail order companies, who, by the nature of their business, rely on a centralised approach to buying and distribution. The extent to which internet retailers are going to be able to cope with regional or individual preferences has yet to be established. The principle of geographic or individual tailoring of the product offer is relatively straightforward, but the logistical support to fulfil orders is more complex (see chapter twelve).

BUYING ORGANISATION MANAGERIAL ROLES

This section describes the managerial roles at each level within a 'typical' multiple retail buying organisation. The discussion begins with the core personnel within a buying department, as shown in Figure 2.2, and then goes on to consider the auxiliary teams that may be included within the buying office structure or play an influencing role in the buying decision process (see section on buying committees, pp. 32–5).

Buying director

There may be more than one buying director in a retail organisation, but it is not likely to have more than one represented at main board level. The multinational grocer J. Sainsbury plc for example, has a 'Group Commercial and International Buying Director' sitting on their ten person strong board of directors (*Annual Report* 1999). Buying directors represent all aspects of the buying organisation within the retail company. Their position corresponds with that of a general merchandise manager within a US buying organisation, although a main board director would be equivalent to a vice-president. Buying directors oversee a large number, if not all, of the product areas, and are responsible for setting the overall aims of the product management teams within the company. They must lead these teams in the pursuit of achieving strategic objectives through product management and be involved in planning decisions that have long term effects on the retailer's ability to perform. A buying director is likely to be involved in the following types of decision-making:

- changing major suppliers;
- introduction of new product ranges (not new items);
- deletion of product ranges or categories;
- concessions arrangements;[1]
- major promotion campaigns;
- strategic aspects of range planning, such as multi-channel retailing;
- adoption of systems and management approaches, within the product management area.

As well as, or instead of a buying director, there may be a merchandise/merchandising director. This will be a similar role, primarily concerned with strategic product planning.

Merchandise managers

Merchandise managers are senior buying and merchandising personnel who oversee a division or a number of interrelated buying departments. This level of management is most likely to be found in variety stores, department stores or in mail order, where it is important to show some degree of co-ordination and consistency in terms of styling, colour range and quality level across buying departments. One merchandise manager may oversee all ladies' wear offer, including clothing accessories and footwear, whilst another might oversee all home furnishings, including furniture, floor coverings, soft furnishing, lighting and household accessories and gifts. This level of manager is sometimes given director status in large retail organisations such as Marks & Spencer plc.

Buying controllers

Buying controllers are situated in the buying and merchandising management hierarchy between buyers and merchandise managers. They usually oversee the buying and merchandising operations of a small number of departments. It may be useful to have a buying controller to help manage large buying departments or to co-ordinate activities of concessions departments; however, in the pursuit of organisational efficiencies and improved communications, many retailers have attempted to create flatter organisational structures, and in such instances this level of management has been removed. In the case of the smaller retailer, buyers might report directly to the merchandise director.

Buyers

The buyer has traditionally been seen as the figurehead of the department that carries out the buying process on behalf of the retailer. He or she may have operational control of the department whereby the rest of the buying team reports to the buyer; however, in some organisations the responsibility for running the department is shared between a buyer (or selector) and a merchandiser (or stock controller). Buyers tend to be more concerned with the qualitative side of buying; they must be aware of all the features of the product that bear upon its ability to give customer satisfaction and they must have an extensive knowledge of what is available within the product market for which they have responsibility. Price negotiation is usually a task for the buyer, but in some organisations this is clearly a merchandiser's responsibility.

Merchandisers

Merchandisers tend to be concerned with the quantitative aspects of buying, and are usually responsible for estimating sales, planning deliveries and distribution of the goods to stores. This role is sometimes referred to as stock controller or stock planner. Most merchandisers also have responsibility for the financial management of the department, including budgeting and profit analysis. Occasionally, a merchandiser also has product selection responsibilities, depending on the use of the title within the organisation, and in some retailers merchandisers plan space allocations. As the merchandise systems used in a buying department have grown in sophistication, so too has the role of the merchandiser: it is now seen as more strategic and as having a greater impact on the product management process. This can have the effect of pushing the buying role further into the area of design, product development and selection, with less control over range planning and direction. Some organisations, such as Gap, do not have buyers at all: they rely on designers to develop products and merchandisers to edit the range (Wills 1999). Next plc, the highly successful UK clothing retailer, traditionally recruited buyers from a design background, relying on merchandisers to carry out analysis and planning.

Assistant buyers

In large retail organisations both buyers and merchandisers are likely to have one or more assistants. It is important to distinguish between an assistant buyer and a buying assistant. An assistant buyer plays a key role in the buying process and may be solely responsible for some buying decisions. They will have a full understanding of the workings of the department and will provide support to the buyer on the operational aspects of the buying department. In many cases an assistant is in training for a full buyership. Assistant merchandisers play a similar role on the quantitative side of the buying process.

Buying assistants

A buying assistant, or buyer's clerk, is a junior member of the team, providing administrative support and carrying out routine duties within the department (frequently performing a combination of buying and merchandising duties). Experience within a buying office is a valued asset in retailing and so a buyer's assistant who shows potential could easily progress to assistant buyer or assistant merchandiser.

DESIRABLE ATTRIBUTES IN BUYING AND MERCHANDISING PERSONNEL

Diamond and Pintel (1997) found that the following qualities are important for a successful career in a retail buying organisation.

Analytical skills

Decision-making is at the heart of any job within a buying organisation. Collating data from many different sources, extracting and assimilating important information, reading situations, making evaluations, predictions and judgements are all things that buyers and merchandisers do on an on-going basis and all require some level of analysis. As retailing becomes faster moving and more competitive, the need for analytical powers increases. The merchandising side of the product management function requires a high level of numeracy, coupled with the commercial acumen to interpret figures as retailing realities.

Communication skills

Working at the hub of a centralised retail structure, a buying office must have lines of communication with all other sections of the retailer. Frequent communication with marketing, logistics, finance and personnel and in particular with stores is vital if the buying organisation is to play its part in the product management process effectively. In addition buying departments constantly liaise with suppliers, therefore communications are both internal and external. Communications that are formal (for example memos, presentations or reports) or informal (answering general queries by telephone or email for example) have to be transmitted in written form or verbally. Related skills such as negotiation, persuasion, assertiveness and diplomacy often have to accompany the basic ability to communicate and, as high profile representatives of the retail organisation, buying personnel should present themselves in a way that is consistent with the corporate image.

Objectivity

Retail buying personnel operate on behalf of the commercial organisation which employs them. Decisions are made for the benefit of the organisation rather than the individual, therefore the ability to divorce personal taste or preference from the business role is an essential qualification. A retailing adage states: 'A retailer must buy what it sells [to consumers], not sell what it [the retailer] buys.' Being objective requires buyers to be flexible, so that they can adapt their powers of analysis and objectivity to an ever-changing retail environment, whether it is changing customer requirements or competitor actions.

Product knowledge

Buying personnel may join a retailer with some formal product training; otherwise it is likely that some on-the-job training will be required to ensure that specific technical product features are fully understood by the retail product manager. Without this knowledge, buying personnel are less able to make appropriate buying decisions. Accumulation of product knowledge is part of the training process of an assistant buyer. The difficulties of buyers making decisions without technical product knowledge are highlighted in Box 2.2.

BOX 2.2   COLOURED BY LACK OF EXPERIENCE

A young buyer working at a women's wear multiple retailer demanded that a supplier reprint a piece of fabric to obtain an exact colour match with their corporate colour palette. Under duress, the supplier reprinted the fabric three times for the unhappy buyer. Eventually the supplier managed to get the buyer to understand that no matter how many times the fabric was reprinted, the colour would never match exactly because the base fabric had a 'nap' (a directional surface, as in satin or velvet), which reflected light in a different way to the standard shade.

(Source: Miller 1997)

Formal qualifications

Although it is possible for junior associates in a retail organisation to make their way into a product management position, a more likely route today is to enter the buying and merchandising part of a retail business as a graduate.

Many of the large retailers will consider graduates from any degree discipline, but it is acknowledged that some business training is very useful for this area of retailing. Increasingly, specialised retail courses are being offered at universities around the world, and a graduate with a good degree in retailing is likely to be extremely attractive to a retail organisation wishing to recruit trainee buying and merchandising team members. For some buying positions, such as clothing or food, a degree with a relevant technology base, such as textiles or food science, may be more important than a business background; however, buying is a commercial role, and therefore strong business acumen must be developed alongside technical product knowledge.

In addition to the qualities outlined above, it may be necessary or desirable for a buyer to be proficient in a second language, so that they are better equipped to negotiate with overseas suppliers. Above all, buying personnel need to have the flexibility to address promptly all the challenges that retailing presents to them.

ADDITIONAL BUYING DECISION-MAKERS

As well as the people working within each product or buying department, other people or sections within a centralised retail buying organisation may play a central role in buying decision-making, including technologists, product development teams and corporate design teams.

Technologists

Although most of the buying decisions are centred on the ability of a product to satisfy a customer need at a price the customer is willing to pay, a retailer has to ensure that it meets its legal obligations with regard to the products it sells. It also has to consider its long term image in the eyes of the public. It is therefore necessary to ensure that a product conforms to legal standards and provides value for money. A buyer is usually a marketing orientated person, who may need some advice when it comes to assessing certain product features and criteria. This is where a technologist can be a useful member of the buying team. Technologists will be up to date on product standards, manufacturing process innovations, raw material properties and so on. They are not primarily concerned with sales and profitability of individual items but, by ensuring that product standards are met and maintained, they play a key role in the long term success of retail product management. The quality of products such as Heinz baked beans or Phillips light-bulbs is assured by the brand, and in such cases the manufacturer takes the responsibility for maintaining the trust in product quality of the customer. However, from the retailer's point of view, it is especially important that their own-labelled products do not violate any product law or tarnish the retailer's reputable name.

The product development team

Where a retailer is involved in putting together a product offer which is unique to its own company, and where suppliers are not able to provide the required level of input into product innovation, it may be necessary for the retailer to set up a development team for a particular product area. For example, J. Sainsbury plc have an experimental kitchen whose staff work on new food products. Many fashion retailers, such as Oasis, have a team of designers, pattern cutters and sample machinists who make garment prototypes for their suppliers to copy.

Product development is a time consuming and costly process; for example, it takes approximately nine months for Tesco plc to develop a new product (Wills 1999). However, in a business environment where customers react favourably to new product ideas it is a way in which a retailer can be sure of offering a wide choice of contemporary products to the customer. In the case of small electronic goods, products can have a life-cycle as short as 6–9 months, therefore the speed at which product innovations are brought to market is crucial to the success of both retailer and supplier.

Corporate design

If a retailer is own-label active, then establishing a department to manage the corporate brand is essential. This is particularly important in packaged goods retailing, where the graphical representation on the outside of the product is what sells the item. The use of logos, corporate style and colours are all of concern here, and a retailer may issue a corporate design manual to ensure that all own-label suppliers conform to the same graphical standard. People who work on new packaging designs, whether outside design agencies or internal design studios, will also use the manual.

THE RETAIL BUYING PROCESS: A TRADITIONAL VIEW

Retail buying is one of a number of instances where an individual is purchasing products on behalf of a business organisation. The activity can therefore be classified as organisational buying and so the traditional theory of organisational buying behaviour can be called upon in order to provide an understanding of the process retailers use when buying products for their stores to sell, and to provide some indication of the likely behaviour of retail buyers in their role as organisational purchasing personnel.

In their extensive study of organisational buying behaviour Webster and Wind (1972) devised a general model of the organisational buying process. An adaptation of this model is shown in Figure 2.3.

Recognition of retail customer needs

Product management contributes to the strategic success of a retail business. As discussed in chapter one, the product range needs to be managed so that

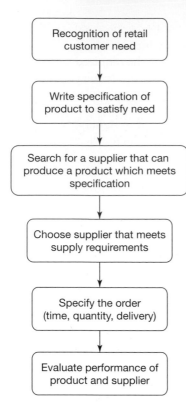

Figure 2.3 **A traditional view of the organisational buying process, adapted to retail buying**

the changing needs of customers can be satisfied. The recognition of new product requirements is the starting point for a series of buying decisions. Tracking customer requirements is part of the buyer's responsibility in many retailers, in terms of 'keeping an ear to the ground'. The following information sources may be used:

- internal sales data;
- trade publications;
- consumer publications;
- suppliers;
- market research (internal or external);
- competitor analysis.

This aspect of product management will be discussed in more detail in chapter four.

Write specification of product to satisfy need

The identified or recognised customer requirement then has to be turned into a product opportunity for the retailer. This stage of the buying process involves the consideration of a set of product features which blend together in the most appropriate way to benefit the target customer. Once this process has been carried out, a record of the product features will be specified, either on paper in the form of a technical specification and/or in the physical format as an approved product prototype (see chapter four for further detail). In reality, this second stage frequently starts the buying process, with a product suggestion (often from a supplier), followed by an evaluation of market opportunity for that product by the retailer. However, refinement of product features is likely to be required even if the product was a supplier's suggestion, particularly if the product is to be marketed under a retailer's own-label or brand.

Search for a supplier

Even though one particular supplier may have made a product suggestion, this does not necessarily mean that it will be the supplier who ultimately receives an order for that product. It may not have the capacity to produce the product in the quantities required, or the price may not be as competitive as that of another supplier offering similar products. The search for suppliers and the assessment of the potential of suppliers suggests that there are many alternatives for a retailer to choose from. This is often not the case (see chapter five), but a supplier's ability to meet the requirements of the retailer in the supply of an individual product is certainly a decision that has to be made in many buying situations.

Specify order

Once the product and supplier combination has been decided, the supply requirements have to be formalised in terms of how, when and where the product is delivered. It will also be necessary at this stage to determine the quantities needed (see chapter six).

Evaluate performance of product and supplier

Evaluation of the buying process is essential if the product management objectives are to be met. Monitoring performance involves both quantitative measures, such as sales information and supplier performance indicators, and qualitative measures, such as customer research and feedback via retail sales personnel. From a long term view of product management, learning from buying errors is as important as achieving sales success.

One of the drawbacks of the traditional buying process model is that it assumes that for every organisational buying situation the buyer goes through this whole process. Obviously, the cereals buyer at Tesco plc would not need to do this when placing an order for a familiar product like Kellogg's Cornflakes for example. The 'buy-class' framework shown in Figure 2.4 acknowledges that in certain contexts the buyer will omit some of the stages shown in the traditional retail buying process (Figure 2.3).

Buy class	New Task	Modified re-buy	Straight re-buy
Stages			
Recognition of retail customer need	Yes	No	No
Write specification of product to satisfy need	Yes	Maybe	No
Search for supplier to produce specified product	Yes	Maybe	No
Select supplier	Yes	Maybe	No
Specify order	Yes	Yes	Yes
Evaluate performance of product and supplier	Yes	Yes	Yes

Figure 2.4 **Different buying situations and the effect on the buying process**
Source: Adapted from Davies 1993: 66

In the new-task buying situation, all the stages outlined above will be carried out even if, as frequently happens, they do not follow this sequence. An example of the new-task buy is where a retailer has identified a new own-label product opportunity. It is necessary for the retailer to consider the positioning of the product in line with customer requirements, establish the product and supplier criteria, select a supplier, draw up the order detail, and then monitor the performance of the new product.

The modified re-buy is a situation where there is a necessity to change some, but not all, of the product and supplier variables. A situation that could be classed as a modified re-buy is where a supplier has not performed to the retailer's satisfaction, and a new supplier is introduced. Similarly, there may be a problem with a minor product feature, such as the packaging; therefore some of the stages of the buying process have to be revisited, but the whole process does not have to be started from scratch.

In the straight re-buy situation, the retail buying process is routine. The only stage that is involved is specifying the order. For example, when re-stocking an existing product, the only decision would be product quantities and delivery times. All the other variables would stay the same.

BUYING COMMITTEES

The extent to which buyers have authority to place orders on behalf of their organisations varies from one retailer to another. In some retail businesses, buyers must have orders over a certain value sanctioned by their operational superior. In others, buyers have the autonomy to run their departments as they see fit, which enables a more entrepreneurial approach to be taken, but buyers ultimately stand or fall according to the performance of their department in terms of sales and profits (see chapter eight). A balanced approach can be maintained through the use of a buying committee, where both the product itself and the buying plans proposed for that product are scrutinised by a panel of experts within the organisation. The main advantages and disadvantages of using a buying committee are given in Figure 2.5.

The different buy classes shown in Figure 2.4 illustrate how retail buying decisions vary in their complexity and involvement. They can also have a direct bearing on the involvement of buying committee members in the process. In a new-task situation, many buying personnel will be involved either directly or indirectly, whereas straight re-buys may well be carried out by one member of the buying team (the assistant buyer, for example).

The retail decision-making unit

When various members of the buying committee gather to consider a purchase for the retail organisation, they will be acting as a decision-making unit (DMU). The theory of the roles that people play within the DMU in organisational buying have been explored by the traditional organisational buying behaviour theorists, and these can be applied to the retail buying committees when they are used for product management decision-making.

Advantages
- Buying is sanctioned by the highest authority, so the decision is not that of the individual, but of the whole organisation.
- The cumulative experience of many senior people within the retailer is brought to the decision-making process.
- Experts can be called upon to make a contribution on specific aspects of the decision.

Disadvantages
- Gathering the committee takes time, so buying opportunities may be missed.
- Senior individuals may use their status to force their personal opinions through the committee process.
- Different members of the committee will have different areas of expertise and different knowledge gaps, which may make consensus difficult and lead to conflict.

Figure 2.5 **Buying committees: advantages and disadvantages**

Sometimes referred to as the 'initiator', the *user* is the person who directly uses the product item. In retail buying the user is a retailer's customer, or potential customer. It is difficult to involve customers directly in retail buying decisions, so a decision-making unit must consult market research sources and retail sales personnel to obtain an accurate representation of the customer's viewpoint. Some of the larger retail concerns, such as Safeway plc, the UK multiple grocer, have consumer panels as part of their marketing research operations, to provide qualitative feedback on new initiatives.

People who play the role of the *influencer* in the decision process come from various sources. Technologists, designers and engineers provide expert opinion on specific product attributes, whilst merchandisers or stock controllers exert a commercial influence, based on the knowledge of previous sales patterns of similar products.

The *buyer* is the person who organises the day-to-day running of the buying process. Buyers themselves or their assistants usually carry out this role, which is different to the role of the *decider*, who makes final decisions regarding the purchase of products. The decider is normally in a position of higher authority in the buying office, such as a buying director or merchandise manager, and essentially sanctions and approves proposed buying plans; but in a straight re-buy situation buyers, or even their assistants, may act in both the buyer and the decider roles.

The *gatekeeper's* role is to control the flow of information into the decision-making unit. It may be taken by a junior member of the buying team who makes the initial assessments of products and suppliers, and therefore checks the flow of irrelevant information into the group. On the other hand, a buying controller or a merchandise manager, who controls information because of their seniority or experience in product markets, may perform the role.

In order to illustrate these roles, the example of the purchase of a new kitchen appliance by a multiple hardware/homeware retailer is outlined in Box 2.3

BOX 2.3   COLLECTIVE DECISION-MAKING

In response to the growing trend towards specialist kitchen appliances, the kitchenware buyer for a medium-sized homeware retailer has been considering the purchase of a new product item: a home pasta-making machine.

In order to evaluate the likely demand for this product, the buyer analysed a number of secondary sources, including market research reports and suppliers' catalogues. He also canvassed the views of a number of store managers, who turned out to be predominantly in favour of the product idea. In collaboration with the merchandiser, a sales estimate for the pasta-maker was drawn up.

The buyer asked his assistant to call in a selection of sample pasta-makers and to obtain prices from a number of suppliers. When the samples arrived he showed them to the other people working in the buying department, the assistant buyer, the merchandiser and the buying assistant, and between them the buying department chose the sample which in their opinion had the best design and offered the most variety of pasta shapes to the customer. They then considered which products represented the best value for money and they also considered whether one or a range of alternative brands of pasta-makers should be stocked. The merchandiser felt at this stage that one product variation should be trialled: a higher order quantity placed with one supplier would give more scope for price negotiation than small quantities placed with a few suppliers.

The three samples that had been considered the best in the department's informal product evaluation were then passed to the product technologist for an initial assessment of the product's ability to perform and meet safety standards. A brief report was prepared for the buyer. Having read the report the buyer rejected one of the samples on the basis of difficulty of operation; he then presented the two remaining samples to his merchandise manager. The merchandise manager liked the idea, and told the buyer that he had seen a pasta-making machine on a stand at a trade fair which he had attended in Germany the previous week. He retrieved a catalogue from his briefcase and gave it to the buyer, who immediately contacted the unfamiliar company to obtain a sample and price. The product was comparable to the other two samples in the selection and so the buyer presented all three samples at a departmental range review two days later.

The buyers, merchandisers, technologist and senior management all discussed the product features and benefits as well as prices, and in the end the sample from a local distributor was selected as best value for money. The merchandise director, who stated that it was important for the retailer to be innovative providing the stock investment was not too high, sanctioned a trial order.

Group dynamics

The roles fulfilled by buying personnel in their operational day-to-day activities can be generalised to a certain degree. However, each person who contributes to the process is an individual, with his or her own set of characteristics, background and personality. Buyers have often played the role of opinion leader and change agent in the retail organisation, and as such may have a form of authority over those with 'higher' status within the organisation. Group dynamics, therefore, can often influence the way in which individual retail decision-making units operate. In addition, the culture of the organisation in which the DMU operates will also have a bearing on the buying process. For example, some retailers have a highly structured hierarchy in their buying offices, through which product plans have to be dragged in a series of presentations and reviews, whilst others have a flatter, more entrepreneurial culture, where new ideas are quickly trialled and either supported or eliminated. Similarly, the external business environment may also impact on the way in which the group works together; for example, in a growing economy more risks may be allowed, whereas in adverse trading conditions buying organisation personnel may be less confident to implement new ideas without a consensus of opinion. Any person entering the field of the retail buying office, whether as an employee or as a potential supplier, should familiarise themselves with the workings of the various individuals within the buying organisation and how the organisation works as a whole.

LIMITATIONS OF THE TRADITIONAL BUYING PROCESS MODELS

The generalist nature of the two models shown in Figures 2.3 and 2.4, which were grounded in the field of industrial buying rather than retail buying, means that the complexity of the retail buying process is significantly underplayed. Product and market specifics often have considerable influence on the way in which the buying process is carried out. For example, seasonal products such as coats or dresses will be bought in a very different way to a staple product like washing powder (see chapter six). Likewise the relationship between the retailer and the supplier will have a significant bearing on the way in which the buying process is carried out (discussed in detail in chapter five) and this is not acknowledged in the models. Another criticism of the traditional buying process models is that they concentrate on operational tasks and neglect the strategic elements of a buyer's job, such as range planning, supplier development and profitability management. The buying operation itself is described in isolation, without consideration of its relationship with other operational areas of product management, such as space allocation or promotional planning (see Figure 1.4). None the less, proposing product areas to be carried, selecting products and selecting suppliers are the key responsibilities of retail buying personnel (Swindley 1992) and so these traditional models do provide a preliminary introduction to the retail buying process.

BUYING GROUPS

The buying aspect of retail product management is a time consuming process and requires considerable expertise, which are resources that some retailers, especially small, independent concerns, do not have access to internally. One solution that might be viable for a retailer of this type is to become a member of a buying group. Buying groups effectively act as a buying organisation, but instead of acting on behalf of stores that are owned by the same business, they act on behalf of stores that are owned by many different business operators.

Buying groups can be found in most sectors of the retail industry. Many small convenience stores rely on the services of 'symbol' groups, such as Spar and Mace, to give access to product management services and buying economies on a wide range of products through the collation of ordering quantities and the use of wholesaling operations. The extent to which the stores have to conform to a standardised store fascia and mode of operation varies from group to group.

Buying groups are also part of the international retail scene. Some buying organisations have a network of buying offices across the globe, sourcing on behalf of a group of retailers with similar operating methods. Associated Merchandising Corporation, for example, operates on behalf of some of the largest US department store chains and has buying offices in the Far East, Asia and Europe. Other retail groups are formed by key players from a number of geographically separate retail markets getting together to share expertise in buying and other operational areas. Associated Marketing Services is an international retail alliance made up of twelve powerful European grocery retailers who between them operate over 24,000 stores. The main product-related operational benefits gained by members of this affiliation are buying economies and power, and buying expertise in a wide supply market; however, other advantages include the transfer of expertise in areas such as trading formats, technology and systems, brand formulation and other marketing activities. The group also represents a powerful political voice which can be used to lobby governments on issues of concern to members (Robinson and Clarke-Hill 1995).

The use of combined buying power can offer the small, independent retailer many of the advantages of the multiple's centralised buying organisation, whilst retaining a degree of entrepreneurial independence for the retail operator. It can also allow large and powerful retailers to spread their influence on a wider scale in a global retail environment.

Buying alliances

In the competitive world of retailing, the major players have become adept at exploring a whole gamut of strategies to achieve some kind of advantage over their rivals. Buying expertise is a rare and highly valued commodity in retailing and a number of large retailers have explored ways of tapping into each other's area of expertise in the pursuit of their own corporate objectives. One method is to form a buying alliance with a fellow retailer. A recent joint venture between Tesco plc, the superstore giant, and Grattans, the major UK mail order company, is enabling Tesco to further expand its retail format portfolio by entering the direct mail order market.

CONSUMER-LED APPROACHES TO RETAIL PRODUCT MANAGEMENT

One of the problems associated with a large and complex retail organisation is that there is a danger that those people responsible for carrying out the buying for a retailer may get detached from the realities of retailing. Buyers are sometimes criticised by store personnel for 'sitting up there in the ivory tower of head office', and whilst a buyer cannot be expected to be in stores every day, there has been a move to alter product management structures in retailers to link head office buying more closely with store-level activity and to gear all product management activities to the consumer. Reacting and responding to the purchasing requirements of customers and anticipating their future needs and wants, based on market research and analysis rather than 'gut feeling', is at the crux of consumer-led product management. The buying office organisation described in this chapter is changing in the light of this new approach to buying. The merchandiser's role is expanding to reflect the growing reliance on information systems to guide the process and the need to make fast, analytical judgements on how products are performing.

In some retailers the merchandiser's role has emerged as that of a category manager's role, which is seen to be the most appropriate way for a consumer-led approach to be organised. Here, the buyer–merchandiser dyad is abandoned in favour of a broader, cross-functional organisation, with more emphasis on teams than on individual roles. In this approach to product management, areas of product responsibility are likely to be narrower than in a traditional buying department, but the category manager is involved in the performance of a range of products from idea conception right through production, supply, store distribution, to final consumer sales and, if necessary, after-sales. In effect he or she is a central retail manager for a small part of the total retail offer. The success of that part comes from reacting quickly to the changing sales patterns of a particular product area and managing the product most effectively and profitably.

A consumer-led approach makes a direct link between the manufacture and supply of product and the demand patterns found in consumer markets, and therefore relies on close collaboration between product managers in both retailer and supplier organisations. Chapter three explores the role of the category management within a consumer-led management organisation in detail, but Figure 2.6 shows the essential differences between a traditional retail buying organisation and a consumer-led buying organisation.

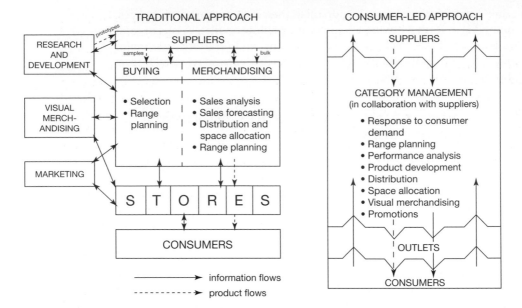

Figure 2.6 **A traditional buying organisation compared with a consumer-led buying organisation**

SUMMARY

In this chapter the way that retailers have traditionally organised for the product management process has been outlined. Multiple retailers, by definition, have to a greater or lesser degree a central buying operation, which liaises with the retailer's supply sources and makes decisions about product variety and assortment on behalf of the network of outlets. Centralisation not only brings the economic advantages of large scale buying, but also allows a retailer to control the implementation of retail brand strategies through the product range.

The importance of the people who carry out this vital and multi-faceted task can be overlooked in the effort to systemise retail operations. Retail product management personnel need to possess a unique combination of high-calibre skills and personal attributes to succeed in a highly responsive and deadline orientated working environment. An organisational structure that supports this role is essential if product management goals are to be achieved.

MINI CASE STUDY 2   ASSOCIATED INDEPENDENT STORES

Associated Independent Stores (AIS) is a non-food voluntary buying group that operates on behalf of around 250 independent retailers. Together the members have around 550 outlets and a combined turnover of £1.2 million, which approximately equates to the turnover of the department store market leader, Debenhams. Although department store retailers account for less than half of the membership, they dominate the organisation in terms of volume bought through the organisation.

AIS is a non-profit-making concern. Members pay an annual subscription to the organisation which varies according to their individual turnovers. By collating their orders, the individual members are able to gain access to a much wider range of merchandise than they otherwise could. The small retailer is often faced with a restricted supply base because of its inability to reach minimum quantities imposed by manufacturers. The buying group's ability to negotiate competitive prices for its members gives the independent an opportunity to compete against the multiple retailers as well as improve profit margins.

Based in Solihull, near Birmingham, geographically central in the UK, the AIS office consists of a series of showrooms that offer the independent buyer the opportunity to view merchandise in four main product classifications: fashion, housewares, furniture and floor coverings. In addition AIS holds around forty sample shows a year in specific fashion and furniture product categories, and provides a clothing buying service to members with limited internal resources. An important and growing part of the service to members is the development of AIS own-branded merchandise by its team of product managers. These ranges are shown alongside supplier branded products at the sample shows, and include 'First Avenue' fashions for both women and men, 'Classmates' school wear, 'First Impressions' linens and cookware and 'Guildcrest' furniture. The ranges are developed with suppliers from a global market. By acting as an administrative intermediary, AIS makes payments to suppliers for the total group shipment, and then invoices the individual stores for their individual purchases.

The structure of the AIS organisation is similar to that found in the buying office of a multiple retailer. Product managers look after specific categories of merchandise and liase with suppliers on behalf of the member stores; however, representatives from the retail members are involved in all aspects of the organisation, including the board of directors. A small committee of store buyer representatives might be called upon to pre-select merchandise prior to an AIS sample show, for example.

As well as the benefits available in buying operations, members also receive a weekly summary of the AIS group sales and regular detailed sales analysis reports on specific product areas, allowing members to compare their own performance with similar retail businesses. They can also access a wide range of marketing support services in areas such as marketing intelligence, visual merchandising, point of sale promotions and advertising. A training service is also offered and networking opportunities are organised with the view to reducing the isolation that independent retailers can feel.

(Source: Mintel 1998)

NOTE

1 A concession is best described as a business within a business, or a shop-within-shop. A set area or a pre-determined amount of space is devoted to a specific range of products, the supply of which is controlled by an entity other than the host retailer. The concessionaire pays the host on the basis of a fixed rental rate, or as a percentage of sales, and may provide their own staff to sell the products.

REVIEW QUESTIONS

1 When recruiting graduates for buying and merchandising careers, what qualities would be deemed essential and desirable for (a) buyers and (b) merchandisers?
2 Discuss the key responsibilities of merchandise directors, buyers and merchandisers.
3 Describe the role of the influencer within a retail decision-making unit.
4 Referring to the case study on Associated Independent Stores, discuss the benefits that membership of a buying group can bring to small retail businesses.

DISCUSSION QUESTIONS

1 Discuss the role played by the organisational structure in the achievement of product management objectives.
2 In multiple retailers, buying decisions are rarely made by one person alone. Discuss the reasons why this is so.
3 Make a comparison between the traditional approach to product management and the consumer-led approach to product management, within the context of one retail sector.
4 Outline the traditional buying process for a chosen product item. Discuss instances that allow some of the stages of the process to be omitted.

REFERENCES AND FURTHER READING

Cash, R.P., Wingate, J. and Friedlander, J.S. (1995) *Management of Retail Buying*, John Wiley, New York

Diamond, J. and Pintel, G. (1997) *Retail Buying*, 5th edn, Prentice-Hall, Englewood Cliffs, NJ.

Freathy, P. and O'Connell, F. (1998) 'The role of the buying function in airport retailing', *International Journal of Retail and Distribution Management* **26** (6): 247–56.

McGoldrick P.J. (1990) *Retail Marketing*, McGraw Hill, Maidenhead, Berks.

Miller, L. (1997) 'The changing role of buyers', *Drapers Record Focus*, October.

Mintel (1998) *Department Stores: Retail Report* (March), Mintel International Group, London.

Robinson, T.M. and Clarke-Hill, C.M. (1995) 'International alliances in European retailing', *International Review of Retail, Distribution and Consumer Research* **5** (2): 167–84.

Swindley, D. (1992), 'The role of the buyer in UK multiple retailing', *International Journal of Retail Distribution Management* **20** (2): 3–15.

Webster F.E. and Wind, Y. (1972) *Organisational Buyer Behaviour*, Prentice-Hall, Englewood Cliffs, NJ.

Wills, J. (1999), *Buying and Merchandising Strategies: New Roles for a Global Operation*, Financial Times Retail and Consumer, London.

chapter
three

CATEGORY
MANAGEMENT

INTRODUCTION

The preceding chapter on buying organisations described a set-up that is
common in multiple retailers, where product management activities are
essentially shared between buyers and merchandisers working in tandem
within a product-orientated department. The decisions of the buyer and
merchandiser teams are subject to scrutiny and influence by specialist experts
and then authorised by a management hierarchy in the central office. The
chapter concluded with a discussion of the emerging approach to product
management that allows for a closer relationship between the supply of
products and the customer, referred to as the consumer-led approach.

Consumer-led product management has become increasingly widespread
since the 1990s. It is the principle behind Efficient Consumer Response (ECR)
and Quick Response (QR), the two main 'management systems' to have
evolved out of the general philosophy of allowing consumer demand to control
all supply chain activity. ECR is the manifestation of consumer-led product
management in the fast-moving consumer goods sector, while QR usually
refers to the supply management of more fashion orientated merchandise.
This chapter concentrates on ECR, in order to illustrate how category
management has evolved as a buying and merchandising strategy and the
effect that this approach has had on buying organisational structures and roles.
Further differences between ECR and QR will be considered in chapter six.

EFFICIENT CONSUMER RESPONSE (ECR)

ECR is an approach to supply chain management which originated in the US and gained support from major European retailers. It is a managerial approach that starts with consumer demand and then gears the whole of the supply chain to responding to that demand. It is a customer-driven, demand-pull product management system: 'a seamless interface from consumer purchase to manufacturing schedules' (Lowson *et al.* 1999: 40); it is different to a supply-push or buying-led approach, which is based on the principles of sales forecasting, with products supplied in preparation for estimated demand. ECR, however, encompasses much more than a stock control system; it involves not only all the operational areas of retail management, but also the way in which retailers, suppliers and third party service suppliers (such as logistics companies) work together to achieve two fundamental objectives simultaneously: maximising customer satisfaction and minimising total costs.

ECR as a concept emerged in the US in the late 1980s as retailers, particularly in the grocery sector, faced increasing price competition from discounters. In order to avoid a downward-spiralling price-orientated battle between suppliers and retailers, all vying for an increased share of diminishing profit margins, a new philosophy emerged which promoted the idea of retailers and their suppliers establishing mutually beneficial, co-operative, cost cutting working practices, with the critical success factor of final customer satisfaction as the key driver of all initiatives. Figure 3.1 illustrates the underlying reasoning of ECR.

Efficient consumer response emerged in Europe in the early 1990s. In the shaping of efficient consumer response a number of high profile retailer and supplier partnerships trialled new management initiatives and systems under the guidance of some well-known management consultancies who had seen how successful the just-in-time philosophy had been in gaining efficiency in the supply chain for manufacturing companies. Just-in-time manages the supply of components according to their usage in a production unit, whereas ECR manages the supply of goods through the retail supply chain according

---

BOX 3.1 ECR INITIATIVES

The following selected retailers and suppliers have been involved in ECR initiatives:

Suppliers Colemans of Norwich (Robinsons Britvic), Kraft Jacobs Suchard, Birds Eye Walls, Procter & Gamble, Nestlé, Coca-Cola.

Retailers Tesco, Safeway, Somerfield, J. Sainsbury, Coop Italia, Dansk, Promodes Caprabo, Delhaize Le Lion, A. Heijn.

In addition the following consultancies have played a major part in progressing the ECR concept: Coopers & Lybrand, Kurt Salmon Associates.

(Sources: Lowson *et al.* 1999; Fernie and Sparks 1998; Fernie 1999; GEA 1994)

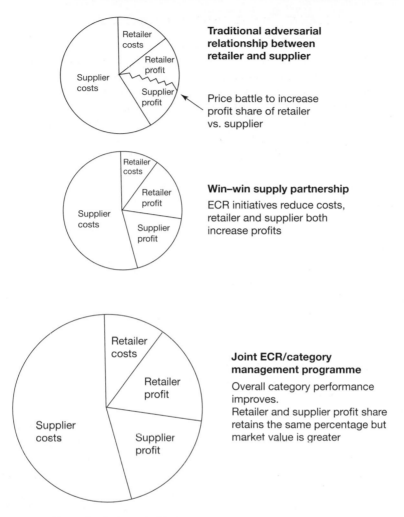

Traditional adversarial
relationship between
retailer and supplier

Price battle to increase
profit share of retailer
vs. supplier

Win–win supply partnership
ECR initiatives reduce costs,
retailer and supplier both
increase profits

Joint ECR/category
management programme
Overall category performance
improves.
Retailer and supplier profit share
retains the same percentage but
market value is greater

Figure 3.1 **The principles of efficient consumer response**

to their demand by consumers. ECR is not a small undertaking, as its various facets, shown in Figure 3.2, illustrates.

Figure 3.2 shows the scope of ECR as an holistic system, encompassing a broad range of activities where improvements in efficiency might be made. These activities might previously have been boxed into 'supply chain' and 'retail management' activities. Within an ECR system, such boundaries become meaningless because all parties work as 'allies' with consumer purchasing power and patterns as the focus for all activities. The level of efficiency gained in the satisfaction of customers is the measure of success of the system, and the rewards are obtainable by all the contributing allies in the system. The first level of activities (efficient store assortment, product introductions, promotions and replenishment) are chiefly concerned with

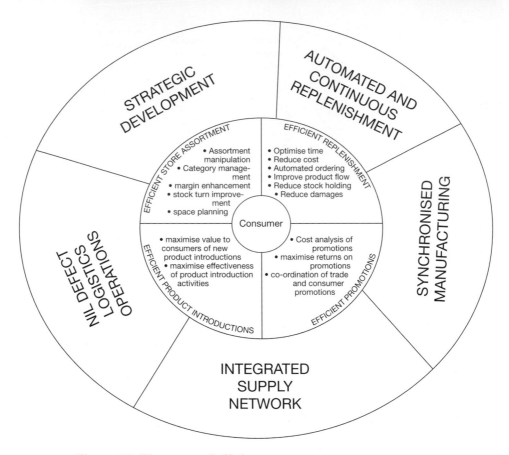

Figure 3.2 **The scope of efficient consumer response**

the management of consumer demand and the initial response to it, whilst the second level (automated and continuous replenishment, synchronised manufacturing, integrated supply networks, nil defect logistics and strategic development) are more concerned with the management of product supply.

Information flow and data technology

A key feature of ECR, which was omitted from Figure 3.2 for the sake of clarity, is the information flow (see Figure 3.3). ECR relies on efficient information flows above all else, and as such the development of ECR systems has relied on the increasing sophistication of 'enabling technologies' such as electronic data interchange (EDI) and the internet. In addition, many of the improvements that needed to be made within an ECR system depended on high levels of data analysis. This would not be possible if data management technologies had not been available to provide the information upon which improvement action could be taken (Fernie and Sparks 1998). The con-

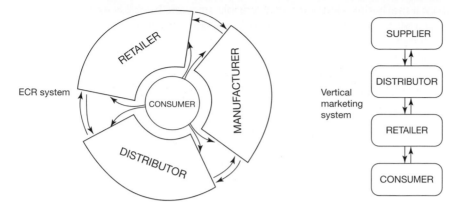

Figure 3.3 **Information flow in an ECR system, contrasted with a vertical marketing system**

tributing allies within an ECR system cannot be efficiently geared to the consumer unless data are managed and shared between all parties. Information flows within the ECR system are complex but, like the operational activities, are centred on the consumer from all angles, rather than solely from the retail perspective, as in a more traditional vertical marketing system.

As data management continues to improve, responding to individual rather than collective demand patterns is the next logical step in the management of supply, as suggested by Lowson *et al.* (1999: 43) in their description of a more 'tailored' form of ECR entitled ACR (automated consumer response):

- linking through alliances and information technology;
- optimal sourcing strategies (not just lowest cost);
- cutting cycle times in replenishment and product development;
- improving distribution systems;
- building new, integrated information architectures for merchandising, micro-merchandising and forecasting;
- category management;
- better targeting of consumer needs;
- new performance measurement systems.

CATEGORY MANAGEMENT

When organising for an ECR system, category management is a useful framework within which the areas of demand management for efficiency improvements can be considered. As such, an ECR initiative embraces category management as a new concept and business role that aims to optimise the range of products stocked in store and the efficiency of promotions, new product introductions and product replenishment. The establishment of a group of products as a category, which essentially have similar demand patterns, are reasonable substitutes for one another and can be viewed from a marketing viewpoint as a sensible strategic business unit on which to base a marketing plan, has been an important contribution to the successful implementation of ECR programmes. According to Harris (cited in GEA 1994), category management is a philosophy, a process and an organisational concept. These three parts of the category management description will be used to frame a further discussion of category management.

Category management as a philosophy

As an approach to thinking about how products are managed within a retail business, category management requires a broader vision than its preceding management orientation, which typically would be buying and merchandising led. Rather than being chiefly concerned about products from a features and procurement viewpoint and then forecasting sales for those products, category managers have first and foremost to consider the performance of the category in relation to consumer demand and then strive for the most profitable way to supply that demand. Consideration of features and procurement therefore become a part of, but not the focus of, the category manager's remit, while forecasting is replaced by responding.

Fundamental to the adoption of a category management philosophy is the way in which suppliers are viewed. Whether they are termed partners or allies, the key to the philosophy is supplier integration. Traditional lines defining functions that a supplier performs are broken down as competencies are shared as well as information. If a supplier is able to perform an aspect of product management more efficiently (for example product development), then it should contribute that part of the process. If a retailer is more efficient, then it should perform the function. The resulting efficiency gains lead to a lower cost product, and the cost savings can be negotiated between the parties.

Category champions

Many of the ECR projects that have helped to develop the category management philosophy have involved large multiple retailers and leading product/market suppliers (see Box 3.1). The suppliers who take on a major role in the category management process are often referred to as category champions or category captains; whilst they are expected to be able to accept the presence of other suppliers and their contribution to the overall success of the category from the consumer's (and retailer's) point of view, they have a major interest in the category and its performance as a whole because their own success is dependent upon it. For example, many category champions produce assortment plans or planograms for retailers that include all products within a category, whether they are their own, another supplier's brand or the retailer's own-branded products. A supplier that is in a very dominant position within a category may even manage the inventory for a retailer (see 'Supplier-managed inventory', chapter six).

THE CATEGORY MANAGEMENT PROCESS

Category management is generally viewed as a step-by-step planning and implementation process that helps retailers and suppliers to achieve both performance-based objectives and longer term strategic aims. This process is outlined in Figure 3.4.

Category definition	Define the category	Determine the products that make up the category from a consumer's perspective. Consider the role of sub-categories or individual SKUs taken in the category. ↓
	Establish the strategic role of the category in the total product assortment ↓	Develop a strategic plan for the category, considering long term trends
Category planning	Establish the performance measures for the category ↓	Determine the way in which the performance of a category will be evaluated. Consider various costing and profitability approaches
	Formulate a strategy for the category ↓	Develop a marketing and supply development plan to achieve both short term and long term category objectives
	Establish the category marketing mix ↓	Determine the various tactics to be used within the marketing and supply plan, e.g. space allocation, promotions
Category management implementation	Establish category management roles ↓	Assign responsibilities for category management implementation within both retailer and supply partner organisations
	Category review	Measure, monitor and modify the category

Figure 3.4 **The category management process**

Source: Adapted from Fernie and Sparks, *Logistics and Retail Management*, (1998: 33), Kogan Page Publishers

Definition of a category

The way in which a category of merchandise should be defined has yet to be fully established, but there is general agreement that it should be established by the way consumers buy the product in question (Wills 1999). Generally, products within a category should be reasonable substitutes for one another (differences being forged by criteria such as brand, flavour or colour variation, product quality and price level), although products within some categories might have an element of being complementary to one another. For example, some grocers might consider 'exotic foods' as a category, into which products such as refried beans, taco shells and salsa might all fall; these are complementary rather than substitute products, but in the purchase of such products it is more logical for consumers if they are displayed together. Some categories may have recognisable sub-categories which may become categories in their own right; for example, a 'hair-care' category might be broken down into sub-categories of shampoo, conditioner, two-in-one conditioners, and styling products. The definition of a category is likely to vary among retailers, according to the size and degree of specialisation in the format used.

The role of the SKU within the product category

When a retail product manager is reviewing the choice within a product category, the individual roles that are played by the different brands or product variations will be acknowledged (McGrath 1997). Some products within a category are 'traffic builders', generating high sales and having a large market share: they draw customers into the store and their absence would risk customer loss. Other products, such as own-label goods, have roles that are clearly concerned with achieving sales or profit objectives. Some stock keeping units (SKUs) create excitement or play a key role in the reinforcement of the retail brand image and some products play roles that are directly confrontational to other members of the category, for example an own-branded product that fights for market share with a brand leader, or a low price own-label variant of a frequently purchased item that defends retail market share and promotes store loyalty. Each member of the category (SKU) should be making an individual contribution to the performance of the category. If a brand or variation does not have a clear role, then a product management decision may need to be taken. For example, could one brand be deleted and the sales successfully transferred to another, more profitable brand? Does the category include enough excitement generators? If the category falls within a growing market, can interest be increased and sales within the whole category further improved by offering more variations of excitement generating products?

The strategic role of the category

Product categories themselves have different characteristics which mean that they have to be managed in different ways in order to achieve optimum profitability. Some categories may be dominated by premium brands whilst others might be more value-driven, for example. If a category is composed largely of premium brands, then most of the brands in the category are, or should be, quite profitable. If, on the other hand, the category is comprised mostly of value and own-label brands, then the opportunity to obtain higher profit margins will be lower for both the retailer and the supplier. There may be opportunities for retailers and suppliers to work together to improve the profitability of certain product categories via product innovation and/or brand repositioning. For example, the ice-cream product category has been upgraded by the introduction of premium luxury ice-cream, ice-cream confectionery, high profile marketing campaigns by companies such as Hagen Daas and the development of premium own-label products. Beer and athletic footwear (trainers) are examples of other categories that have shifted from value to premium (Vishwanath and Mark 1999).

The role of the category within the store

Category management not only looks at the detail of the product SKU 'members' within the category, but is also concerned with the role of the whole product category within the retail outlet and the contribution the category makes to the strategic positioning of the retail brand identity. Retailers are using category management in the pursuit of product differentiation to gain a competitive advantage over their rivals; they need suppliers who understand their retail market positioning and who can help them to improve the performance of their strategic product categories, not only from the point of view of short to medium term profitability, but also to enhance an image of creativity and innovation, excitement and theatre in the store (Din 2000). Category orientated point of sale display materials can reinforce a strategic product category positioning. Figure 3.5 explores the various roles that categories might play within the store's total product assortment.

Establish the performance measures for the category

As an integral part of a management approach that looks towards efficiency in demand management as well as supply management, category management has profitability as its key performance indicator. Chapter eight discusses the different ways in which profit performance can be measured, from the very basic gross margin calculation, through to more sophisticated measures that take a whole gamut of costed activity into account. Fernie (1998: 31) recommends activity-based costing for evaluating category performance because it not only considers the costs of supply (logistics and selling) but it also takes account of the costs associated with demand management, such as the costs of product introductions and the costs of promotional activity.

Retail brand reinforcer	New categories High fashion and symbolic categories High technology product categories Includes strong manufacturer brands Create excitement and theatre in store
Cash-flow contributor	Established categories Non-symbolic categories Consistent value provision
Profit generator	Growing categories Fashion categories Symbolic categories High profit margins
Service provider	Stagnant or declining categories Staple product categories Well established market leading brands Competitive with other category providers – low profit margins
Exemplar	Growing or well established category Contains leading brands Deep and wide assortment Considered the best retail offer by target customer

Figure 3.5 **The role of the product category**

Formulate a strategy for the category

Having defined the category and its role within the retail business and established optimum profitability as the success indicator, the next step in the category management process is to draw up a strategy for that particular group of products. It is at this stage that issues such as promotional activity, product assortment planning, own-brand strategy and proprietary brand support need to be blended together in order to maximise category profit performance. The position of the category within its own life-cycle will impact upon the viability of the strategy (see chapter four).

The category mix

The set of tactics used to achieve the optimum range assortment and to obtain efficiency in promotions, product innovation and replenishment will be determined by the strategy formulated for the category. In essence the category receives its own marketing mix within the parameters of the retail branded identity. For example, by conducting efficient promotions, a retailer does not waste resources by promoting brands whose performance does not pay. Taking a more analytical approach to promotional activity can vastly improve the profitability of a product category by removing costs associated with promotional activities that are not in the best interests of the retailer's product range performance. Many promotions require time and effort to set up, data input amendments and production of special communications and packaging, and may result in deflecting sales to a product with a lower product profit (away from an own-label product for example). Unless promotional activity is going to result in overall better performance of the category or bring some other long term benefit to the retailer (such as loyalty to a store because of its offers), then it may be better to resist the promotion.

Point of sale displays can also be viewed with the same analytical judgement; for example, changes to shelf allocations or the use of point of sale materials should only be undertaken if they have the potential to improve the performance of the whole category for the retailer. Prices may also be manipulated in order to maximise category performance. The use of 'known-value' items, where there is little price elasticity, is important in value-driven categories such as packaged bread, whereas in premium-product driven categories, such as wine, retailers have more opportunity to increase margins and benefit from impulse-based promotional offers.

The way in which a retailer implements category management is best considered in the final part of the category management definition, that of an organisational concept.

CATEGORY MANAGEMENT AS AN ORGANISATIONAL CONCEPT

From the point of view of the category definition, category management requires an understanding of how customers shop; this has traditionally been the concern of marketers rather than buyers within a retail business. Category management, therefore, brings a much stronger marketing orientation to the product management process. Category management has the effect of reducing the role of the buyer and augmenting the role of the merchandiser, but essentially a category management role is a cross-functional one. According to Wileman and Jary (1997: 132): 'the intersection of buying and merchandising and marketing is the heart of retail brand management, and its focus is category management'.

The implementation of category management, like the rest of an ECR approach to product management, relies on collaborative and co-operative supply partnerships (see chapter five). Category management requires a focus team organisation that spans both supplier's and retailer's organisational boundaries.

DRAWBACKS OF CATEGORY MANAGEMENT

Category management as a central tenet of the ECR movement has provided benefits to participating retail–supplier collaborations. As an example, the mini case study at the end of this chapter documents the experience of a leading frozen food producer and an Italian retailer. However, according to Wills (1999), ECR has remained an impenetrable concept, relying too much on theory and jargon, with the costs of achieving efficiencies outweighing the resulting benefits. In addition, many of the initiatives have reflected what many well-run retailers were already doing. However, the far-reaching facets of ECR and the new philosophy of category management certainly support the more analytical approach to product management, discussed in chapter two. The full-scale adoption of category management requires a considerable amount of reorganisation within the retailer and has met with a number of inhibiting factors such as: skills shortages (for example, in enabling information technology management); the difficulty in accepting suppliers as allies or partners with whom information should be shared; the reluctance to change inappropriate organisational structures; and the lack of clear strategic plans for product ranges (Wills 1999).

Another concern with the implementation of category management is the resulting lack of variety offered to customers. Concentrating on efficiency in logistics and merchandising may result in highly efficient retailing; however, there is a risk that the consumer experience is being given lower priority. This could be a dangerous strategy when store-based retailing is becoming increasingly threatened by much more efficient (from the customer viewpoint) home-based retailing formats. Category-managed product ranges are safe and offer the majority of customers in the majority of purchase decisions 'efficient' selections of market-leading products; however, these selections may start to appear boring and over-managed. Even though there is a suggestion that information technology may help to prevent retailers drifting too far in this direction (see Box 3.2), the view that retail product assortments can become boring under category management is reinforced by Webb (1999), who asserts that retailers who put an emphasis on the profitability of the category rather than considering the holistic appeal of the store are contributing to the 'banalisation of retailing' in which product ranges are 'uninspiring and ubiquitous'.

A further drawback of category management is the threat to smaller suppliers. The practice of establishing category captains to improve the performance of the entire product category runs the risk of putting larger suppliers in a position where they can abuse their power by improving their own market share at the expense of the other suppliers within the category. It has been suggested that retailers benefit from leading suppliers fighting to contribute the most to the category management process, whilst the second and third tier brands are squeezed off the shelf. In some countries retailers are required by law to allocate a percentage of shelf space to smaller suppliers; for example, in France approximately 10 per cent of shelf space has to be given to local suppliers (McCawley 2000). Forcing smaller suppliers out of the category adds to the banalisation of retailing, resulting in the multiple retailers and major suppliers managing a category for their own purposes, whilst shoppers are driven away in the process. It is significant that retailers such as Selfridge's department store have retained a buying-led organisational structure rather than a category management structure in the pursuit of a clearly defined product differentiation strategy (Wills 1999).

BOX 3.2   INFORMATION OVERLOAD?

Information overload can seriously dent the confidence of any buyer who has used intuition and flair to tap into the kind of trends that no amount of data analysis would support. Merchandise management systems may have a positive restraining effect, but they can also stifle entrepreneurship and creativity, words that are increasingly being used in a positive sense in business management.

There is no doubt that integrated information systems have improved the availability of products in stores and have given a product manager a much more detailed view of their business. Has the product itself, however, become drowned by information overload? Responding to consumers quickly and efficiently will certainly reduce shopping frustration levels: shoppers can have what they want, when they want and where they want, as new marketing channels and retail formats open up a multitude of ways in which goods can be acquired. Does all this rapid response produce more wonderful, exceptional, inspirational 'must have' products?

Many consumers still seem less than satisfied with the product ranges on offer, criticising retailers for offering too much of the same thing and for blandness. Information technology has taken most of the laborious number crunching out of a merchandiser's job, allowing the product range to be managed more closely and strategically; but for buyers, information overload concerning past sales can prevent them looking forward with enthusiasm for new ideas. The enabler has become the controller. However, the answer to this problem may lie in the use of information technology itself (of course!).

Data mining is a process whereby captured customer data are manipulated to find linkages between people and the products that they buy, and this technique may prevent product range rationalisation going too far. One supermarket chain found that although feta cheese was a slow-selling item, a target for elimination in a category management drive perhaps, this type of cheese was predominantly purchased by customers who formed the highest-spending group. The slow seller was therefore allowed to maintain its presence within the category because of its 'high class' clientele. Like the EPOS information that went before it, data-mined information only tells a retailer about current customers and their purchases, but it does give a deeper understanding about the role that individual products play in the individual customer's shopping basket, and supports the need for 'exceptional' products.

(Source: Tredre 1995; Wills 1999)

MINI CASE STUDY 3   SAGIT–UNILEVER*

Sagit is part of the multinational conglomerate Unilever and is the leading frozen food supplier in Italy, where frozen food is a growing market; traditionally it has had a low market penetration because of the availability of fresh alternatives and a lack of consumer interest. However, as the quality of frozen foods has improved, Italian consumers have started to favour their convenience from the points of view of storage, meal preparation and waste avoidance.

Sagit has been involved in a number of category management projects with its retail trading partners. As in other projects, Sagit, as the supply partner, has been able to bring a wealth of information to the category management discussion on the way consumers behave. This information, derived from a number of marketing research projects, is summarised below:

- impulse purchasing of frozen foods is low;
- many customers in general grocery shopping trips do not buy frozen food at all;
- customers who buy frozen foods buy very few products (for example only two or three products are selected from a product assortment of over 250).
- frozen food buyers are store loyal rather than brand loyal;
- store promotions are found to be the most effective form of product promotion, due to the lack of brand loyalty.

The objective of Sagit's category management project with Italian retailer GS was to improve the performance of the whole category, thereby offering mutual benefits to both retail and supply partners.

The starting point was to establish which products were to be grouped as a category. To perform this task adequately, the way in which consumers approached frozen products with a view to selection was investigated. This resulted in products being grouped according to their primary ingredient (for example, meat, fish or vegetable) and then according to their function (for example, ready prepared meals, pre-prepared meal components, fancy sweet dishes and fancy savoury dishes).

The second stage of the project involved a review of the product assortment. This resulted in some changes to the product range:

- a more prominent selection from leading brands, including key product items;
- elimination of non-profitable items and those with a very marginal contribution to sales or profits;
- introduction of sixteen new products and the removal of fifty-seven existing products.

The third stage involved space management – the layout, fixturing, display and allocation of shelf space to products:

- displaying the product according to the categories of merchandise described earlier in the category definition stage, by natural product and then by use;
- a vertical presentation of products, as opposed to their lying flat;
- clearer product information;
- alternative placement of high turnover and low turnover goods to encourage shoppers to consider all products within the assortment;
- placing products with a high propensity to be impulse-purchased in more visible and busy display areas;
- placing products that are more inclined to be pre-planned purchases in areas that require customers to cover a larger proportion of the display;

- other space allocation decisions were determined by sales and profit objectives, the size of the SKU, stock-turn and lead times.
The final stage involved in-store communications:
- point of purchase material helped to define the category as a pleasant environment, for example a welcome garland was place at the start of the department;
- clear price marking was applied throughout;
- the sub-categories were clearly marked in the section of the display;
- specific product orientated point of purchase material was used to reinforce the brand leadership of Sagit's (Findus) products.

The results of the project were very encouraging, in particular for Sagit and their retail partner SG. Annual sales for the whole category improved by 5 per cent (compared to a market growth for frozen foods of 2 per cent). Sales of Sagit products increased by around one-third, and sales of GS's own-branded products increased by nearly 40 per cent. Other brands within the section experienced stable or decreased sales volumes.

There were additional benefits that were identified by qualitative research after implementation of the category management initiatives. Generally the visibility of the category had been greatly improved: 98 per cent of customers noticed the new displays and in-store communications, and were very positive about the ease and pleasantness of the shopping experience within the department. They also considered the general organisation of the department to be improved, along with the clarity of the displays, the visibility of items, prices and promotions.

* This mini case study is based on a paper published in the Proceedings of the 10th International Conference on Research in the Distributive Trades, Institute for Retail Studies, University of Stirling, 1999, and has been adapted with the kind permission of the authors Gennaro Cuomo and Alberto Pastore.

REVIEW QUESTIONS

1 Describe how category management contributes to the efficient consumer response approach to product management.
2 Outline the main objectives of category management
3 How does the role of the category manager differ from that of a buyer and a merchandiser?
4 Outline the category management process, referring to the Sagit case study to illustrate your discussion.
5 What are the main drawbacks of category management? What steps can a retailer take to overcome these?

DISCUSSION QUESTIONS

1 Compare and contrast the buying process (chapter two) and the category management process (chapter three)
2 Analyse a product category of your choice in a large supermarket according to the roles played by the various product items.

3 To what extent do you think that category management will become widespread in centralised retail buying organisations?

REFERENCES AND FURTHER READING

Din, R. (2000) *New Retail*, Conran Octopus, London.

Fernie, J. (1998) 'Relationships in the supply chain', in J. Fernie and L. Sparks, *Logistics and Retail Management*, Kogan Page, London, ch. 2.

Fernie, J. (ed.) (1999) *The Future of UK Retailing*, Financial Times Retail and Consumer Reports, London.

Fernie, J and Sparks, L. (eds) (1998) *Logistics and Retail Management*, Kogan Page, London.

Gattorna, J.L. and Walters, D.W. (1996) *Managing the Supply Chain*, Macmillan, London.

GEA Consulenti Associati di Gestione Aziendale (1994) *Supplier–Retailer Collaboration in Supply Chain Management*, Report published by the Coca-Cola Retailing Research Group – Europe.

Lowson, B., King, R. and Hunter, A. (1999) *Quick Response: Managing the Supply Chain to Meet Consumer Demand*, John Wiley, Chichester, Sussex.

McCawley, I. (2000) 'Small suppliers seek broader shelf access', *Marketing Week* 17 February.

McGrath, M. (1997) *A Guide to Category Management*, Institute of Grocery Distribution, Letchmore Heath, Herts.

Tredre, R. (1995) 'Thread barons', *Observer* 19 November.

Vishwanath, V. and Mark, J. (1999) 'Your brand's best strategy', in *Harvard Business Review on Brand Management*, pp. 169–87.

Webb (1999) in J. Fernie (ed.) *The Future of UK Retailing*, Financial Times Retail and Consumer Reports, London.

Wileman, A. and Jary, M. (1997) *Retail Power Plays*, Macmillan, London.

Wills, J. (1999) *Merchandising and Buying Strategies: New Roles for a Global Operation*, Financial Times Retail and Consumer Reports, London.

chapter four

SELECTING PRODUCTS

INTRODUCTION

Getting the right product, in terms of type and quality, might seem an easy task to the outsider, and for some products the powers of the individual may not be stretched too far in order to do so. For example, a product such as Kellogg's Cornflakes has been around for a number of decades, it has a steady demand from a loyal customer base, the recipe does not change significantly, and so the decision to buy more of this product is much more concerned with the quantity required and the time of delivery than with what the actual product is. On the other hand, it only takes a short walk around a European shopping centre in the last week of January to see examples of products that are the result of poor decision-making regarding type and quality, sitting in large quantities on shelves for the world to pick up and put down; products that will not shift, no matter how much the price has been reduced.

Making decisions about exactly what the product range should include, down to the minutest detail, has always been the crux of a buyer's job. Whether the range is selected from a manufacturer's range or is developed in-house, the final version that arrives in store is the responsibility of the buyer or selector. This chapter examines the procedures buyers go through in order to minimise those late January pile-ups. As mentioned in chapter two, many retail organisations break the buying task down so that one team of people is predominantly concerned with the qualitative aspects of a purchase (the selectors) and another team is predominantly concerned with the quantitative aspects (the merchandisers or stock controllers). In other retailers a category manager assumes the role of product selector. However, the term buyer will be used in this discussion because it is the most commonly used title for this operational task.

IDENTIFICATION OF PRODUCT NEED

Marketing theory suggests that the needs of the customer should be the trigger for a retail buying decision. However, in reality consumers in developed countries are motivated by wants and aspirations rather than physical need (Maslow 1970) and so shopping motivations include many psychologically based individual and social needs other than the basic necessity of product retrieval. A shopping trip may present the opportunity for a day out, a relief from boredom, or an opportunity to find out about new trends with a group of friends (Tauber 1972). Selecting the right product requires an understanding of the complexity of the modern shopper and an ability to blend product detail in a way that satisfies both the physical and the psychological needs of that shopper. This must be carried out within the context of the retailer's positioning strategy, referred to in chapter one.

NEW PRODUCT DEVELOPMENT

Product innovation is becoming increasingly necessary for retailers to keep customers interested in their product range. In a retail market that is saturated and competitive it is especially important to provide customers with the interest and excitement that newness engenders (Bruce and Biemans 1995). It is therefore important for retailers to be able to use product development and innovation to their best ability. Some of the larger retailers have built a facility for product innovation in-house. For fashion retailers it may be a design studio that produces sample garments using new fabrics and styling ideas. For a food retailer it may be a development kitchen that blends new combinations of ingredients for pre-prepared food products. For other products research, design and technology departments produce prototypes using the latest materials and technologies. Clearly this type of operation carries considerable overhead costs, but without the facility retailers are reliant on suppliers for new product development. Some suppliers see their competitive advantage lying in their innovative approach, but others are much less proactive, tending to follow product trends and saving costs. As the need grows to bring new products on to the market quickly, retail buyers have less time to devote to new product development, and so suppliers who are innovative will become increasingly sought after (see chapter five).

PRODUCT CATEGORY LIFE-CYCLES

When selecting products retail buyers need to be aware of the cyclical sales pattern that both individual products and product categories tend to follow. The product life-cycle theory has been a great source of debate over the years, but it is generally accepted that it has some value when it comes to understanding the sales and profit implications of products over time (Brassington and Pettitt 2000; Baker 2000).

Although the product life-cycle, which relates to a specific product item or brand, may be of some value to the buyer of branded fast-moving consumer goods, the category life-cycle is perhaps a more useful concept for many buying decisions, although it may be necessary to consider both.

The position of a product or category within its life-cycle (see Figure 4.1) can guide a buyer when making decisions about the depth of their product assortment, as shown below.

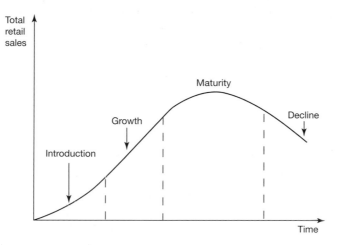

Figure 4.1 **The category life-cycle**

Introduction

In the introduction stage, a retailer offers a limited assortment, for example one brand. A new product can create excitement and could be the start of an important product category. When mobile phones were first introduced there were was little brand choice and the product was functional.

Growth

In this stage the retailer has the opportunity to increase assortment, introducing more brand alternatives and more product variations. As more consumers become interested, product variations to fulfil the needs of different target groups become viable. As the mobile phone market grew, the brand choice proliferated, alternative designs became available, and the choice of associated service packages increased, tailored to different types of user.

Maturity

A large assortment is offered in the maturity phase, including many brands and many product variations (including own-label in most product categories). The category becomes established and more competitive between retailers. As the mobile phone market matured, price became a key selling feature and distribution became extensive. Additional product features such as text messages and internet access were introduced to extend the life-cycle.

Decline

Here, the product category loses appeal, to be replaced by another growth category. Retailers should cut the assortment back to leading brands and the best-selling variation. In the case of mobile phones, health concerns may cause the product to lose appeal; otherwise the product will eventually reach saturation, when replacement and upgrading become the main opportunities for new sales.

Although the general concept of the life-cycle pattern can be useful as a basis for the understanding of consumer purchasing patterns, many products have a life-cycle that is completely different to the standard. Some products have a highly seasonal cycle which may or may not occur within an overriding category life-cycle (see Figure 4.2).

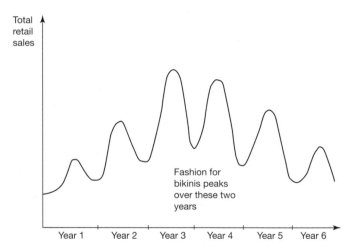

Figure 4.2 **The category life-cycle for bikinis**

Seasonality brings great sales opportunities to retailers, both in terms of the opportunity to offer new ranges of products and the opportunity to maximise sales volumes. It also presents the risk of overstocking, as outlined in chapter six.

Some products have a very steeply curved life-cycle at the growth stage and at the decline stage, with a very short period of maturity. These products can be described as fads and are particularly prevalent in the toy and teenage fashion accessories market. Again fads offer the retailer the opportunity to generate high sales over a short period of time, but the risk of having a stock-pile of an outdated fad are very high. Other products, which can be described as staple products, do not conform to the life-cycle pattern because the demand is more or less continuous, for example for sugar or orange juice.

THE INFLUENCE OF CONSUMER TRENDS ON THE RETAIL OFFER

The influences on the life-cycle of a product category are many and varied. If buyers are to use the life-cycle as a predictive tool, they must appreciate the underlying consumer trends that affect the rate of growth of the associated product market. Consumer trends include demographic trends, consumer economic trends, technological trends and societal trends, including lifestyle and fashion.

Demographics

As consumers pass through the various stages of their own personal life-cycle, the products that are relevant to their needs change, beginning with diapers and milk products, passing through the world of toys and home enter-tainment, fashion accessory fads and music orientated products in the teenage years, home furnishings and aspirational products in the twenties and thirties, followed by bulk supermarket purchases, holidays and healthcare as we reach our own maturity and decline! Thus the demographic profile of market populations, given by the unavoidable influence of birth rates and death rates, affects the potential for growth in age-relevant product markets. Demographic changes are slow moving and general and are only really relevant to a buyer in terms of the overall potential of a product category, but the extent to which retailers and producers invest in or support a particular product category may be determined by demographic trends. For example, in the late 1980s and early 1990s a number of women's wear retailers launched children's wear ranges in response to the increased birth rate at this time, for example Gap in 1986 (1990 in the UK), Next in 1988 and Principles in 1995 (Mintel 1999).

Consumer economics

The amount of personal disposable income that consumers have available to spend in retail outlets is influenced by a number of general economic factors including:

- unemployment levels;
- regional employment patterns;
- interest rate levels;
- inflation levels;
- earnings levels.

In spite of the effect of cyclical variations in economic growth, the general trend in the level of consumer expenditure in developed countries has been upwards for the last century, and so an increasing proportion of our expenditure is on discretionary purchases as opposed to the necessities of life such as food and housing. As we enter the twenty-first century, growth in many of the traditional retail sectors (such as food and clothing) is relatively stagnant, while spending levels on travel and leisure services are continuing to rise.

Like demographic trends, the effects on product choices of consumer economic health are relatively long term and general, yet it is vital for retail buyers to be sensitive to consumer confidence in the light of real and perceived economic change. In the fairly rapid onset of the economic recession of the late 1980s to early 1990s, many UK retailers reacted too slowly to a downturn in consumer expenditure, resulting in the need for heavy discounting to shift large quantities of discretionary purchase items, such as clothing, jewellery, household furnishings and appliances, which impacted upon the financial results of leading retailers of the time, notably Ratners, MFI and the Burton Group. Meanwhile, in the UK grocery sector, traditional supermarket retailers like Tesco, J. Sainsbury and Safeway launched Value, Economy and Saver ranges (respectively) in response to the constrained consumer purse and opportunistic market entry by European discount retailers such as Netto and Aldi. These own-label products, with basic packaging and rock-bottom prices, became prevalent in many food product categories in the early 1990s, yet by the end of the decade were restricted to a small number of staple items.

Social trends

Alongside demographic and economic trends, the ever-changing nature of the society which we inhabit impacts strongly on the products we choose to live amongst and consume. 'The products that we buy are a reflection of ourselves' and 'We are what we eat' are statements that reflect the relationship between people as social beings and how they spend money. The connections between societal trends and the demand for product categories and brands have been explored adequately elsewhere (for example, Corrigan 1997; Fernie 1999) and so this book will isolate a small number of product examples in order to illustrate how product managers have exploited opportunities presented by societal change (see Figure 4.3).

The influence of technology

Changes in technology can have a very serious effect on the life-cycle of a product. Retailers like Dixons and Kingfisher who have considerable interest in the electrical and electronics product markets are faced with rapid product innovations and updates. In such a market the timing of product launches and product deletions can be crucial to maximising sales volume. For example, a new product innovation that improves the quality of a computer printer would ideally be introduced at a time when the stock of the previous printer model is low. Once the new product is launched, the price of the previous model drops and there is a real danger of obsolescence. If the timing

Product example:	Washing powder in ready measured 'tablets'.
Societal trends:	Increased numbers of working women; the time-constrained consumer.
Product example:	Organic foods
Societal trends:	Health consciousness and fears; environmental and ethical concerns.
Product example:	Mobile phones
Societal trends:	Multiple occupations, time-constrained lifestyles; increased use of communication technology; safety concerns.
Product example:	Sushi – ready to eat Japanese food
Social trends:	International travel and diversity; fashionable lifestyles; health consciousness.

Figure 4.3 **Products that reflect societal change**

BOX 4.1 THE RISE AND RISE OF CONVENIENCE FOODS

The growth in pre-prepared foods over the last decade illustrates the extent to which social trends have influenced the grocery market. Products such as pre-washed salads, vacuum packed soup, frozen pizza, ready-to-eat chicken tikka masala, salad bars, and even ready-prepared bangers and mash are all available in supermarkets.

The following social trends have all played their part in moving this industry forward: longer working days; part-time (sometimes multiple part-time) occupations; increasing numbers of working women; less free time for the majority; ability and willingness to 'buy time'; increasing number of single households; fragmentation of the family nucleus; increasing participation in leisure activities; an ageing population and more elderly people living independently.

The ready-meals market was worth £786 million in 1999 (Mintel 2000). In particular, pizzas and ethnic food, which compete head-to-head with take-away food outlets, have shown strong growth recently. Grocery retailers are very enthusiastic about this trend as it allows them to develop premium product ranges, such as Tesco's Finest, Asda's Curry Pot and Stir Fry Bar, and Marks & Spencer's Organic range. A lifestyle orientation is being used to identify product variations, for example Marks & Spencer's 'Café Specials' come in stylish black packaging.

(Source: Mintel 2000; Clements 2000)

of the launch is delayed, however, the retailer runs the risk of losing first-to-market sales to a competitor.

Technological developments are not only important for the electrical sector; they can play an important part in the continuous improvement of product features, from the raw material, the production processes, the packaging – even to the method of retailing the product itself. For example, Styleyes is a service offered by the UK optical retailer Dollond & Aitchison that allows customers to see what they look like in alternative styles of glasses by using a camera lodged within a PC terminal in the store. Likewise, internet customers can send in a photograph and then overlay different styles of spectacles on to their face on a web page.

The legal requirement

Product managers have to ensure that, as well as offering consumers products that are appealing and interesting to the changing body of consumers, they are also acting within the law. The law (for example the Sales of Goods Act 1979 in the UK) states that a product which is sold has to be fit for sale and the purpose for which it is being purchased, and so a retail buyer must have detailed knowledge of the product legislation that is associated with the ranges they sell. The product may need to comply with a relevant quality standard, with respect to compatibility of technology or consumer safety for example. There may be a requirement for detailed product information, particularly with respect to claims made by product descriptions or brands, for example in 'healthy eating' or 'low fat' products. Standards and legal requirements may also apply to packaging, and the methods used for storage, display and handling of goods may be subject to health and safety regulations (meat products for example). Compliance with the law with respect to the product range may be necessary at both domestic and international levels, depending on the geographical spread of the retailer's outlets.

TRACKING PRODUCT / MARKET TRENDS

In order to ensure that product/market trends do not go undetected or their effect on the product management process ignored, a retailer may instigate some form of auditing or tracking process; however, in many instances the information gathering process is on-going and informal. Nevertheless, the following stages should be included in this process whether or not the process is formalised:

1 **Consumer trend analysis**   Identification of changes over time that allow predictions to be made about future product preferences. Will include analysis of demographic, economic, societal, technological, lifestyle and fashion trends. Information will be used from a variety of sources, including both internal records and external agencies.

2 **Product sector analysis**   In this stage of the analysis, the changes identified above should be interpreted into specific predictions with regard to the product category in question. The action of competitors should also

be taken into account; for example, is a competitor likely to be proactive or reactive in response to a product market opportunity or threat? Information gained from suppliers, with regard to new product innovations in particular, may be useful in this process.

3 **Catchment area analysis** The previous stages may reveal changes that will happen at different times in the markets that the retailer serves, or their effect may be restricted to specific geographical locations. At this stage, therefore, the consumer trends and the product sector changes must be interpreted at the local level, taking catchment area, store size and store format into consideration. Information can be gleaned from marketing data base agencies and existing store comparisons.

4 **Product range analysis** Here, the current product range is reviewed in the light of the preceding set of analyses, and decisions regarding new product category additions, category extensions and product deletions are made. Internal performance data will be scanned to show evidence of emerging sales trends.

BOX 4.2   ON-LINE TRACKING

Worth Global Style Network is an on-line news and information service for the fashion and style industries. For a subscription fee, fashion retail buyers are able to obtain a continually up-dated and extensively researched report on fashion trends. The service includes photographs of the window displays in trend-setting shops all over the world. It provides reporting from all the fashion trade fairs, right from the yarn and fabric shows that predict colours and textural trends, to the designer catwalk shows, picking out the styles and details that trigger new fashion trends. Design forecasting fashion retailers have used agencies for many years, but the web-based service provides an all-encompassing and ongoing fashion tracking service that buyers can tailor to the product area that they are responsible for.

(Source: Worth Global Style Network 2000)

THE PRODUCT SELECTION PROCESS

The product selection process starts with a product range review, in which the performance of all the products is evaluated. This may result in some being deleted or the identification of the need for a product amendment. Gaps in the range may also be established, providing opportunities for new product. Following the review, it is then necessary to establish what features the amended or new product should possess in order to satisfy consumer demand fully.

The product range review

Within the general appreciation of the long term trends that affect the product classification for which a buyer has responsibility, the product range must be regularly reviewed in order to ensure that it continues to offer the customer products of interest. Although the performance of the products within a range are monitored on a continual basis, usually via an EPOS system, most retailers carry out formal and in-depth range reviews on a regular basis to consider the performance of products and decide upon any necessary remedial action. The range review will consider both quantitative and qualitative aspects of a product's performance. Figure 4.4 illustrates the likely inputs into a range review and the kind of decisions that are made during the review.

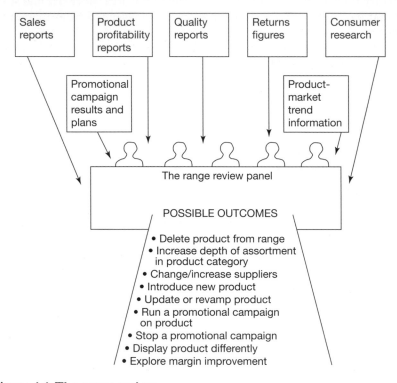

Figure 4.4 **The range review**

The range review is an all-encompassing, detailed discussion of the performance of a range of products, therefore issues such as supplier performance, promotions and in-store merchandising have to be considered alongside issues which are directly to do with the physical product. However, consideration of these indirect aspects of a product's performance are considered in other chapters of this text, leaving those aspects which are directly concerned with a product's entity to be discussed within this chapter.

PRODUCT SELECTION CRITERIA

When making decisions about introducing a new product or brand or making changes to an existing product, to update it perhaps, a buyer has to consider a product in fine detail. Each individual criterion that bears upon the product's ability to satisfy a consumer has to be considered, as well as the totality of the features.

Physical properties

These are the tangible aspects of the product, represented by size, weight and volume and by the components or ingredients. They are likely to be critical to the appeal of the product (although not always to the immediate shelf appeal, in the case of packaged goods) and will have a direct bearing on the consumer's evaluation of the product. Some products need special properties in order to perform their required function, for example a quilt has to have the property of warmth, or 'tog value', in order to be of any use, and a raincoat has to be waterproof, whilst ice-cream needs to taste sweet and delicious. Getting the physical property correct may require the help of a product technologist, employed by the retailer or a supplier.

Packaging

For many products it is the packaging that initially attracts a potential customer, and so the design of the package in which a product is enclosed is as important as the formulation of the product within. Packaging performs a variety of functions including aesthetic appeal to customers, protection of the product, added value for the customer (for example a container that can be used when empty), an aid to product use (such as a spray container), a contributor to brand identity and a vehicle for promotional messages.

Increasingly, packaging must also conform to company environmental policy and/or consumer expectations in the light of their personal environmental concerns. In addition, the design of a pack can be influenced by logistical requirements for space efficiency. For example, the boxes in which fruit juices are packaged have become increasingly tall and slim, so that more 'facings' of product can be squeezed on to supermarket shelves.

Style

Product styling has always been relevant to clothes, accessories and home furnishings, but increasingly style is finding its way into many product categories (see Box 4.3). Although difficult to define, the style of a product is generally dependent on the blend of shapes, colours and materials and has more to do with aesthetics than functionality in the product's design. For example, Apple broke the mould in computer styling when they launched the iMac; using colour and transparent materials, the product looked stylish and fun, whilst retaining top technical performance. Style is related to fashion and 'taste'; a fashion is the following of a trend in the style elements that are incorporated into a design, and the taste level is connected to the extent to which the design elements do or do not conform to established fashions. In addition, style may be manifested in the features that stimulate our sensory channels, for example the texture, smell, taste and sound of a product. The style of a product includes what Loosschilder and Schoormans (1995) refer to as 'abstract attributes', which are subject to substantial differences with respect to their recognition and perception by consumers and are therefore difficult to quantify.

Utility

A product's utility is concerned with how it performs in use. This will depend on how it is designed and produced. The following variables all bear upon the utility of a product: function; maintenance; durability; versatility; health and safety; and environmental issues.

The number of functions and their operations will be important criteria, especially for labour saving appliances and other technical goods. For example, in the purchase of a food processor, the number of functions available may make one competitor's product superior to another. The extent to which a product needs to be maintained also influences its utility. The ease of cleaning and the need for servicing are both issues that consumers will be concerned about. Leather furniture, for example, needs to be accompanied by maintenance instructions, and after-sales service provision may be a key feature for technical goods like computers.

Durability, or how long a product lasts in use, is another facet of utility. Toys, for example, need to be able to withstand considerable wear and tear without collapsing in a heap of dangerous components. The number of uses that a product offers also contributes to utility; for example, a plain dark suit is a much more versatile garment than a vibrantly coloured dress; on the other hand, the dress may have more utility for special occasions. Health and safety considerations also impact on utility: if a product proves to be dangerous to customers in normal use, then it has no utility; and the extent to which a product supports environmental concerns may bear strongly upon utility for some customers. For example, a washing machine that uses less water and power may be the differentiating factor between one appliance and another for the environmentally concerned customer, rather than the number of functions that can be performed. Utility therefore is based on the physical properties and the design of the product, and has a close relationship to quality. For example, something that is made with high quality materials and is manufactured to a high standard is more likely to be durable and to perform its functions well. However, utility, like style, is often subject to the motivations and interpretations of individuals. The ability to customise products according to individual requirements is an increasingly important trend in product design (see Box 4.3).

Product quality

Product quality is determined to a certain extent by its physical properties. However, the components or ingredients used may themselves be subject to physical variation that determines the level of quality. For example, a jumper

---

BOX 4.3 WHITE GOODS?

The term 'white goods', which was once used for refrigerators, cookers, washing machines and smaller kitchen appliances, has become something of a nonsense, since kitchen products are becoming widely available in chrome and a variety of colours, including fashionable fluorescents. The boom in lifestyle and home improvement media interest has encouraged producers and retailers to add fashion and aspirational elements to their products, instead of focusing purely on the functional aspects. Zanussi, for example, offers over 4,500 different combinations of cooking system, tailoring oven size, hob layout, fuel type and colour finish to the requirements of individual customers. Functional elements are not being ignored, however: Samsung has developed a model of microwave that can read the bar code on a frozen meal and, linking into the manufacturer's database, carries out the cooking instructions automatically.

(Source: Porter 2000)

---

may be made of 100 per cent wool, but the quality of the wool used may determine how soft and smooth the garment feels. The quality may also determine how long the garment lasts, which is an aspect of the product utility, as discussed above. The raw materials and the production processes used therefore will bear a direct influence on the overall quality level of the finished article. For some products it is important to comply with a European or international product standard in order to attain a specified level of performance or safety in use. These product standards have a numerical reference that denotes the particular performance level or safety level. Carrying the standard denotes compliance with this quality level.

Product quality is not just about performance. Customers are increasingly concerned from a social and ethical stance about what goes into a product and how it is made. For example, increasing numbers of consumers want reassurance that the ingredients of food products are grown without genetic modification or by organic farming methods. Likewise there is increasing concern about the use of child labour and sweatshop conditions for production workers in manufacturing units around the world. As consumer requirements become increasingly sophisticated attention to this type of product criterion detail will increase and retailers will need to provide reassuring information about the product for customers (see Box 13.1 in chapter thirteen).

Product quality assurance

Achieving consistency in the level of quality in the product range is very important to retailers, in order to maintain customer trust and satisfaction. Although retailers do not usually have a direct influence on the quality of product, because their role is normally buying and selling rather than manufacturing the product, it is such an important part of their own retail marketing strategy that they may feel it necessary to invest in a system of quality assurance to make sure that goods of inferior quality do not reach the customer. After all, a retailer can take all kinds of steps to gain redress from a manufacturer over faulty goods, but losing a customer and damaging the retailer's image may be an irrevocable consequence. Quality assurance systems aim to maintain a consistent level of quality in the flow of goods, and quality control systems aim to halt the progress of faulty products in the supply chain.

A definition of quality is: 'the whole set of features and characteristics of a product or service that are relevant to meeting requirements' (Baily *et al.* 1994). The important notion regarding product quality, therefore, is having satisfactory outcomes; it is not an enduring battle to raise standards. In fact, the pursuit of a quality level which is higher than is necessary to satisfy customers has as many drawbacks as setting a quality level too low. Some likely consequences of setting the quality level too low are:

- not all faulty products are detected;
- customers are faced with faulty products in store;
- customers may be lost for ever;
- high level of complaints;
- high level of returned merchandise;
- have to reduce price of merchandise to shift stock, or have to remove product from sale.

Likely consequences of setting quality level too high are:

- production costs increase, resulting in higher prices to customers;
- too many products are rejected, resulting in low stock levels;
- only a limited number of suppliers may be capable of reaching the quality level, thereby reducing choice of potential suppliers;
- high quality level may not be apparent or relevant to customers; another product feature may be more important to them, for example the fashion element.

One way in which suppliers can reassure their retail customers regarding quality standards is by becoming registered for the Quality Assurance Standard (denoted by EN 29000 or ISO 9000). This standard assures retail customers that the supplier is implementing the necessary procedures within the organisation to be able to ensure that a consistent level of quality is produced. If this quality level is not maintained, then the buying organisation can sue the producing company. Theoretically, if a supplier is ISO 9000 registered retailers do not need to implement any quality control measures themselves.

Quality control

Retailers using a supplier who does not have a quality assurance scheme may need to set up procedures of their own to prevent any faulty products reaching the customer. Quality control can take place at any point in the supply chain, and it may involve retailers' quality control personnel working closely with the supplier's production technologists to resolve any problems. The usual places for quality control to take place are:

- *factory*: goods may be inspected during production and/or when finished at the production site. This has the advantage that any problems can be investigated immediately and (hopefully) resolved quickly;
- *distribution centre*: goods may be inspected on a random basis as they enter the warehouse. This is the final point at which faulty products can be detected in non-store retail formats;
- *store*: store personnel can be trained to watch out for faulty merchandise, especially if delivery is direct from supplier to store.

The product specification

A product specification is an important document in the quality control process as it provides the link between the end result of a buyer's negotiations with a supplier and the delivery of bulk purchases. It ensures that the goods that arrive in the retailer's outlet exactly match the buyer's requirements. The product specification is a detailed description of the product and will include:

- relevant product coding information;
- labelling and packaging instructions;
- component materials;
- production method details;
- dimensions (with full size specification for alternative sizes);
- sketch or blueprint (a technical representation of the item).

In theory, a supplier should be able to make a product having read the specification, but of course a sample of the product to copy is preferable. If the product does not meet the specification, then a quality control problem arises, and needs to be resolved through action or negotiation (or both). Product specifications are particularly useful when a product has been developed exclusively for a retailer. Prior to delivery, negotiations may have revolved around a set of prototype samples. The specification will be a written summary of the final approval sample, which itself might be 'sealed' to indicate that approval. The sealed sample and the specification therefore become the 'standard' for quality control purposes.

Having an appreciation of the acceptable level of quality for a particular retail outlet is part of the understanding that a retailer's supply partners need to have of their customer's positioning (see chapter five for further discussion on supplier relationships). As the level of understanding increases, the retail buyer will be able to depend on the supplier to use its own initiative when it comes to quality matters, and rely less on the role of documents and procedures to maintain quality levels. Many large retailers have a zero defect policy, which means that there is no tolerance of faulty goods within the supply chain. If a supplier is unable to maintain this commitment, it runs the risk of incurring financial penalty or being de-listed.

Brand

Although the 'brand' is an intangible product feature, for some consumer purchase decisions it might be the only attribute that counts. For example, if a convenience store does not stock Nescafé instant coffee, one consumer may substitute tea or another beverage until s/he can shop for the brand elsewhere, whilst another consumer may happily switch brands to Maxwell House coffee. The brand therefore can represent a product in its totality and it becomes currency for the quality level expected. In the case of manufacturer brands, the value (or equity) is built up by the supplying organisation rather than the retailer, whereas in own-label or retailer's own brands, the brand value is a complex blend of the product and the consumer's relationship with the retailer, referred to by Davies (1993: 125) as the 'process brand'.

Other indications of quality level or guarantee of consumer satisfaction which could be applicable to products include: a trademark; an industry certification (for example, a guild of craftsmen); approval by an association (for example, the Soil Association for organic produce); and a designer name.

Imitation or innovation? The management of a retailer's brand portfolio

Retailer branding has grown in line with the increasing dominance of the multiple retailer and it has been one of the manifestations of the shift in power from the manufacturer to the retailer. By taking control of the product from idea conception (even if it is the idea to copy) through product development to order specification, retailers have been able to sell keenly priced own-label (private label) versions of products whilst retaining similar or improved profit margins. Once viewed by consumers with scepticism regarding quality (McGoldrick 1990), own-label products are now happily accepted as reasonable substitutes in many product categories.

Own-label products have penetrated deeper into some sectors of the retail market than others. In Europe, they are particularly prevalent in food and clothing sectors and less important in the DIY and electrical sectors (Euromonitor 1999). As a whole the UK is the most retailer-branded dominated country, with around one-third of retail sales, whilst in the US own-label accounts for only 20 per cent overall.

Managing the brand portfolio is at the heart of many retailers' product strategy. Between the extremes of 100 per cent own-brand (for example, Gap or Marks & Spencer) and all manufacturer- or supplier-branded (which might be found in an independent electrical retailer for example) a retailer might use one or more of the following approaches to own-label merchandise.

- *exclusive brands*: made for a retailer by a manufacturer, which bear a brand that identifies neither party. Aldi, for example, uses this approach;
- *own brands/house brands*: brands in their own right whose association with a retailer is clear; for example, Sainsbury's Novon clothes wash products, or House of Fraser's Linea women's clothing range;

- *own label*: products that simply bear the retailer's name. They may have their own identity (Waitrose, for example, use a very individual own-label brand identity) or they may have an identity that mimics a brand leader;
- *own label sub-brand*: these carry the retailer's name but the products have a unique positioning, indicated by similarity in packaging themes. For example, Tesco's 'Finest' range of convenience foods have silver packaging and a flowing typeface, whereas their 'Value Lines' have distinctive blue and white stripes with a bold red typeface.

A commitment to the retail brand in product management has a number of advantages in addition to the financial implications alluded to earlier. Retailers are able to control the brand's identity and image, innovate and target products to maximise market opportunities, and extend and contract the branded ranges as they see fit. Manufacturers' brands, however, bring prestige and strong positive consumer associations to the retailer's outlet and have the benefit of product development and marketing support which need no contribution from the retailer.

Price/value as a product feature

Although the price is a tangible feature of a product, the extent to which the price attached to a product represents value is, like the style and the brand, subject to different perceptions and interpretations by different customers. Pricing is such an important part of product management because in the setting of a price a retailer has to consider both the value perceptions of the consumer and the financial objectives of the business, that the whole of chapter eight is devoted to profitability issues in the product management process.

SUMMARY

In a crowded retail market place, having the best product range for your target customer is still one of the most effective ways of achieving competitive advantage. Selecting the right products involves keeping track of customers' preferences, anticipating demand for new products and ensuring that each product lives up to customers' expectations in all its various features and attributes. Reviewing the product range on a regular basis will ensure that the offer continues to interest and satisfy the experienced and discerning shopper. Achieving competitive advantage via the product range none the less is impossible without the contribution of product suppliers, who are the subject of the next chapter.

REVIEW QUESTIONS

1 Review the influences on category life-cycles. Where possible, give some examples to show how these influences have shaped the demand pattern for the product category.

2 Examine the role of the range review within the product management process.

3 Outline the various approaches to retailer-controlled branding. Why is there so much variation in retailer-branding strategies?

4 Describe how branded goods provide quality assurance to retail buyers. What steps can a retailer take to assure quality in their own-branded products?

DISCUSSION QUESTIONS

1 Choose a product item and discuss the consumer trends that have influenced the demand for that product. Also, consider whether consumer trends have influenced any part of the product's presentation, for example packaging, product formulation, marketing communications about the product, or method of selling.

2 Find four products that you consider to be in different stages of their category life-cycle. Justify your findings.

3 For a product of your choice, examine the product selection criteria that would be important in its selection process.

4 Discuss the following terms in relation to products: utility, style, fashion, customisation, ethical.

REFERENCES AND FURTHER READING

Baker, M.J. (2000) *Marketing Strategy and Management*, Macmillan, London.

Baily, P., Farmer, D., Jessop, D. and Jones, D. (1994) *Purchasing Principles and Management*, 7th edn, Pitman, London.

Brassington, F. and Pettitt, S. (2000) *Principles of Marketing*, Pearson Education, Harlow, Essex.

Bruce, M. and Biemans, W.G. (1995) *Product Development: Meeting the Challenge of the Design-marketing Interface*, John Wiley, Chichester, Sussex.

Clements, A. (2000) 'Can't cook? Don't bother', *Retail Week*, 21 April.

Corrigan, P. (1997) *The Sociology of Consumption*, Sage, London.

Davies, G. (1993) *Trade Marketing Strategy*, Paul Chapman, London.

Euromonitor (1999) *Private Label in Europe Report* (March), Euromonitor Publications, London.

Gilmore, J.H. and Pine, B.J. (1997) 'Four faces of mass customization', *Harvard Business Review* 75 (1): 91–102.

Loosschilder, G.H. and Schoormans, J.P.L. (1995) 'A means–end chain approach to concept testing', in Bruce and Biemans, op. cit.

Maslow, A.H. (1970) *Motivation and Personality*, Harper & Row, New York.

McGoldrick, P.J. (1990) *Retail Marketing*, McGraw-Hill, Maidenhead, Berks.

Mintel (1999) *Children's Clothing Retailing Report*, Mintel International Group, London.

Mintel (2000) *British Lifestyles Report*, Mintel International Group, London.

Pellegrini, L. (1993) 'Retailer brands: a state of the art review', *Conference Proceedings of the 7th International Conference on Research in the Distributive Trades*, Institute for Retail Studies, University of Stirling, September, pp. 348–63.

Porter, J. (2000) 'White heat', *Retail Week*, 25 February.

Rafiq, M. and Collins, R. (1996) 'Lookalikes and customer confusion in the grocery sector: an exploratory survey', *International Review of Retail, Distribution and Consumer Research* **6** (4): 329–50.

Tauber, E.M. (1972) 'Why do people shop?' *Journal of Marketing* **36** (4): 46–9.

Worth Global Style Network (2000) <http://www.wgsn.com> (accessed 27 March).

chapter
five

SUPPLY
SOURCES

INTRODUCTION

Most retail businesses do not manufacture the goods that are sold through their outlets. Even though there are some notable exceptions to this statement, such as Benetton (fashion) and Thorntons (chocolates), outside supply sources as the producers of the product range are the mainstay of most retailers' success. Access to a wide supply base that delivers products at an acceptable level of quality, on time and in the right quantities goes a long way towards achieving a retailer's product management objectives, and stocking products from sources of supply which have particular meaningfulness for the final consumer, in terms of brand recognition or product expertise, can be a source of competitive advantage. If the product range at one retailer is perceived by customers to be better than that of a rival, it might be because a retail buyer has chosen the products with more skill and understanding of customers' needs; but it might also be the result of the buyer having better product ranges to choose from because the suppliers were more proficient at their jobs too.

This chapter explores the topic of supply sources. It considers the different types of suppliers that retailers may use, and how they go about locating them. It establishes the way in which suppliers are selected by retailers and what goes into a supplier evaluation. The way in which a relationship grows and develops between a retailer and a supplier is traced, and the contribution that supply partners can make to the supply chain management process is examined.

TYPES OF SUPPLIER

There are a number of different alternatives that retailers might consider to be suitable sources of supply. The choice will depend on factors that are principally associated with the size of the purchasing retail company. For example, a large multiple retailer such as J. Sainsbury will require huge quantities of mainstream products such as Heinz Tomato Ketchup to be delivered on a regular basis and so suppliers must have sufficient production capacity to satisfy the order level required by the retailer. Heinz, on the other hand, would not be interested in supplying Holmbridge Post Office (see Mini Case Study 1 at the end of chapter one) with their weekly order of one dozen bottles of Ketchup directly, so these products have to be obtained by small retailers via a wholesaler. The challenge for both retailers and producers is to find a suitable match between supply source and distribution channel.

Power

Many studies of the relationships between retailer and suppliers have been based around the concept of distribution channel power and control (see, for example, El Ansary and Stern 1972; Butaney and Wortzel 1988). The assumption is that the greater the market share of an intermediary or producer, the greater the power of that channel member and therefore the more control they have over the exchanges that take place within that distribution channel. The rise of retail power through the process of market concentration and increased own-label product development has been well documented (see, for example, Davies 1992). This power, combined with the more recent phenomenon of the category champions (see chapter three), is polarising the consumer goods markets into a combination of power retailer–supplier partnership emporiums and regional specialists, with the medium sized business finding it more and more difficult to offer meaningful retail experiences in between.

Market share is not the only determinant of power in the distribution channel, however. Strong brands are also able to exert considerable influence over retailers' supply selection strategies irrespective of their market ranking. The strength of a brand's appeal to consumers may override other product selection criteria, such as quality or price, and so the retailer effectively has no choice in terms of supply source other than to deal with the branded goods manufacturer or a distributor for that brand. In mail order catalogues, for example, a brand such as Levi's might be allocated one whole page for their denim products, but the final product selection is left to the supplier rather than the retailer.

Manufacturers

Large retailers frequently deal directly with a product manufacturer. That manufacturer may own one or more production units, which in turn could be geographically spread on a national or international basis. Manufacturers will normally have a sales office or a showroom, either attached to a production unit or in a location that is convenient for the retail customers. From the sales base the liaison between retail buying and merchandising teams and the supplier's sales and product development teams can take place. Even in today's world of e-commerce, close physical proximity can help a supplier to achieve a higher sales service level, which can be a source of competitive advantage.

Retailers who deal directly with manufacturers are likely to be placing orders that are so large that they could be considered to be booking production space as opposed to ordering items, therefore most direct buying is restricted to multiple and mail order retailers. A small retail concern may be able to buy directly from a small manufacturing concern but is likely to use indirect sources of supply, such as an agent or wholesaler, when ordering goods from large producers. The growth of the multiple retailers has largely contributed to the contraction of the wholesaling industry throughout Europe, especially in the food and clothing sectors.

Agents

An agent acts as a selling intermediary for a product manufacturer. By collating orders from smaller retail organisations through a network of agents, a manufacturing concern is able to supply efficiently a large number of smaller customers. Together, their orders make up quantities that are economical to produce. Agents are likely to work from a sales office/showroom that is located as conveniently as possible to the retail customers. They usually work on a commission basis and may represent more than one producer. Agents are particularly useful for retailers in the early stages of global sourcing.

Wholesalers and distributors

Wholesalers and distributors work in a similar way to agents, in that they will accept small orders from retail customers. The difference is that wholesalers actually take ownership of the goods between the producer and the retailer. They therefore supply the retailer from their stock as opposed to the producer's stock, as in the case of the agent. They will apply a profit margin to the products they sell to the retailer, usually determined by themselves rather than the producer. There are advantages and disadvantages associated with the use of intermediaries such as wholesalers or distributors. A key advantage is that the retailer can buy goods in small quantities thereby reducing the financial investment in stock. Additionally, by purchasing small quantities frequently, the retailer uses less space for storage, allowing the conversion of as much of their premises as possible to selling space. Intermediaries allow small retailers access to leading brands and an increased selection of suppliers. Small retailers would not have the resources to search out these suppliers, nor would their individual orders be worthwhile for the larger manufacturer to supply. The main disadvantage is the retailer has to pay the wholesaler's profit margin on top of the cost price of the product. Cutting out intermediaries allows large retailers to sell at lower prices whilst generating the same profit margins for themselves. Another disadvantage is that intermediaries are not normally able to guarantee exclusivity, apart from perhaps on a very small geographic scale.

'Grey market' sourcing

This term refers to the practice undertaken by retailers to obtain branded merchandise from traders who do not have a 'licence' awarded by a manufacturer to sell their goods. The legal issues associated with this type of sourcing are complex, but 'grey' goods have been sold in reputable retailers such as Tesco and Asda, who effectively have challenged the legality of requiring a 'licence' to sell consumer goods such as clothing and toiletries. One of the problems with dealing in grey goods, however, is guaranteeing the authenticity of the product.

BOX 5.1 THE EROSION OF THE WHOLESALE MARKET: A MAJOR THREAT TO THE SMALL INDEPENDENT RETAILER

Holmbridge Post Office is a small independent retail concern, selling convenience and basic grocery products to a small catchment area. Its product offer includes a selection of fresh fruit and vegetables. Five years ago, James Davis, the proprietor of Holmbridge Post Office, had a choice of three wholesale fruit and vegetable suppliers in the nearby town of Huddersfield. Now there is only one wholesaler trading. Up until last year, this wholesaler delivered fresh produce on a daily basis, but now it considers it uneconomical to deliver daily and has cut the round to three times per week.

James is pleased that the best wholesaler has remained in business, but he feels it can now dictate terms, as it has no competition, which is not in his interest. He also has to take more risks in terms of ordering quantities and has to find the space for the extra produce to cover an additional day's supply. This is not easy when the total selling area amounts to 180 square metres.

The demise of wholesale markets is generally attributed to the large supermarket groups which have grown to dominate the producers and have caused the closure of so many of the small and medium sized grocery retailers upon which wholesalers depend.

THE SUPPLIER SEARCH

How does a retail organisation find suitable suppliers? The probable answer to this question given by many retail buyers would be 'not very easily', but the problem is not so much about the lack of suppliers in the market, but about finding the right kind of supplier. The search for good suppliers is therefore an important and on-going task for retail product managers and is likely to fall within the remit of the buyers, who have the best product and market knowledge.

In reality, retail buyers find that it is the suppliers that seek them out most of the time. Suppliers consider retail buyers notoriously difficult to reach, but it is generally acknowledged that taking a complacent approach to the supply base is dangerous. If retail buyers are not up to date and expertly informed about the supply possibilities in their product field, then they are not performing their role as organisational buyer adequately. An innovative supply source rejected by a busy retail buyer could become the next source of competitive advantage for the competition. It is frequently the task of an assistant buyer to make the initial assessment of a supplier's suitability for a retail business. Many multiple retailers source on a global basis, therefore the supplier search can involve extensive travel to producing areas of the world. Dealing through agents or buying groups is a way of accessing a wider supply market (see chapter two for a discussion on buying groups).

Global sourcing

Direct sourcing of products from around the world requires considerable expertise and resource expenditure, so it is only worthwhile if large volumes of product can be bought at much lower prices than would be available from local suppliers. However, there may be reasons other than costing constraints that prompt retailers to source from the global market. Some products are indigenous to certain countries, and therefore have been sourced abroad for centuries. Coffee, bananas and spices are examples of this type of products. Unique products may only be available in some countries, such as hand-crafted items which use a combination of raw materials and skills that are only available commercially from low production cost countries. Finally, certain branded items may only be available from an overseas source. Global sourcing usually requires retail buyers to make a trade-off between more variety in the supply base and longer lead times. Domestic suppliers may not be able to offer the lower costs and product diversity of a global supply base, but they should be able to respond more quickly to changes in consumer demand.

Of course, items from a variety of international sources are available through agents and wholesalers, but if a retailer is hoping to develop its own exclusive products from an overseas source, there may be little alternative to getting on to a plane with a banker's draft. Global sourcing is considered in more detail in chapter thirteen.

In an apparent contradiction to the trend towards a more widespread search for suppliers, retail suppliers, whether they are wholesalers, agents or the sales force of a direct supplier, are frequently geographically concentrated. This provides convenience and efficiency for the retail buyers, and a higher density of retail buyers are attracted by the critical mass of supply sources in one area. The wholesale market at New Covent Garden in the UK is a well-known example of this concentration of retail supply, whilst the show-rooms of many of the retail clothing suppliers are located in the area north

---

BOX 5.2   THE GLOBAL SEARCH FOR BODY PRODUCTS

Anita Roddick, founder of the Body Shop, has been famous for her trips around remote parts of the globe in the search for unique body-care product ingredients. Her travels have resulted in a highly differentiated product range, in-store promotional product information opportunities, and extensive press coverage of her endeavours to establish trading links with developing countries.

---

of Oxford Street in London's West End (the 'Rag Trade' area). In the US, market weeks take place twice a year in Los Angeles and New York, which provides geographical and time concentration for both retailers and suppliers. The retailers know that the suppliers will have their full ranges of the latest products on show, and the suppliers are able to gain scale efficiencies by taking a large proportion of their orders at one time. Ultimately geographical clusters of suppliers bring efficiencies which make the end product cheaper for the final consumer and provide the necessary means of distributing products to a wider customer base.

Trade shows

A trade show is an organised gathering of suppliers, who present samples of the products they are able to supply to retailers and take orders against those samples for supply at some stage in the future. Trade shows are organised on a product specific basis, and are usually held in a purpose built exhibition hall, such as the National Exhibition Centre in Birmingham, UK.

Literature

The busy environment of the buying office is not exactly conducive to reading, but retail product management personnel make time to read relevant trade journals and peruse any product catalogues that may be sent to the buying office. These secondary sources may therefore provide more supplier information for the buyer.

THE CHOICE OF SUPPLIER

In the traditional model of the buying process, shown in chapter two, the stage following the supplier search is the selection of the supplier. Having made the initial contact by way of an interview, or perhaps by meeting at a trade show, the retail buyer then has to assess a supplier's suitability to his or her company's needs. A product sample may appear very attractive in a showroom, but a retailer needs to be assured that the product will look as attractive to its customers when the product is on display in the store or when the product reaches a consumer's home. Normally, a retailer will put a supplier through a number of assessment stages in order to appraise its suitability and will evaluate and monitor its performance.

Initial selection factors

A supplier's initial assessment will be made according to its ability to satisfy a retailer in four main areas. Figure 5.1 shows a range of supplier assessment criteria, together with the kind of indicators that would determine the likelihood of a supplier meeting these criteria.

Product range and quality The variety of products available, the quality standard achievable, the quality standard for the price, and the ability of the supplier to assure product quality (see chapter 4).
Indicators: Technical capability of machinery and workforce, production specialisation and flexibility, access to raw materials, design capability, quality assurance procedures, nil defect delivery, ethical working practices and environmental assessment.

Price The value of the product for the price, the discounts available for large quantities and for rapid payment, the profit margin envisaged on the product.
Indicators: Scale economies, experience effects, low cost raw materials and components, financial stability, willingness to negotiate.

Delivery The ability of the supplier to deliver according to the retailer's specification in terms of timing, quantities and product variety.
Indicators: Capacity, minimum order quantities, lead times (for initial and repeat orders), willingness and ability to collaborate on consumer-led response initiative (see chapters three and six), workforce stability.

Service This could refer to a number of ways in which a supplier adds value through service to their retail customers; it would include both before- and after-sales service.
Indicators: Innovation, speed of new product introduction, sampling service, marketing support, handling of queries and complaints, exclusivity deals (regional or national).

Figure 5.1 **Supplier assessment criteria**

   Much of this appraisal is really only possible once a supplier is 'live' and actually fulfilling an order. It makes sense, therefore, to begin a relationship with a supplier by conducting a low risk trial in the form of a small order or an order of a basic item that the retailer may already be sourcing from a number of existing suppliers. Before embarking on a trial order the retailer may take further steps to appraise a supplier. This might include: taking references from other retail customers (not always feasible due to competitive constraints); conducting an analysis of the supplier's current customer list; visiting the production units where the goods will be made; and inspecting and testing samples of products from the production line. Suppliers may have specific expertise, and therefore offer value for the production of part of a range whilst being inappropriate for others. For example, the machinery needed to sew fine fabrics for blouses and shirts would not be suitable for the production of heavy jeans.

In a multiple retailer a technologist is likely to become involved with the supplier appraisal in order to assess the capabilities of the machinery and processes, to predict the likely product quality outcome. A small retailer may not have the resources to inspect a supplier in this way; therefore, a small trial order could be the most cost effective method of assessing supplier suitability. A retailer does not generally pay for goods until they have been received and inspected, so no immediate financial loss is incurred if the goods have to be returned to the manufacturer. Some large retail organisations contract out their supplier assessment monitoring to third parties, as illustrated in Boxed 5.3.

Supplier development

Multiple retailers who produce product ranges under their own labels or brands will be interested in assessing a supplier's ability to be 'developed'. Most retailers will have within their portfolio a supply base that includes suppliers at different stages of development. Some will be relatively new, undergoing trial orders. Others will have completed their trial orders successfully and the volume of their orders will be increasing, or they might be asked to supply a greater variety of product for the retailer. Other suppliers will be very well established, perhaps having grown with the retail business, and may be supplying a wide variety of products to many different buying departments.

SUPPLIER EVALUATION AND MONITORING

If a supplier has been dealing with a retailer for a long time, it can be assumed it is reaching a high level of satisfaction with the retailer on the main assessment criteria of product quality, price, delivery and service. However, suppliers to major retailers are subjected to regular evaluation or continual monitoring to ensure that their standards do not fall. The buying department may carry out this analysis or it may be the task of a separate department or third party who is responsible for supply chain management (see Box 5.3). The most common method of supplier evaluation is the weighted multi-attribute evaluation system. Figure 5.2 shows how this system of supplier evaluation works.

Supplier monitoring

Rather than performing a one-off evaluation, many retailers monitor their suppliers on a continuous basis. The supplier's performance is rated as a percentage on a set of performance indicators. If the rating starts to fall a significant way below 100 per cent, remedial steps need to be taken by the supplier, otherwise penalties will be incurred, as described above. Performance indicators may encompass all the main evaluation criteria shown in Figure 5.1.

Suppliers to be evaluated: A, B and C

Supplier evaluation criteria to be used	*Importance weighting (out of 10)*
Innovative products	8
Short lead times	7
On time delivery	9
Nil defect delivery	9
Low prices	8

Marks (out of 10) for each supplier are given on the above criteria

	A	B	C
Innovative products	5	7	9
Short lead times	6	7	9
On time delivery	9	5	7
Nil defect delivery	8	6	7
Low prices	7	8	7

Composite ratings (multiply criteria weighting by individual score)	A	B	C
	291	268	317

Result: Supplier C has the highest evaluation and supplier B has the lowest evaluation. Suppliers who do not achieve the required level of evaluation are likely to be subjected to financial penalty or reduced orders in the future.

Figure 5.2 **Supplier evaluation: the multi-attribute rating system**

BOX 5.3   DEBENHAMS OUT-SOURCE SUPPLIER ACCREDITATION IN EUROPE

Whilst Debenhams have used a third-party quality control organisation for some time in the Far East, a recent move has led them to out-source the process of assessing a supplier's suitability for accreditation by the leading department store. The accreditation involves quality checks which assess not only suppliers' machinery and technical capability, but also that the factory is able to follow a code of conduct and reach acceptable ethical standards. Once a factory is accredited it can be used to supply any of the buying departments, and will be quality audited on a regular basis by the quality control organisation. The release of in-house technologist resources will enable a greater emphasis to be placed on product costing and price point engineering in the early stages of product development.

(Source: *Drapers Record*, 5 June 1999)

The evaluation of a supplier's performance does not stop at the point where the product is delivered to the retailer's premises, whether that is at a distribution centre or at a store. A supplier is also evaluated according to the sell-through rate of the product. This refers to how quickly a product sells, how much volume is generated in a time period and how much of that volume is sold at full price. These factors have a direct relationship to the ability of a product to generate profit, and the greater the profits generated for the retailer from a particular supplier's product range the more favourable the product manager will be towards that supplier in the future. The volume and value of returned goods, whether they are faulty or not, may also be used in the evaluation of suppliers.

RETAILER–SUPPLIER RELATIONSHIP DEVELOPMENT

Most transactions that a retail buyer makes are not carried out with a new supplier. The majority of the transactions will be carried out within the framework of an ongoing business relationship between a retail organisation and a supply organisation. This reality causes problems when attempting to equate what actually is normal practice in the buying office with the traditional buying process theory outlined in chapter two. Very often it will be a supplier who makes a new product suggestion or who comes up with a product improvement; suppliers who wait passively to be found by a searching buyer will probably wait forever! This lack of emphasis on the influence that the supplying firm could have on the way in which organisational buyers actually behave prompted a group of researchers in the early 1980s to revisit the buying process. The resulting interaction model (IMP Group 1982) of organisational buying behaviour is adapted to the retail buying situation in Figure 5.3.

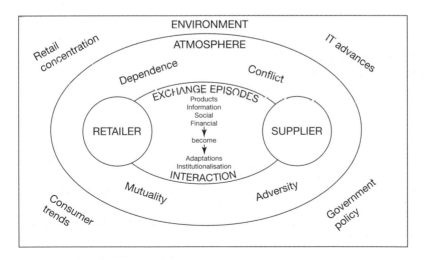

Figure 5.3 **The interaction model of retail buying**

THE INTERACTION APPROACH

The interaction approach recognises that transactions or exchanges between a retailer and a supplier occur in a number of different formats. The most obvious is the transaction of goods for money. In a straightforward purchase of a box of one dozen cans of baked beans from the local wholesaler, money for goods might be the only transaction that occurs. In the case of a biscuit supplier developing a new chocolate biscuit bar for Tesco plc, however, it is likely that a number of prototype products will pass to and from each company, together with packaging ideas, promotional plans, costing information and sales estimates. The main purchase will occur at the end of a significant amount of discussion and negotiation. In this type of transaction there is a great deal of interaction between the two companies, involving personnel from a number of different departments. A technical issue may need to be resolved between Tesco's technologist and the supplier's product engineer. The supplier's packaging designers will liase with Tesco's corporate design department to ensure that the packaging conforms to the corporate image and carries all the necessary product information. Once the biscuit is on the store shelves and selling, Tesco's stock control team will discuss delivery schedules with the production controllers at the biscuit manufacturer, and the buyer will discuss any promotional price offers with the supplier's sales director.

Naturally, as time progresses the individuals from the two companies get to know each other and the exchange changes from being purely business orientated to involve social exchanges. These social exchanges do not necessarily involve non-business communications nor do they have to take place off the work premises. They simply refer to the way in which people get to know each other in their work roles, which facilitates communication and eliminates the need for formalities that can take up valuable time and resources. The retailer expects the supplying company to learn how they like to work and if necessary to adapt to their working methods. Once these procedures have been adopted they become what is referred to as institutionalised within the business, so that any other working methods become obsolete. In such a situation, individual exchanges or exchange episodes (as they are referred to in the original model) merge to become facets of the relationship.

Atmosphere

The IMP Group found that interactions between supplying firms and buying firms generally took place within a discernible atmosphere. The atmosphere could be one of trust and mutuality or it could be one of conflict and antagonism. The atmosphere was seen to have an influence over the way exchanges were carried out. Where the dealings between two companies were geared to discrete transactions, it was more likely that the atmosphere would be confrontational, with little expectation of continuity in dealings. Where the relationship had developed over time, however, the atmosphere tended towards being trusting and co-operative, with an emphasis on continuity of a business relationship between the two companies.

Environment

Whilst the traditional buying process models (such as Webster and Wind 1972) did acknowledge that business environment influences, such as technology, societal change, economic well-being and the political framework, could affect the buying process, these influences were only acknowledged to be of relevance to the buying organisation. In fact a buying company and a selling company operate in the same business environment, and so it is the combined response of the two organisations to environmental threats and opportunities that will have the most significant bearing on the interaction between the two. For example, in an economic downturn, a retailer is faced by more price sensitive shoppers. One response could be for the retailer to cut back order quantities as demand falls for products, with the possible result that a production plant may have to be closed and skilled operators laid off. When the economy improves, those skilled workers are no longer available for work, so the factory cannot be re-opened and the retailer has to source elsewhere. An alternative response could be a combined effort between retailer and supplier to investigate ways of reducing the cost of the item, thereby offering the consumer a lower priced product. Demand is therefore retained, the factory stays open, and the relationship between supplier and retailer is maintained. Co-operation between the two interacting companies allows threats to be challenged and overcome.

STAGES OF DEVELOPMENT IN RETAILER–SUPPLIER RELATIONSHIPS

Earlier in this chapter, it was suggested that a retailer may have suppliers at different stages of development within their supplier portfolio. Some retailers may have a supply base dominated by producers who have been supplying the retailer for many years. On the other hand some retailers may never develop very close relationships with suppliers, and may continually deal with all their suppliers on a one-off basis. The extent to which the relationship between a retailer and a supplier has developed can be depicted on a continuum, as in Figure 5.4.

One-off transactions	Repeated transactions	Long term relationship	Partnership	Alliances	Vertical integration
		Ongoing transactions	Collaborative systems	Franchises Licences	Owning suppliers

Figure 5.4 **A continuum of retailer–supplier relationship development**
Source: Adapted from Webster 1992: 1–17

Although there are a number of retailers who are vertically integrated, many became so by moving forward into the distribution channel, that is, by manufacturers opening up retail outlets. The tendency these days is for retailer and manufacturer to retain their autonomy yet move the businesses together by forming supply 'partnerships'. The characteristics of a supply partnership are contrasted with the characteristics of transactional supplier dealing in Figure 5.5

Transactional
- Short term or one-off
- Many suppliers and buyers
- Disloyalty and lack of commitment
- Low switching costs, little or no investment made in relationships
- Loose or no procedures
- Exchange centred on single person in firm
- Changes in customer/supplier make little difference

Partnerships
- Long term and on-going
- Few suppliers and buyers
- Loyalty and commitment
- High switching costs, significant investments will have been made in the partnership
- Strict procedural guidelines
- Many people and departments involved in exchanges
- Change in customer/supplier causes disruption

Figure 5.5 **The transactional vs the partnership approach in retail supply**

There are some relationships between retailers and their supply sources that are best described as alliances; in these there is some kind of legal arrangement that binds the channel members. An example of this kind of relationship is a franchising operation, where a central organisation allows an individual to run his or her own business, but has a legal right to insist that the business is conducted in a particular way, conforming to a central policy with regards to standardised product and service offers. Another example is a licensing arrangement, which is particularly prevalent in character merchandising (see Box 5.4).

SUPPLY CHAIN MANAGEMENT

Supply chain management has provided retailers with the opportunity to obtain higher levels of operational efficiency through the alignment of suppliers' logistical systems with their own. This is only possible when a partnership approach is taken and both parties stand to benefit from the

---

BOX 5.4   CHARACTER MERCHANDISE

Licensing refers to an arrangement where manufacturers produce goods that have some reference to a popular character. In effect it is the character, for example Mickey Mouse or Barbie, that becomes the brand and it overrides both the retailer and the supplier. Character merchandise can be found in almost every retail sector, with food and clothing being the most important in a global market worth £76 billion (Mintel 1999). Primary-school children, currently an age group experiencing a demographic boom, are the main market for character merchandise. The children recognise the character and subject their parents to 'pester power' for the product.

Although popular with the target market, licensing does have a number of drawbacks: the characters may become unpopular or be perceived as 'too childish', restricting its appeal to a narrower age band; parents may feel children are being exploited, or they may disapprove of the character. In addition, character merchandise is usually premium priced because of the extra cost of royalties paid to the licensees, who may intervene in the retailer–supplier relationship in order to maintain their own quality standards.

(Source: Day 1999)

---

results, as described in chapter three. The trend towards supply partnership development and the use of integrated information technology systems through the whole supply chain has resulted in retailers placing an increasing responsibility on suppliers for ensuring product availability. Retailers are also placing increasing responsibility on their existing suppliers to increase the variety in the product offer. Rather than searching for and developing new suppliers when a product opportunity is identified, retailers are more likely to increase the business within the existing supply base, which has already made the adaptation and institutionalisation investment to service the retailer as they require (see Mini Case Study 4 at the end of this chapter). This strategy for new products should result in lower priced products from an experienced supplier.

Increased marketing and distribution efficiency as a result of supply chain management has been the focus of much of the strategic development of large retailers and their supply partners in the last decade, but retailer–supplier partnering is not only available to large organisations. Examples of initiatives that will improve retailer–supplier relationships in any size of business are shown in Figure 5.6

SUMMARY

The supply base is increasingly being used to contribute to the value added to the product range by the retailer. Access to product sources around the globe and advances in logistics and supply chain integration have allowed retailers to improve choice and availability. The trend towards partnerships between retailers and their suppliers is allowing the two parties to combine

- An understanding of the retailer's target customer and the brand image that the retailer is trying to build, by the supplier as well as the retailer.

- Detailed feedback on sales from the retailer to the supplier. This might include transmission of sales data via EDI. Qualitative feedback on poor sellers is likely to reduce mistakes in the future.

- Co-operation and co-ordination in marketing activities. Examples would include co-operative advertising, provision of promotional material by supplier for retailer's campaigns, and store support for supplier's media campaigns.

- Sharing of information on relevant consumer trends and product/market trends and innovations.

- Commitment of businesses to one another, including combined forward planning, store space dedicated to supplier's ranges, provision of point of purchase materials and fixtures for the retailer, retailer involvement in product development.

- Systems integration to facilitate information sharing, including sales data, stock and delivery information.

- An understanding of the retailer's quality standard requirements, including product quality and compliance on delivery and administration.

Figure 5.6 **Factors that will improve relationships between retailers and their suppliers**

their expertise to provide more flexible product assortments and faster new product innovations. Even small retailers are working more closely with their suppliers to gain a mutual understanding and a combined customer orientation. The next chapter focuses on product quantity decisions in product management, which are a primary source of concern for suppliers and retailers alike, as they strive to minimise stock investment and respond quickly to consumer demand.

MINI CASE STUDY 4   MARKS & SPENCER AND DEWHIRST

The partnership between Marks & Spencer and Dewhirst is perhaps one of the longest standing business partnerships of all time. It began in 1894 when Michael Marks, a stallholder in Leeds Market Hall, formed a partnership with Tom Spencer, who had previously worked as a cashier for a wholesale company I. J. Dewhirst. The two companies have continued to trade, and Dewhirst is now a world-class manufacturing company in its own right, as well as being the second largest non-food Marks & Spencer supplier.

Dewhirst has its roots in supplying textile products to M&S, but product expansion into areas such as toiletries has given Dewhirst the opportunity to diversify. In 1998, Marks & Spencer launched a salon-formulation hair-care range in response to the growing interest in healthy hair and consumers' willingness to purchase upmarket hair products. The following account follows the introduction of the new product range, highlighting the relationship between supplier and retailer as they work together to bring a product idea to market.

Richard Fawdry, merchandiser for toiletries at Marks & Spencer, talks to his contact, Sales Director Lorraine Crosby at Dewhirst, every day. Dewhirst is one of six suppliers to the toilettes department and has a toiletries product development team who work exclusively on Marks & Spencer products. In the spring of 1997, Lorraine suggested to Richard that Marks & Spencer could develop a premium priced 'salon formulation' hair-care range. Richard was interested and asked Dewhirst to make some proposals.

The initial stage of the product development was the generation of themed story boards, pulling together ideas on product ingredients and packaging designs including bottle shapes, caps and openings, labels, colours and product textures. These were used in product brainstorming sessions involving designers, selectors and merchandisers from M&S and product designers and marketers from the Dewhirst organisation.

The next stage involved intensive discussion on the size of the range and target price points. A few bottles of shampoo would not make an adequate presence, but space constraints within the store meant that a new product launch would result in less space for other products. Once the range had been agreed in principle, the task of producing a product prototype began. For this, a product development representative from Dewhirst visited laboratories in California, where the best hair-care formulations are made, using all the latest ingredients and technology.

Marks & Spencer did not get heavily involved in the formulation of the hair products, trusting Dewhirst as the product experts to come up with a product suitable for the Marks & Spencer customer.* Lorraine, meanwhile, kept Richard informed on all aspects of the product's progress. When the formulation had been agreed between the toiletries technologist at M&S and Dewhirst technicians, it was blind tested with consumers. In the meantime, product features such as packaging and product information were considered in detail, with the aim of producing a product with worldwide appeal at price levels considered to be value for money, especially to the largest customer group, the UK. Exchanges of design information were facilitated by an EDI/CAM link up between the two companies. Every detail of the product was discussed in depth, with the final selling price as a key influence in the negotiations.

Finally Richard worked on a detailed sales estimate for the range. He considered how wide the gap in the market is for this range, how strong is the competition from other hair care brands and retailers, and how much market share Marks & Spencer could expect to take. Lorraine provided some information to Richard on the market structure and competing retailers to help with this task. Richard also needed to decide if all the M&S stores would take the hair-care range and, if they do, whether they would take all the different product variations. The final sales estimate was given to Dewhirst, so that they could start planning production in the factories to meet the delivery schedule.

Point of sale material to support the launch was generated by Marks & Spencer's graphics department, using product prototypes supplied by Dewhirst in the photography. The finalised range planning was presented at a merchandise review and was endorsed by the Marks & Spencer board of directors. Once the product launch was successfully underway, Lorraine and Richard went for an after-work celebratory drink!

* Nevertheless, M&S would have ensured that the formulations were safe and fell within the chemical industry based legislation, and that their policy that products are not tested on animals was being followed.

REVIEW QUESTIONS

1 Review the alternative sources of supply available to retailers, indicating the advantage and disadvantages of the different sources.
2 Outline ways in which a supplier's potential and actual performance can be assessed.
3 Using the interaction approach (Figure 5.3), describe the relationship between Dewhirst and Marks & Spencer.
4 Discuss the notion of a supply partner within the retail industry.

DISCUSSION QUESTIONS

1 Discuss the various types of supplier that are available to retailers, indicating which type of supplier would be more suitable for the following retailer types: (a) a superstore group such as Tesco or Asda; (b) an independent gift shop; and (c) a medium sized regional department store chain.
2 A partnership approach to retailer–supplier relations usually involves a reduction in the number of suppliers that a retailer uses. Suggest reasons for this trend.
3 Suggest ways in which a retailer's supply base can bring competitive advantage to the company.

REFERENCES AND FURTHER READING

Bowlby, S.R. and Foord, J. (1995) 'Relational contracting between UK retailers and manufacturers', *International Review of Retail, Distribution and Consumer Research* 5 (3): 333–60.
Butaney, G. and Wortzel, L.H. (1988) 'Distribution power versus manufacturer power: the customer pole', *Journal of Marketing* 52 (Jan.): 52–63.
Davies, G. (1992) 'The two ways in which retailers can be brands', *Journal of Retail and Distribution Management* 20 (2): 24–34.
Dawson, J.A. and Shaw, S. (1990) 'The changing character of retailer–supplier relationships', in J. Fernie (ed.) *Retail Distribution Management*, Kogan Page, London, ch. 1.
Day, J. (1999) 'Building a strong character', *Marketing Week*, 25 November.

El Ansary, A.I. and Stern, L.W. (1972) 'Power measurement in distribution channels', *Journal of Marketing Research* **9** (Feb.): 47–52.

Ford, D. (1998) *Managing Business Relationships*, John Wiley, Chichester, Sussex.

Hogarth Scott, S. and Parkinson, S.T. (1993) 'Retailer–supplier relationships in the food channel: a supplier perspective', *International Journal of Retail and Distribution Management* **21** (8): 11–18.

IMP Group (1982) 'An interaction approach', in D. Ford (ed.), *Understanding Business Markets: Interactions, Relationships and Networks*, Academic Press, London.

Kline, B. and Wagner, J. (1994) 'Information sources and retail buyer decision-making: the effect of product-specific buying experience', *Journal of Retailing* **70** (1): 75–88.

Miller, L. (1998) 'It's a very grey area', *Drapers Record Focus*, 4 July.

Mintel (1999) *Character Merchandising Report*, Mintel International Group, London.

Valsamakis, V. and Groves, O.G. (1996) 'Supplier–customer relationships: do partnerships perform better?', *Journal of Fashion Marketing and Management* **1** (1): 9–25.

Webster, F.E. and Wind, Y. (1972) 'A general model for understanding organisational buying behaviour', *Journal of Marketing* **36** (April): 12.

Webster, F.E. (1992) 'The changing role of marketing in the corporation', *Journal of Marketing* **56** (Oct.): 1–17.

chapter
six

PRODUCT QUANTITY DECISIONS

INTRODUCTION

One of the most fundamental questions for the retail product manager, whether carrying the title of buyer, merchandiser or category manager, is how much of a particular product line should be brought in to the business? To begin with, this apparently simple question needs further clarification. For example, does the question refer to the individual quantities required by each store or the amount needed by the whole organisation? Does it refer to how much product should be bought for a day's trading or for a whole season? In addition, there may be other issues, such as discount availability for certain order levels, that would bear upon a quantity decision. Retail product management decisions involving product quantities require the same analytical approach as decisions about 'what product?'.

Getting the right quantities delivered into the retail organisation is necessary to satisfy basic customer needs and retail management goals. If there is not enough of a product item, then there is a risk of unsatisfied customer demand, which means lost sales for the retailer. The extent of this loss is difficult to determine and may account for a much greater value than can be accounted for by the one product item. Not only can a stock-out affect the sales of complementary goods (for example, a jacket may sell much better when matching trousers are available), dissatisfied customers may decide to take their custom to another store and never return. On the other hand, the penalties of having too much of a product item are also great. The retailer has to bear the costs of carrying excess stock, in terms of financial investment, operational maintenance costs and the use of valuable space to store unproductive merchandise. It may also result in the retailer having to lower prices to stimulate demand for the overstocked item, resulting in reduced profit margins on the product.

This chapter presents an overview of the principles and practices retailers use to control product quantities. It reviews the traditional periodic review approach to stock control, before moving on to explore more contemporary methods such as sales based ordering and automatic replenishment, efficient consumer response (ECR) and quick response (QR).

STOCK CONTROL

An ideal situation in retailing would seem to be that stock is replenished at exactly the rate at which it sells. But even this does not always hold true: for example, which retailer would like to replenish Christmas decorations at the rate they were sold in the week commencing 19 December? Management of the quantity of product items in retailing is often referred to as stock control, because the flow of stock is controlled at a rate that is appropriate for the level of sales. However, the management of stock is also about managing the finance tied up in stock and so considerations other than the basic rate of sales have to be taken into account when determining buying quantities.

STOCK MANAGEMENT FOR STAPLE ITEMS

Within the product range offered by most retailers, there are some products that are termed staple items. These are the kind of products that need to be replaced at regular intervals. The consumption of these products is consistent, and so the derived demand is also consistent. Examples of this type of product are family shampoo, milk, bread, furniture polish, dishcloths, basic underwear and light bulbs. Over time the expected sales of this type of product become very predictable and could be expressed as a function of average per capita consumption and the number of customers who visit a particular retailer.

Stock management by periodic review

Control of stock, in the case of staple products, is relatively straightforward and the use of systems based on the periodic review process is commonplace for this kind of merchandise. The periodic review, as the name suggests, relies on the stock position being reviewed within a specific time period. The frequency of review depends on the shelf life of the product and the demand for the item. For example, a review by a grocer of the stock position of milk would take place at least once a day, whereas an electrical retailer may review the stock position of light bulbs once a week (see Figure 6.1).

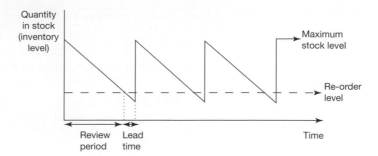

Figure 6.1 **Periodic review: light bulb example**

When the electrical retailer reviews the stock position and realises that more light bulbs need to be ordered, an order is given to a supplier. The retailer then waits for the delivery. In the meantime light bulbs continue to sell, so the review period should be set at a time when the goods are unlikely to have completely run out, and the remaining stock, known as the safety or 'buffer' stock, will cover customer purchases until the new light bulb delivery arrives. This might be a matter of days or it might be a week or so. The time between placing and receiving an order is referred to as a supplier's lead-time. The longer the lead-time, the higher the safety stock level needs to be. The advantages of the periodic review system are that it is simple and easy to administer (and can be carried out at both store and warehouse level), but it is not very useful for fast selling merchandise or when large fluctuations in demand occur. For this type of merchandise, an ordering system that is based on the rate of sales, or the estimated rate of sales, might be more appropriate. These approaches are discussed later in this chapter.

The longer the review period in the stock control system described above, the larger the quantity required in order to prevent stock-outs. However, a large order quantity is likely to present the retailer with other problems, such as storage and handling costs, as well as those of financing such high stock levels. It may seem more cost effective to order more frequently and in smaller quantities. The retailer therefore has not yet solved the problem of how much product to order at any one time. A principle that may help a retailer decide how much product to order is the economic order quantity (EOQ).

The economic order quantity

One of the basic principles of stock management is that of the EOQ, and whilst the EOQ may not be theoretically relevant to many retail buying situations nowadays, for reasons that will become apparent later in this chapter, an appreciation of its principles will help product managers to see some of the hidden costs associated with their decisions about order quantities.

In the process of buying a product, there are a number of costs involved, some of which may be more apparent to the retail organisation than others. The costs involved with acquiring a product can include:

- the administration cost of placing an order, such as labour, paper, telephone bills. Many companies have been able to reduce this cost substantially by using electronic data transfer;
- the costs involved with supplier search and selection (see chapter five). This might include overseas sourcing trips, as well as the day-to-day costs of information exchange and negotiations between the retail buyer and their supplier base;
- once an order is placed, further costs might be incurred when expediting the order. This involves checking that the order is going to arrive on time and making alternative arrangements if there are problems with the delivery;
- the retailer may feel it necessary to inspect the product once it arrives, which can be an extremely costly exercise (see chapter four).

Clearly, some of these costs are easier to allocate to individual product lines than others, and often they will be absorbed under the general fixed costs of the buying department. However, the smaller the quantity ordered, the more orders will need to be placed in any period of time, and therefore the higher the costs involved will be (Figure 6.2).

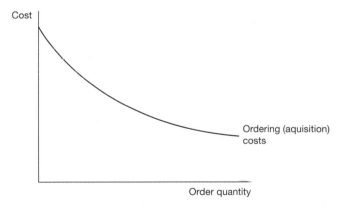

Figure 6.2 **The costs of ordering**

On the other hand, there are also costs involved with the possession of products. The largest cost to a retailer of possessing stock is the capital tied up in it, which is only released at the point of sale. This cost is relatively easy to allocate to individual product lines. There are other costs associated with the possession of goods that are less obvious and harder to allocate. Once the goods have been received, they will need to be handled, warehoused, picked, be prepared and packaged to be sent to stores, delivered to store and possibly be maintained in store (Figure 6.3).

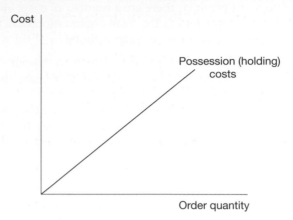

Figure 6.3 **The costs of possession**

The economic order quantity is the point at which the cost of ordering equals the cost of possessing the stock. It is the point at which the total cost of buying is at its lowest (Figure 6.4).

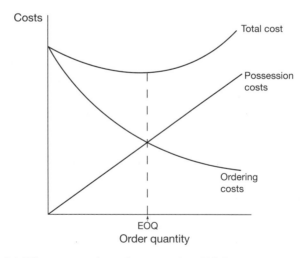

Figure 6.4 **The economic order quantity (EOQ)**

The practicalities of retailing that invariably lead to making decisions based on compromise, especially in the case of the small retailer, means that the EOQ is better approached as a theoretical concept rather than as a buying aid for retailers. This is because in most product instances, the demand for an item is not constant, the shelf-life of many products is very short, and the cost of maintaining and holding stock has risen much more steeply than the costs of acquiring stock.

BOX 6.1   THE MECHANISMS OF THE EOQ

The following example illustrates the mechanisms of the EOQ. A hardware retailer places orders for cleaning products from XYZ supplier. The cost of acquiring the cleaning products is £6.00 per order. The cost of possessing the products is 7.5 per cent of the monthly stock value. The total order value for cleaning products for the year is £6,000 (12,000 items at an average price of £0.50).

Table 6.1   Quantities and costs in the economic order quantity (EOQ) calculation

Order frequency	Order quantity	Value of order (£)	Cost of ordering (£)	Cost of possession (£)	Total annual costs (£)
24	500	250	144	18.75	162.75
12	1,000	500	72	37.50	109.50
10	1,200	600	60	45.00	105.00
8	**1,500**	**750**	**48**	**56.25**	**104.25**
7	1,715	857	42	64.29	106.29
6	2,000	1,000	36	75.00	111.00
4	3,000	1,500	24	112.50	136.50
2	6,000	3,000	12	225.00	237.00

The economic order quantity, or the amount that retailer XYZ should order to minimise its costs, is 1,500 items, at an order value of £750, and the order should be placed eight times a year.

The economic order quantity principle does have a number of drawbacks:

- EOQ does not consider the need to react to unexpected sales fluctuations.
- EOQ does not consider seasonality or perishability factors which could lead to product obsolescence.
- EOQ does not consider the discounts that might be obtainable for ordering larger quantities.
- EOQ does not consider the quantities a product is available in (for example, the product may only be available in dozens or in crates of 100).
- The retailer may not have available space for the EOQ. It may not have any storage space.
- The retailer may depend on the delivery of suppliers or distributors whose own delivery schedules may determine the order quantity placed by the retailer.

Over the last decade, many retailers have found that they have been able to lower substantially the cost of ordering, whilst the costs of holding stock have increased. This has meant that a much larger cost saving can be made by lowering the amount of stock held in the retail system than could be made by reducing the number of times orders are placed. Lower stock holdings have been one of the major benefits of the implementation of consumer-led approaches to product management (see chapter three).

Some of the methods retailers have adopted to reduce the costs of ordering are:

- centralised ordering;
- the use of an order programme at the start of the season. This is similar in principle to a materials requirement plan (MRP) used in purchasing for production companies; it outlines the order quantities required for a future time period, and then schedules deliveries from suppliers to meet those requirements;
- the use of EDI and network systems to cut out paperwork and provide collated information quickly to other members of the supply chain;
- the use of sales-based automatic replenishment systems (discussed later in this chapter).

SERVICE LEVEL

In chapter 1 the concepts of variety and assortment were introduced as determinants of the retail offer. However, the third facet of the retail offer, which plays an important role in determining the customer's perception of the product offer, is the service level that a retailer offers. In this context service level does not relate to the level of personal service a customer receives in the shop, but refers to the stock service level or the amount of certainty customers have of finding the items they wish to purchase in stock. The ideal stock service level is of course 100 per cent, so that no matter how many customers come into an outlet for a product item, a stock-out will not occur. It therefore follows that the service level has a bearing on the financial and physical capabilities of the retailer. A very high service level maximises sales opportunities but runs the risk of having too much stock, which the retailer may not be able to pay for or have room for. The more recent approaches to retailer stock control aim to satisfy the following aims simultaneously:

- keep stock holding low, thereby keeping stock investment and handling costs low;
- maintain high stock service levels for the customer.

SALES FORECASTING

The way in which a retailer can achieve the seemingly conflicting objectives outlined above is by being able to respond quickly to consumer purchase patterns, so the demand for fast-selling lines is fulfilled and the need to mark down prices to sell slow merchandise is avoided. In reality, from a stock control viewpoint very few product items have really stable demand. Even very basic items such as milk, bread and eggs tend to sell more towards the end of the week in anticipation of increased consumption at the weekend.

Perishable products have the added challenge of a short shelf-life and so products such as these are usually ordered on the basis of estimated sales for the forthcoming period.

Electronic point of scale (EPOS) systems have contributed enormously to a retailer's ability to improve stock control. Detailed information about past sales of each stock keeping unit (SKU) has facilitated the job of predicting the future sales of each product line, which enables the retailer to be prepared with enough stock to meet sales. The data are captured at the point of sale and transmitted electronically, and therefore almost immediately, to a central data storage point, usually located in the retailer's head office. The retailer therefore can build up a very accurate picture of what is selling and how quickly in its stores. The retailer can see sales patterns emerging on a seasonal basis, a weekly basis or even at different times throughout the day, as shown in Figure 6.5.

Early morning	6–9 am	Newspapers, milk, cigarettes, bread products
Morning	9–12 am	General groceries, household goods, stamps, fresh fruit and vegetables
Lunchtime	12–3 pm	General groceries, soft drinks, fresh fruit and vegetables
Afternoon	3–5 pm	Confectionery, milk, bread, cakes, tinned foods, fresh produce, soft drinks
Early evening	5–8 pm	Bread, confectionery, lottery tickets, pre-prepared meals, wines and spirits, video rentals
Evening	8–10 pm	Alcoholic drinks, confectionery, video rental, lottery tickets

Figure 6.5 **Convenience store typical daily sales pattern**
Source: Mintel 1997

An understanding of how products sell is the best basis for an effective stock control system within a retail business, and analysis of past sales to make predictions about future sales is the starting point for a sales forecast. Indeed for a staple product such as butter or flour or cereal, the fluctuations in demand over time may be so small that past sales alone could be enough to obtain an accurate sales forecast. In reality, the sales of most products are influenced by a greater or lesser degree by a number of factors:

• seasonality;
• fashion;
• likely product substitutions;
• price fluctuations;
• product endorsement.

Seasonality

The seasons in the year influence product availability and demand. At one time customers accepted that seasonal fruit and vegetable availability fluctuated through the year and consumption patterns reflected what was locally available. Global sourcing and improvements in logistics and transportation have allowed retailers to extend the selling season of many items, such as strawberries and mange-tout, by importing the produce from various countries around the world throughout the year. Despite the improvement in availability, however, demand for products still tends to peak at the time when the product was originally available in the local market because of the seasonal associations, such as bowlfuls of strawberries and cream eaten during the Wimbledon Tennis Championships held in London in June.

Seasonal influences can be product specific or they can have a broader effect. The sales pattern for pumpkins, for example would be quite dramatic, as shown in Figure 6.6. The most important seasonal influence on the UK retail market is Christmas. Marks & Spencer, for example, break their annual sales reporting into three key seasons: spring, summer and Christmas. There are very few categories of merchandise that do not benefit from the Christmas season sales uplift. Even sales of swimwear increase at this time because people who can afford winter sun are likely to be giving their wardrobes an overhaul at this time of year. Figure 6.7 shows some other seasonal peaks in various product categories.

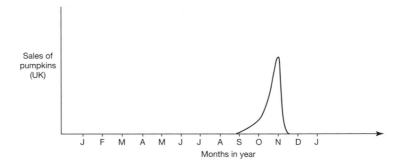

Figure 6.6 **Annual sales trend for pumpkins**

Product classifications	Seasonal peak
Gardening and DIY	April–June
Barbecue products	May–September
Toiletries	February (Valentine's Day), March (Mother's Day) and November/December (Christmas)

Figure 6.7 **Seasonal peaks in different product categories**

Fashion

Although seasonal features and fashion features of products, whether clothing or otherwise, have a combined influence on sales patterns, the effect that fashion has on a product becoming outdated, and therefore obsolete, stimulates demand for new products in retail businesses. Fashion trends can be quite dramatic, causing a high peak in sales, followed by a steep drop as the 'fad' passes on to something new. Other fashion influences last one or more years, for example a trouser leg width or a shirt collar shape. Here are some examples of fashions and fads in different product categories:

Home furnishings	Translucent acrylic bathroom accessories; Brabantia-type pedal bins
Food/drink	Roquette salad; sushi; sun-dried tomatoes; flavoured vodka; smoothies
Toys	Cyberpets; yoyos

Product endorsements

When the famous TV cookery presenter Delia Smith showed the British nation how to cook a boiled egg in 1999, she used white hens' eggs. A day later the BBC was inundated by calls from viewers demanding to know where they could buy white eggs. Supermarkets had long since phased out white eggs in favour of the more homely looking brown egg. Such is the effect of product endorsement by a famous and trusted figurehead. The effect of Delia Smith's following is so great that supermarkets are notified in advance of the ingredients used in her recipes so that huge quantities of the items can be distributed to stores. Product endorsement in itself can create a fashion, such as the stack-soled trainers and combat trousers endorsed by girl bands such as All Saints and the Spice Girls.

Other influences

The three factors, seasonality, fashion and endorsement, can stimulate demand for specific products within a time period. However, demand for products can also be stimulated by other factors. Price reductions are introduced to stimulate sales, whether they take the form of a short term and product-specific reduction, or a longer term, general reduction, as in the case of an end of season sale. The role of price in the product management process is examined in detail in chapter eight, but the effect on sales patterns of price changes and the expectation of seasonal price reductions cannot be overlooked at this stage. Product substitutions also have a role to play in sales forecasting. Lack of availability of one product or brand of a product is likely to increase the likelihood of a competing item being purchased as a next best alternative. Even though the nation was not able to buy white eggs after the Delia Smith demonstration, the demand for brown eggs increased substantially.

The involvement of branch stores in determining quantities

Although it is unlikely that branch managers in most multiple retailers will habitually place orders directly with suppliers, in many retail situations sales forecasting has a significant input at local branch level. It is the branch managers who know the characteristics of their catchment area and their influence on customer needs and preferences. They will also know the effect of local competition on sales and how this may affect the sales estimate for different product categories.

The method of formulating a forecast that is amalgamated from the forecasts of individual stores is the 'bottom-up approach' to sales forecasting. The forecasts from the stores may then be collated at regional level (possibly distribution centre region) and then split down according to departments, from this the buyers or merchandisers will forecast the business for the whole retail company.

An alternative method is the 'top-down' approach where the higher echelons of retail management make an overall company target and subsequently split the forecast by department and by store, and then set the buyers and branch managers the challenge of meeting their targets by whatever means they can. Difficulties with the top-down approach are:

- *motivation*: associates at all levels prefer to be consulted about their own performance. If they have set their own targets, they are likely to feel more motivated to achieve them;
- *lack of knowledge about local catchment's profiles*: it is the person who has the knowledge about the opportunities and threats within the local business environment who is most likely to give an accurate picture of what the outcome will be for the retailer;
- *lack of appreciation of category life-cycles or trends*. These factors, which have a bearing on the long term growth or decline of a product category are best assessed by the buying departments, which are the most likely to have immediate product and market expertise.

Top-down forecasting does allow a retailer to benefit from the judgement of experienced managers, and may prevent the over-ambitious buyer or branch manager being dangerously optimistic in forecasting.

Forecasting at distribution centre level

In most large retail companies, orders from the stores are sent electronically to a distribution centre which replenishes the stores on a regular basis. The use of distribution centres in the supply chain has a useful smoothing effect on sales forecasting. By combining the sales forecast for a number of stores in a retailer's network, a more accurate forecast at regional level is established.

SALES-BASED ORDERING

For goods with a relatively stable demand multiple retailers can use a system of automatic ordering based on previous sales, which is amended according to current situational factors. This system is based on the principle of exponential smoothing. Sales in previous time periods are weighted to forecast the future period. The weighting allows for the influence of exceptional demand patterns to be removed. Sales-based ordering can then be managed by exception, according to the current trading environment. For example, the demand for bottled water is relatively straightforward in that it is stable until warm weather occurs, when demand rises and falls according to the heat. As the temperature rises the sales-based order is amended upwards until the heat wave breaks, at which point the branch manager swiftly amends the sales-based order downwards to slow the flow of bottled water product. Managers of grocery stores in university towns have to increase swiftly the sales-based orders for pizzas and cheap wine when term begins!

Sales reactive replenishment systems

The most recent approaches to stock control are those that aim to cut all stock holding by retailers to the absolute minimum. This is achieved by having a replenishment system that only responds to actual sales. A stock plan is prepared in advance for a time period, but instead of stock being ordered according to forecast, it is called up in response to actual sales. These systems are the basis of efficient consumer response (ECR) systems in the food and fast-moving consumer goods sectors and quick response systems in non-food sectors.

ECR and quick response

The principles of an efficient consumer response approach to product management were outlined in chapter three. The alignment of supply management with demand management in product categories relies on information sharing and collaboration between retailer and suppliers, and so an efficient sales reporting system is a fundamental requirement for setting a responsive supply system in motion.

The key difference between an ECR system and a QR system is determined by the nature of the products involved: ECR systems generally concern food and fast-moving consumer goods, which have relatively stable demand patterns and higher volumes. The demand management is normally performed at distribution centre level and in higher unitisation than the single product item, for example the 'crate-load'. Quick response systems on the other hand deal with units, and therefore are concerned with higher value, lower volume product (typically clothing and home furnishings). They also involve supply techniques that allow retailers to respond more effectively to fashion and seasonal sales variations (Fiorito *et al.* 1995).

In quick response systems sales information is sent electronically to the supplier without intervention from the buying office, so the supplier is as up to date as the retailer on what is selling. The supplier replenishes the item directly to the store in accordance with a predetermined stock assortment plan (see chapter seven). A quick response system means that stock is eliminated from the retailer's holding system (apart from what is on display in the store) but it does rely on the willingness of the supplier to hold a small amount of stock in order to enable them to react immediately. This is supported by swift and flexible manufacturing systems, which are planned according the sales information received.

In an ECR system, the need for a predetermined stock assortment plan is effectively eliminated; the assortment plan exists, and then is subject to constant fine-tuning in response to consumer demand patterns.

The advantage to suppliers who are involved in a sales reactive system is that it gives them real-time sales information, which helps them to plan production for the back-up stock. The supplier will be able to spot fast and slow sellers and react swiftly by swapping production from slow to fast sellers. The sales information will also help the supplier to schedule orders for raw materials more effectively (see Mini Case Study 5 at the end of this chapter)).

A considerable commitment is required to make a sales reactive replenishment system work:

- the supplier and retailer must have compatible information systems to allow for electronic transmission of data;
- distribution from supplier to retailer must be reliable and cost effective;
- in a QR system, suppliers must perform functions that might otherwise take place at a retailer's distribution centre. These functions are often referred to as pre-retailing and include: ticketing or labelling; preparation of stock (folding, hanging on retailer's hangers, pressing, stacking into predetermined quantities and so on).

In addition to these operational requirements, sales responsive systems only work properly if retailers and suppliers work together in an atmosphere of co-operation and trust. For example, the retailer must trust the supplier to treat potentially sensitive sales information in confidence, and they must have faith in a supplier's willingness to hold stock or be able to replenish very quickly. The supplier adapts its systems to the requirements of the retailer in the belief that the business relationship will continue into the next season and beyond.

Drawbacks of sales reactive replenishment systems

One of the drawbacks of the QR system is associated with the small, frequent delivery pattern. The extra transportation costs and pre-retailing function will eventually be paid for in the cost of the goods to the retailer and this may outweigh the benefit of the leaner stock holding levels. The logistical problems encountered when a number of suppliers are responding quickly may make store operations difficult. Where retailers have a very large product range and an associated large number of suppliers, the quick response philosophy has only been partially adopted. In this case automatic replenishment in response to sales is still part of the system, but instead of delivering direct to stores, the distribution centre retains its role and ready-prepared store deliveries from suppliers are collated onto lorries.

Other drawbacks relate to both QR and ECR and include the difficulty in establishing real partnerships between retailers and their suppliers, and the lack of appropriate structures within the retailer and supply organisations to allow the systems to operate to their full potential (see chapter three).

SUPPLIER-MANAGED INVENTORY

It is possible that, where appropriate, a retailer may relinquish the stock management operation completely to suppliers. In its true form a supplier or vendor managed inventory (VMI system) passes the responsibility for managing stock levels within the store to the supplier, with the retailer providing the information that allows the supplier to schedule its production and finished stock level so that automatic replenishment is guaranteed. In certain instances, it makes sense for a supplier to provide a stock filling service. For example, with small item merchandise, such as batteries or spices, it is not unusual for the supplier to offer a shelf stacking service as part of their cost price to the retailer. The supplier simply invoices the retailer for the stock that is replenished on each visit. However, VMI is a more complex arrangement, with a supplier taking on the strategic development of a product category as well as providing the operational stock-servicing role. In a VMI system the retailer and the supplier agree to a forward planned assortment, and then the supplier is provided with real-time sales information so that it can replenish automatically and spot the sales trends. This allows the supplier to plan production in a way that means fast-selling goods can be replenished without delay and the build-up of unwanted merchandise at the end of the season is reduced. In principle, VMI is similar to a QR system, but the supplier has more control over range development. In effect suppliers rent shelf space, and if they see a trend developing for a particular type of merchandise, then it is expected that they, rather than the retailer, will make the decision to offer increased variety in that type of product. As with other highly integrated stock management systems, VMI cannot work without a true partnership existing between retailer and supplier; it takes the role of category captain one stage further. Without this, VMI is open to abuse and some so-called VMI systems simply push the stock holding burden up the supply chain to the supplier, relieving the retailer of any end of end of season over-stock. Information is, again, the key and must be shared openly if suppliers are to take on such a strategic role in product management. Only when suppliers can see the pattern of sales developing can they react efficiently to demand. If they are not able to supply efficiently, then the costs will end up being passed back to the retailer in higher prices for future merchandise.

PROMOTIONAL PRODUCT PLANNING

Many retailers rely on promotional activity to increase sales. A promotion may be part of an offensive strategy in which advance planning, budgeting and forecasting will take place in order to maximise a specific selling opportunity, for example, a cosmetics promotion for Mother's Day in a department store. Other promotions, however, may be part of a defensive move to get a retailer out of trouble. If, for example a retailer finds that an exceptionally warm autumn has reduced demand for coats and heavier weight outerwear, it may decide to run a promotion on those particular merchandise categories to stimulate sales to the forecast level. By reducing prices, demand is restored to the planned level and, whilst the short-term profitability is hampered, the retailer is not faced by an overstock situation which may cause even more serious logistical problems in the very important pre-Christmas selling period.

Planning a promotional campaign may involve a host of in-store and out-of-store activity. A campaign may include the co-ordination of TV and print-based media advertisements, coupled with additional space allocation and point of purchase material within the store. In a successful promotion, the increase in gross profit (an increased turnover with reduced profit margin is the likely formula) should ideally outweigh the costs involved with the promotion, but a retailer may be content with a break-even result on a direct profit/promotional cost basis because of the increased footfall and therefore sales in other departments.

The retailer must be sure then that the increased sales turnover is possible. If there is not enough stock, then the money invested in promotional activity will have been wasted. Long term, well supported promotions will strengthen the image of the store in terms of product assortment, but too many minor promotions, where the benefit to the customer is not very credible, can be damaging to the store's reputation, and a communicated 'offer' which cannot be found in the store is likely to cause high levels of customer dissatisfaction.

SUMMARY

Many retailers have found that the significant investment into a stock control system which couples a sales forecasting programme with highly reactive stock replenishment has paid enormous dividends in areas such as the reduction of product obsolescence and mark-down, reduction of stock cover and therefore investment, and the ability to maximise sales of fast-moving lines. However, stock control challenges for retailers start to become more difficult when products have a high seasonal or fashion factor. Forecasting becomes more difficult, sales patterns become more varied and extreme, and the risk of having too much or too little product becomes much greater. The forecasting process is more subjective; the external influences often come from a diversity of sources, some of which may be quite unexpected.

The development of integrated information and distribution systems that allow retailers immediate access to the knowledge of where and how much of any product is available at any point in the supply chain has made a really important contribution to the process of effective stock management. Any activity taken on by a retail organisation that is likely to affect a product's sales performance should be built into the forecast, because a retailer cannot generate sales without stock, and stock bought for sales that do not happen constitutes a retailer's nightmare. This chapter has given an insight into some of the practices used by retailers to determine the quantities of stock required by the business. Steps that retailers can take to manage the qualitative elements of the product range so that the offer to the customer is, at any one time, appropriate to their needs and wants are discussed in the next chapter.

MINI CASE STUDY 5   QUICK RESPONSE IN FASHION RETAILING: BENETTON AND OASIS

One of the first protagonists of the quick response approach to retail supply was Benetton. As a vertically integrated manufacturing and retailing company they were quick to see the benefits of setting up systems which enabled the manufacturing end of the business to react as swiftly as possible to consumer sales patterns. Forward ordering of stock can make stores vulnerable by causing them to carry styles and colours that prove to be less popular whilst running out of the best sellers quickly, with long lead times for replenishment. Traditionally, sweaters and cardigans are produced by knitting up coloured yarn; however, the Benetton's quick response system uses a 'garment-dyed' process, whereby uncoloured (grey) yarn is knitted up into the garment style. The finished article can then be 'piece-dyed' to whatever colour is selling well. In some cases two-colour effects can be introduced using dye-resist and dye-attract yarn in the garment. The system prevents the build up of unwanted stock of both garments and yarn, as the finished article is produced according to the need for replenishment and can be delivered to stores within a matter of days. The transfer of sales data via EDI to the manufacturing units speeds up the process even further.

Oasis also uses quick response systems in its fashion supply chain. These include ordering fabric as late as possible, and then only finalising the style of garment to be cut out of the fabric 2–3 weeks before delivery is due into the stores. Using multiple suppliers for one product helps to prevent gaps in a range of co-ordinating pieces, whilst fast turnaround of goods in the distribution centre ensures that the product is not stuck in non-retail space. Suppliers need to be able to understand the way Oasis works, and be able to provide the flexibility and quick changes that fashion retailing requires. Joint planning helps, but ultimately the suppliers have to understand that reacting to sales is always going to be necessary, and no amount of pre-planning will tell you what the fashion-led customer will end up buying. Past sales patterns only give an indication, and relying too heavily on what has done well in previous seasons runs the risk of producing stale product ranges. A high-fashion product has a shorter shelf-life than a packet of biscuits, and so needs to be treated as a perishable item.

Many of Oasis's suppliers have grown with the company from its early days, and so they have a keen awareness of the retailer's needs and have adapted their production facilities accordingly. They are rewarded for their service by loyalty from the retailer. Negotiations between the retailer and its suppliers are tough, but they are conducted with a mutual understanding that both are continually striving towards the same aim, which is to sell more garments in Oasis stores to Oasis customers.

(Source: Jack 1995)

REVIEW QUESTIONS

1 Explain the principles of the economic order quantity. Suggest reasons for the diminishing use of the EOQ in retail stock control operations.
2 Discuss the notion that understanding consumer purchase patterns is the underpinning of any efficient stock control system.
3 Discuss the contribution that sales reactive stock control systems have made to leaner stock holding in retail organisations.
4 To what extent do retail–supplier partnerships facilitate the implementation of a quick response system?

DISCUSSION QUESTIONS

1 Consider the seasonal, fashion and endorsement influences of the demand for the following product categories: (a) soft drinks; and (b) wines.
2 To what extent can a periodic review system of stock control be compared with a sales-based stock management system?
3 Using the information given in Table 6.1, plot the ordering and possession costs on a graph and show the economic order quantity. Refer to Figure 6.4.
4 Referring to Mini Case Study 5 at the end of the chapter, explain how a quick response system can help a fashion retailer to have the 'right' quantity of products in its stores.

REFERENCES AND FURTHER READING

Baily, P., Farmer, D., Jessop, D. and Jones, D. (1994) *Purchasing Principles and Management*, 7th edn, Pitman, London.
Fernie, J. (ed.) (1999) *The Future of UK Retailing*, Financial Times Retail and Consumer Reports, London.
Fernie, J. and Sparks, L. (1998) *Logistics and Retail Management*, Kogan Page, London.
Fiorito, S.S., May, E.G. and Straughn, K. (1995) 'Quick response in retailing: components and implementation', *International Journal of Retailing and Distribution Management* **23** (5): 12–21.
Harris, D. and Walters, D. (1992) *Retail Operations Management: A Strategic Approach*, Prentice-Hall, Hemel Hempstead, Herts.
Hart, C., Kirkup, M., Preston, D., Rafiq, M. and Walley, P., (eds) (1997) *Cases in Retailing: Operational Perspectives*, Blackwell, Oxford.
Jack, S. (1995) 'All together now', *Drapers Record*, 11 February.
Lowson, B., King, R. and Hunter, A. (1999) *Quick Response: Managing the Supply Chain to Meet Consumer Demand*, John Wiley, Chichester, Sussex.
Lysons, C.K. (1991) *Purchasing*, Pitman, London.
Mintel (1997) *Convenience Retailing* (January), Mintel International Group, London.
Wills, J. (1999) *Merchandising and Buying Strategies: New Roles for Global Operation*, Financial Times Retail and Consumer, London.

chapter seven

PRODUCT RANGE MANAGEMENT

INTRODUCTION

The principles of product range management are underpinned by the understanding of the concepts of variety and depth of assortment. As discussed in the opening chapters of this book, the extent to which a retailer positions itself as a specialist or a generalist and how the retailer is able to add value to the consumer shopping experience by meeting their current and anticipated needs are key determinants of a successful product strategy. Within this overall product based strategic position, however, the retailer still needs to make detailed plans in order to manage satisfactorily the operations required to fulfil their strategic objectives. This chapter provides some guiding principles and management aids that will help retailers to achieve the balanced stock position that they are looking for.

In addition to the variety and depth in the product offer, stock availability also plays a part in achieving a balanced product range. The methods used by retailers in order to achieve a satisfactory stock service have been outlined in the previous chapter. However, the discussion was generally restricted to the decisions made about single product items. Product managers in retail businesses are generally responsible for a whole group of related merchandise, rather than single product items, as discussed previously in chapters two and three, and so quantity decisions have to be made about each line or stock-keeping unit (SKU) in the context of a *range* of products. The size of product ranges managed by individual product management teams varies according to the degree of specialisation within the retailer, and the process of splitting the total product offer into manageable and logical ranges of products is a fundamental step in retail product management.

THE PRODUCT RANGE

A number of approaches can be used to determine how products are placed into ranges:

- *End use* A DIY superstore like B&Q, for example, has bathroom, kitchen and garden sections, with products clustered into 'projects'.
- *Product features and technology* For example, an electrical retailer may have ranges split according to the relevant technology, such as CD, minidisk and DVD.
- *Price of the item* Variety stores may have a 'budget range' that is bought separately from other ranges. Alternatively, a premium range of luxury foods in a supermarket may be managed in its entirety by a team operating separately from the other food categories.
- *Brand* It may be more sensible, for example in a department store like Debenhams which has over fifty own-brands alone, for ranges to be managed by brand rather than by product category. In this way the identity of the brand (sometimes referred to as its 'handwriting') remains strong, consistent and co-ordinated.

Within each range it may be possible to break the products down further into groups that show distinct similarities in sales patterns. For example, the dress range at women's wear retailer Principles will include party dresses, summer dresses, business dresses and occasional dresses. Each of these different types of dress has similar sales patterns and may have similarities in other product features such as fabrication, colour and styling (see Figure 7.1). As discussed in chapter three, the term product category is used to denote a manageable collection of products that essentially have comparable sales patterns and are considered to be reasonable substitutes for one another from a customer's viewpoint.

At any time within the retail year, a product range is likely to include some categories that are growing, some that are stable and some that are contracting. Therefore it is the job of the buyer to ensure that not only are the right number of products available, but that the right kind of products are on offer. Achieving the correct balance of offer within a product range is a challenge to any buyer, but, as with sales forecasting, achieving balance when dealing with fashion orientated and seasonal products is particularly challenging.

In many retail situations, product ranges can be broken down into core ranges, which have a consistent sales pattern throughout the year, and

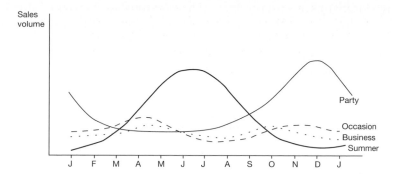

Figure 7.1 **Sales patterns for dress categories within a women's clothing retailer**

seasonal ranges, which have an irregular sales pattern over time with peaks and slower selling periods. For core ranges, stock planning and control can be based on the sales-based ordering principle outlined in chapter six, but for seasonal goods, which present heightened risks and rewards, the retail buyer needs to pre-plan or forecast the season's sales and stock position. In order to minimise the risks and maximise the potential rewards, product range management must be approached from two angles: the financial angle, to ensure that the stock investment is not too great for the flow of income from sales; and the physical angle, to ensure that whenever a customer enters the store there is an appropriate choice of relevant merchandise on offer.

The product planning aids that are described in this chapter apply in essence to both large and small retailers. In a large retail company, merchandise planning will use a computerised system, which will eliminate laborious calculations. However, as managerial judgement is still required to make the exceptional qualitative decisions that can mean the success or failure of a product range, an understanding of the underlying principles of merchandise planning systems is necessary for any retail product manager.

THE MERCHANDISE BUDGET PLAN

Merchandise budget plans are concerned with the financial planning of merchandise ranges. For any retailer (of any size) it is vital that a balance is achieved between the amount of money going out of a business to pay for supplies of stock and money coming into the business from sales to customers. Even though there are various accounting methods that allow a little flexibility (for example, extended credit terms), this balance is essential to the liquidity of the business. A merchandise budget plan is difficult to accomplish without the benefit of previous experience and internal records; however, relying on historical data alone can lead a buyer or product manager into repeating previous mistakes, including missed opportunities.

The first step of the plan is a realistic sales forecast, the principles of which were discussed in chapter six. The time period for the plan will vary according to the individual needs of the retail business, but a six-monthly plan is common for many seasonal products. The sales forecast shown in Table 7.1 is for a relatively seasonal product – women's toiletry gift packs. The sales are above average in January, because of all the reduced Christmas stock, in April because of Mother's Day and Easter, and in June due to pre-holiday purchases. The forecasted sales are shown as a percentage of the total season's sales estimate and at retail selling value.

Table 7.1 **The first stages of a merchandise budget plan**

	Category: Toiletry gift packs (womens)						
	Jan	*Feb*	*Mar*	*Apr*	*May*	*Jun*	*Total*
Forecast sales							
%	19	13	14	24	14	16	100
£'000	11,400	7,800	8,400	14,400	8,400	9,600	60,000
Beginning of month							
Stock: Sales ratio	2.8	3.3	3.2	2.6	3.1	3.0	3.0[a]
Stock (£'000)	31,920	24,960	26,880	37,440	26,040	28,800	N/A

Note: [a] Average ratio.

The second step of the plan is to consider how much stock is needed in the stores in order to achieve the forecasted level of sales. Arriving at this stock to sales ratio will need consideration of the following:

- How fast can replacement items be supplied?
- How fast will the item sell out, and how important is it to keep the product in stock?
- How much choice does the customer expect to find in the store in order to make a purchase?

For a relatively slow-selling, specific product item that can be restocked by a local distributor (power tool, for example), the stock to sales ratio can be kept low; but for party dresses, where lead times might be three weeks or more and customers require an extensive selection of styles and sizes to choose from, the stock to sales ratio needs to be higher. Usually these factors are considered collectively for the category of merchandise being planned, and an average stock to sales ratio is arrived at for the planning period. Thus, an average ratio of 2 might be sufficient for power tools, but may be as high as 10 for party dresses. This average is then raised or lowered through the selling season to reflect the effect of differing sales rates on the stock position: when sales peak, the stock runs down quickly and the stock to sales ratio drops down from the average; but when sales are slow, the stock to sales ratio rises. For seasonal goods it might be necessary to 'stock pile' in order to cope with subsequent surges in demand; again this is reflected by an increasing stock to sales ratio. In the example of women's toiletries, the average stock ratio is 3.0 and is raised and lowered according to the rate of sales.

The stock required to achieve the sales during the month should ideally be present at the beginning of the month; therefore the stock position refers to the beginning of month (BOM) stock level. As sales progress through the month, the stock level drops, so by the end of the month the stock position could be expressed as (BOM stock – sales). However, in reality, as well as selling stock, the retailer will also be receiving stock, in order to build the required level of stock for the next month, so the stock position at the end of a preceding month should be the required BOM stock of the next month. The difference between the (BOM stock – sales) figure and the end of month (EOM) stock figure will be the purchases that have arrived during the month. Figure 7.2 illustrates this process.

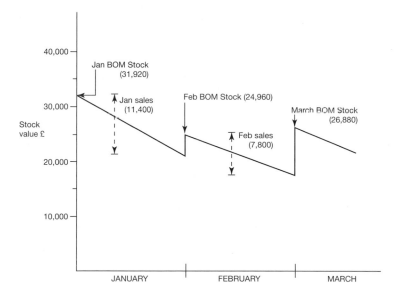

Figure 7.2 **Illustration of stock levels**

If the plan started in Table 7.1 is continued, we can see how this process works through the season. Expressed as an equation:

Planned purchases = EOM stock + sales – BOM stock

The planned purchases for each month represent the value of stock (at retail price) that the buyer needs to bring in from suppliers. Some goods may need to be ordered in advance of the season, whilst others can be topped up immediately; therefore it is likely that some of the planned purchase figure will have already been committed to pre-ordered goods suppliers. The remaining funds are what are left 'open' for the buyer to spend on fast lead-time stock. In this way the stock level for the next month is achieved.

Table 7.2 **Arriving at the planned purchase figures**

	Jan	Feb	Mar	Apr	May	Jun	Total
	Category: Toiletry gift packs (womens)						
Forecast sales							
%	19	13	14	24	14	16	100
£	11,400	7,800	8,400	14,400	8,400	9,600	60,000
Beginning of month							
Stock: Sales ratio	2.8	3.3	3.2	2.6	3.1	3.0	3.0[a]
Stock (£)	31,920	24,960	26,880	37,440	26,040	28,800	N/A
End of month stock (£)	24,960	26,880	37,440	26,040	28,800	—	N/A
Planned purchases (£)	4,440	9,720	18,960	3,000	11,160	—	N/A

Note: [a]Average.

Open-to-buy

Buyers do not pay their suppliers retail selling prices, however, and so the planned purchase figure must have the gross profit margin removed in order to give the buyer the true 'open-to-buy' figures. For planning purposes, an average gross margin for the category might be used, even though the retailer may vary the margin on the products within the range (see chapter eight). The sales and stock figures in the plan should always be planned at retail selling price, so that actual and planned figures can be easily compared.

Reductions in stock value

Unfortunately, sales are not the only reason for the removal of stock from retail businesses. There are a variety of reasons why a stock value position falls, and these have to be accounted for in order to give a true reflection of value of stock. Stock reductions include:

• external theft;
• internal pilferage;
• shop soiling and damage;
• mark-downs.

Discounts may also be given to customers (for example to store card holders) and to staff (as an incentive), and so all these reductions in the value of stock have to be reflected in the budget plan. Historical figures are useful in terms of setting a realistic reductions level for a category of merchandise. However, the following guidelines should be used when it comes to detailed planning:

• *shrinkage* (theft and damage) tends to follow the same pattern as sales: the more people in the store, the more shop soiling and damage of goods is likely to occur, and the easier it is for thieves to operate amongst the crowds. In addition, a thief's needs tend to coincide with those of an honest shopper, so the retail crime rate peaks in the Christmas build-up (see Box 7.1);

- *markdowns* may be taken as part of a planned, offensive promotional strategy or as a defensive reaction to competition or poor sales performance. If the general economic forecast is poor, it may be prudent to plan a higher than average markdown figure, for example;
- *staff discounts and customer discounts* tend to be taken slightly ahead of the normal sales peak. This is because it is more likely that staff and regular customers will be enticed by new merchandise offerings at the start of the season. They may also be swift to take advantage of end of season price-cutting.

If these various reductions to the value of stock were not taken into account, the stock value on the retailer's stock control system would be very different to the actual value of the physical stock present within the retail business. The only way to reconcile the two would be to undertake a physical stock-take. This would confirm whether or not the planning and monitoring systems show an accurate representation of business reality.

In terms of dealing with reductions in the merchandise budget plan, they have to be planned into the stock equation as shown in Table 7.3; in effect a retailer has to buy extra stock into the business in order to compensate for the falling value of stock through reductions. In this case the total reduction in stock value through the season averages 10 per cent of the total estimated sales for the category. The equation for calculating the planned purchase figure, taking reductions into account is:

Planned purchases = EOM stock + sales + reductions – BOM stock

Table 7.3 A full merchandise budget plan

	Jan	Feb	Mar	Apr	May	Jun	Total
Category: Toiletry gift packs (womens)							
Forecast sales							
%	19	13	14	24	14	16	100
(£)	11,400	7,800	8,400	14,400	8,400	9,600	60,000
Forecast reductions							
%	21	13	12	24	15	15	100
£	1,260	780	720	1,440	900	900	6,000
Beginning of month Stock: Sales ratio	2.8	3.3	3.2	2.6	3.1	3.0	3.0[a] (Average)
Stock (£)	31,920	24,960	26,880	37,440	26,040	28,800	N/A
End of month stock (£)	24,960	26,880	37,440	26,040	28,800	—	N/A
Planned purchases (£)	5,700	10,500	19,680	4,440	12,060	—	10,476[a]

Note: [a] Average.

BOX 7.1 UNDERSTANDING THE CRIMINAL CONSUMER

Retail crime is big business. In 1999, retailers spent £612 million on crime prevention, which was 11 per cent more than the previous year; 4.17 million offences were recorded against retailers, and whilst the majority of these were external theft by 'customers', an increasing proportion of retail crimes involve retailers' own staff, at just over 32 per cent of the total cost of crime, which was calculated to be £1.61 billion in 1999 (BRC 1999).

One of the ways to help to prevent retail crime is to understand the 'customer' behaviour of the thief. For example, in December a large number of crimes involve 'typical' gifts, such as toys and nightwear. Many criminal customers use a 'shop and steal' tactic, purchasing some but not all items taken out of the store; they may even return to steal or buy later in the same shop. Like other consumer behaviour, aberrant consumer behaviour is influenced by external factors (Bamfield and Tonglet 1999); for example, in terms of demographics, a 'swell' in the under 25 age group is likely to increase crime rates, because males under 25 are the group most prone to steal. Also, shops that are well stocked with merchandise attract thieves. But it is also important to recognise potential problems within a store layout, such as displaying expensive merchandise near exits and using tall and solid fixturing that prevents an open view.

Understanding customers' actions also helps retailers to spot criminal behaviour; for example, excessive handling of goods, over-careful trolley packing, gazing in an inappropriate direction, and adopting strange stances to conceal stolen merchandise are all indications that might alert a retail manager to wrongdoings.

(Sources: Bamfield and Tonglet 1999; Clements 2000)

THE ASSORTMENT PLAN (MODEL STOCK LIST)

The assortment plan is a valuable aid: not only for the management of products from a buying perspective, but also as a very useful document for store management, because it denotes what, in physical product terms, should be on display within the store at any particular time period. In essence, the assortment plan starts where the product range review, described in chapter four, finishes. In some retail businesses the assortment plan will not change throughout the year, but in others a new model stock list may need to be drawn up for each major selling season. It may also be necessary for retailers to issue a number of different assortment plans if they have a wide variation in size of store.

The model stock list will usually break down the merchandise within a product category, but it will not normally be carried out at SKU level, unless the merchandise is extremely specialised and/or of high value.

On the assortment plan for core (staple) ranges, the product detail may specify brand and product variation; in fact the model stock list begins to take the form of a written planogram (see chapter nine). However, in order to allow the buyer of fashion orientated goods more flexibility the plan will carry less detail. The kind of variable shown on the assortment plan will be:

- styling design themes;
- colours;
- flavours;
- pack size;
- fabrication/type;
- price level (not exact prices).

The assortment plan for the red wine category in a convenience store might look something like Table 7.4.

Table 7.4 **Assortment plan for red wine**

	Price level	*Type*	*SKUs*
French	High	Beaujolais, Claret, Cabernet Sauvignon	7
	Medium	Cabernet Sauvignon, Côtes du Rhône	5
	Low	Vin de table	1
Spanish	High	Rioja, other	3
	Medium	Tempanillo, other	2
	Low	'Spanish'	1
Italian	High	Chianti, other	3
	Medium	Valpolicella, other	2
Other regions	High	Australian	4
	Medium	Chilean	2
Litre bottles	French		2
	Spanish		1
Boxes	French		1
	Italian		1

By specifying particular attributes on the assortment plan, the buyer ensures that the product range offers the customer a good variety from which to choose. However, the plan also allows flexibility so that buying opportunities can be maximised. For example, a wine from a new producing region such as Argentina can be incorporated into the range (other regions, medium price).

Fashion assortment plans

The product assortment plan is fundamental to the range planning of fashion merchandise and is built up gradually and in more detail as the planning for the season progresses. Fashion buyers need to make sure that they cover all the key colours, silhouettes and design themes which they identify as being important for the coming season. Design ideas and themes are generated in a number of ways:

- the 'directional' shopping trip, looking in trend-setting retailers' for fresh ideas;
- using the services of a design information service (see Box 4.2);
- keeping track of the media used by the target customers, to spot trends and product endorsements by peers;
- tapping into the target customers' lifestyles (observational and structured research).

Practical considerations for the assortment plan

There are a number of practical considerations that buyers have to take into account when drawing up their assortment plan.

Store size and characteristics

The buyer must have an idea of how much space should be devoted to each category (the expansion or contraction of categories will be evident on the different seasons' assortment plan). The display fixtures available also have to be considered. If no suitable fixtures are available and investment in new fixtures is not appropriate due to financial or physical constraints, then it may be better not to buy that category of merchandise (see chapter eleven for a discussion of the flexibility of display fixtures). For example, a buyer might feel strongly about a trend for full-length evening dresses for the Christmas party season. However, the number of fixtures available for full-length garments may be limited because the store usually concentrates on separates.

Complementary merchandise

In creating an assortment plan the buyer must consider the balance of merchandise, so that transaction values can be raised as high as possible. An obvious example would be the balance between suits and shirts or blouses, but it could also be applicable to foliage and flowers in a florists, or pasta and pasta sauces in a grocery store.

Profitability of merchandise

Whilst the anticipated profit margins may be a valid consideration for the retailer when drawing up the assortment plan, the customer is not interested in a retailer's profitability, and so profit expectations should be considered alongside all the other requirements of a balanced offer and not be allowed to dictate the plan.

Corporate objectives

For some retailers it may be top priority to be able to guarantee a very high stock service level for the customer. With other retailers, customers understand that the offer is more diverse, that they as individuals may not be guaranteed the exact product item required, and that a number of very similar substitutes will be available. In fact in such a situation the customer may well be heartened if they do not see a rack of the same items if their purchase item needs to show a high level of individuality, such as a gift. Marks & Spencer, for example, takes a product line off sale if they cannot offer a full range of sizes to the customer. Such shortages may occur because the product is selling so quickly that the manufacturers are unable, temporarily, to keep up with demand. Marks & Spencer, however, would not compromise the service promise to the customer, even though possible short-term gains could be associated with selling broken size ranges of 'hot' items. Upmarket retailers like Jaeger, on the other hand, deliberately do not display all the available sizes so that stores retain an uncluttered and spacious feel (Buttle 1993).

Fine-tuning the assortment plan will utilise all of a buyer's knowledge and experience gained from a variety of external sources. One of the most valuable sources of information is the stores and their personnel; in the majority of successful retailers, buyers have a specified amount of time dedicated to store visits. Store visits enable the buyer to hear at first-hand from the sales associates what the customers like and do not like about the product range and perhaps what they expect to find in the range on offer: this will highlight the strengths and weaknesses in the total product offer. Feedback systems may be formalised, for example by using surveys, or 'want slips' that are completed by the sales team, but these methods have the risk of bias and low response, therefore building a rapport between the buying and merchandising teams at head office and the store managers and sales teams is an ongoing and necessary challenge. Many enlightened retailers admit that this two-way communication is one of the key challenges of retailing and are prepared to devote time and resources to maintaining a satisfactory information flow. Zara, the international fashion retailer, for example, encourages its store personnel to talk directly to its design teams about garment styles that work well with customers (Clements 2000b).

Some assortment plans include the size distribution that will be available for each type of merchandise; whether or not this is included, it is a product manager's responsibility to make a sizing decision when placing an initial order. Whether the order is for nightdresses or for corn flakes, the size variation offered to the customer must still be considered. For many products size distribution is not an issue, but other product variations have to be accounted for:

* *sizing*: body size for clothing, bed size for linens, cubic capacity for refrigerators;
* *body sizing variations*: ladies: 8, 10, 12 and so on, trouser inside-leg length, waist size; men's: chest size, waist size, trouser inside-leg length; children's: by age, height;
* *pack sizing variation*: weight, volume, multi-pack variation.

For many retail businesses a highly disciplined approach to merchandise planning has been the underpinning of their success. However, for a number of retailers, part or all of the product range is acquired on the basis of opportunity. For example, the buyers at T.J. Hughes, the highly successful discount department store, allocate around one-third of their budget to opportunity purchases (Wills 1999), which might be second goods, ends of lines or excess factory stock.

CONCESSIONS

Concessions are a way of allowing a retailer to extend the product range offered within the outlet without experiencing some of the risks associated with buying merchandise. The basis of a concession, which may be referred to as a 'shop-in-shop', is that a retailer allows a supplier of a particular brand of merchandise a designated amount of space within an outlet from which those goods are sold. The actual terms of the agreement will vary from retailer to retailer. In some agreements the supplier will provide staff to sell the merchandise; in others it is simply a matter of using dedicated fixturing. In some deals the retail product manager has to buy a minimum quantity of merchandise in order to secure the in-store promotional support (fixtures and point of sale material), whereas other concessions operate on a sale or return basis, which carries a lower risk for the retailer. The rewards gained by a retailer from using concessions also vary: for example, it might receive a flat rate 'rent' for the selling space, or it might receive a percentage of the sales income. If the agreement is based on the retailer actually purchasing the stock, then it will gain the full amount of sales income, but the profit margins may be lower than those on other merchandise. Usually the branded supplier will want to dictate the selling prices to the retailer in order to establish consistency with its other stockists (it may have its own retail outlets, for example).

Running concessions is a good way of supporting a strong brand which may encourage customer traffic and therefore sales of other merchandise, but a retailer must ensure that the agreement with the concessionaire is flexible enough to prevent valuable selling space being devoted to inappropriate merchandise. The brand must have an image that is consistent with the retailer's image and the other merchandise on offer. Concessions that work well have the potential to offer the retailer benefits of healthy supply partnerships, such as receiving priority treatment for re-orders and special orders, as well as joint marketing campaigns.

SUMMARY

Establishing the detail of the product range offered by a retailer is part of the strategic product management process involving a balancing act between the need to meet financial objectives and the need to present an inspiring product offer to the customer. Product ranges on offer have to reflect the changing requirements of consumers and should offer customers added value so that they do not choose to shop with a competitor. The assortment plan shows how this is going to be achieved, in the light of decisions taken during the range review process. However, range planning must be managed according to the resources available to the retailer. The merchandise budget plan helps the retailer plan ahead for seasonal merchandise so that sales opportunities can be maximised and the dangers of over-investing in stock are minimised.

EXERCISES

1 Refer back to Table 7.3 when attempting this exercise.

Some additional information concerning the orders provisionally booked by the buyer of the women's toiletry department with suppliers for the spring season has been provided:

Beauty Pack Ltd   £3,000 order, delivery February, March, April
Handy Gifts & Co   £6,000 order, delivery February, March, April
Gift Bag Ltd   £4,000 order, delivery January, February March
Scents and Sense   £2,000 order, delivery March, April

Note: Deliveries are split evenly across the months, unless otherwise stated.

The average gross margin for this category is 45 per cent.
Task: Calculate the open-to-buy figures that will be left for each month, when all the orders have been confirmed.

2 Refer back to Table 7.3 when attempting this exercise.

In order to show how the open-to-buy changes when actual sales do not exactly meet forecasted sales, make the following actual figure substitutions on the plan shown in Table 7.2:

(a) The April promotion was more successful than anticipated, and sales peaked at £15,000.
(b) May was very cold, which slowed holiday purchases, resulting in sales reaching only £8,400.

3 The following exercise involves drawing up a merchandise budget plan, based on an abstract from the merchandisers report for the 'novelty socks' category, which falls within the hosiery department of Harvey & Aldred department store:

As one might expect, the sales of this type of merchandise are highly seasonal. Socks are favourite stocking fillers at Christmas, and are often bought at the last minute when no better idea has emerged! In fact, we take almost half the season's money in the month before Christmas. We do, however, keep a small range to sell the year round, with an average beginning of month stock/sales ratio of three. There are two reasons for this; there are Birthday gifts, of course, and it also enables us to join in any 'themed' promotion that is being planned storewide. This year, for example, we are doing a 'Tartan Promotion' in early October, which will be good for all men's accessories. In the week of November 5th, the whole men's wear floor has a celebration event, where we offer a 20 per cent discount on all customer purchases over £50. Socks often do well in this week as they are used to 'top up' the sales to get the discount. This year our total season's sales forecast is £18,500, and reductions normally average out at 10 per cent of sales.

4 Choose a product category within a local supermarket store and draw up an assortment plan that you think is appropriate for that particular category in that particular store. Then, take a visit to the store and find out how your plan differed from the actual assortment on offer. Explain or justify any differences between the two.

REVIEW QUESTIONS

1 Explain the differences between the merchandise budget plan and the assortment plan.
2 What does the term 'reductions' refer to in merchandise planning? Explain why it is necessary to allow for reductions when planning a merchandise budget.
3 Identify the various practical considerations that retailers should take into account when drawing up their assortment plan.

DISCUSSION QUESTIONS

1 Discuss how the following planning aids help retail product managers to achieve their objectives:

(a) the assortment plan;
(b) calculation of monthly open-to-buy.

2 For a number of chosen categories, think of the sales distribution over the year. To what extent are your products seasonal, and when would be a good time(s) to launch a product-related promotion in each category?
3 Why does the amount of detail in assortment plans vary between product sectors? Give some product examples where you think it would be possible to have a very detailed assortment plan and where the assortment plan would benefit from being more flexible.
4 On a merchandise budget plan, what would be the significance of a negative figure in the open-to-buy figures, for example, if confirmed orders in April in Table 7.3 amounted to 5,000 instead of 4,000? Suggest how a buyer might deal with this situation.

REFERENCES AND FURTHER READING

Bamfield, J. and Tonglet, M. (1999) 'Understanding consumer behaviour: how shoplifters shop the store', *Proceedings of the 10th International Conference on Research in the Distributive Trades*, Institute for Retail Studies, University of Stirling.

British Retail Consortium (1999) *Retail Crime Survey*, British Retail Consortium, London.

Buttle, F. (1993) 'Jaeger ladies', in P.J. McGoldrick (ed.) *Cases in Retailing Management*, Pitman, London.

Clements, A. (2000a) 'Light-fingered staff challenge the shoplifters', *Retail Week*, 7 April.

Clements, A. (2000b) 'Zara leads conquering armada', *Retail Week*, 14 April.

Levy, M. and Weitz, B.A. (1998) *Retailing Management*, 3rd edn, McGraw-Hill, Maidenhead, Berks.

Wills, J. (1999) *Merchandising and Buying Strategies: New Roles for a Global Operation*, Financial Times Retail and Consumer Report, London.

chapter eight

PROFITABLE PRODUCT MANAGEMENT

INTRODUCTION

Profitability is essential if a retail business is to survive, but achieving profitability is a complex task, given the variety of transactions that take place within the retail arena. Profitability is a short term, a medium term and a long term issue. For example, in the short term enough profits have to be generated on the sales of items to cover the costs of buying in the product; and in the medium term, enough profit has to be generated to pay the costs of running the business (rent, staffing costs, distribution costs and so on); but in order to develop the business a further chunk of profits will need to be set aside for reinvestment, for example, into an additional or larger outlet.

Ultimately, there are two methods of increasing retail profitability; one is to increase the profit margins made on the products that are sold, and the other is to reduce the costs involved with selling the products. Chapter two outlined the role of the buyer and merchandiser who, in a traditional organisational structure, share the responsibility for profitability management within the department. In some organisations the merchandiser takes on the bulk of profitability issues, such as managing margins and price reductions, but the person who negotiates cost prices with suppliers will also make a significant impact on departmental profitability. Trade-offs between product features and prices will be the selector's concern. The role of the category manager, discussed in chapter three, puts a great emphasis on profitability in the guise of efficiency improvements, throughout the efficient consumer response system. A full consideration of all the issues that affect profitability is beyond the scope of this text. However, a retail product manager who does not have a basic understanding of how profitability is achieved and how it can be measured will not maximise the potential of his or her responsibilities. In an era of retail saturation, trading profitability becomes an increasingly important strategic goal for retailers.

SETTING RETAIL PRICES

The price that a customer pays for a product is made up of two main components: the cost of the product, or the price than the retailer pays to a supplier, and the gross profit margin, which is the selling price minus the cost of the product (see Figure 8.1)

Figure 8.1 **The retail selling price**

An expression that is often used in retailing is the 'mark-up', and normally this refers to the gross margin. The mark-up can therefore be expressed as a total amount in monetary terms (£4 in Figure 8.1) or as a percentage of the cost price (25 per cent in the figure) or as a percentage of the selling price (20 per cent in the figure). The most common use of the term-mark up is as a percentage of the cost price; however, because of the various uses of the term, it will be avoided in the following discussion and the term profit margin will be used.

Having discussed the various uses of the term mark-up, it would seem appropriate at this stage to discuss the use of the term mark-down. A mark-down is a price reduction and relates to the difference between an original selling price and a new selling price. A mark-down can be expressed as a monetary figure or as a percentage of the original selling price (see Figure 8.2).

It would not be useful to express the mark-down as a percentage of the cost of the product, but the new price will of course now have a different (reduced) mark-up (12.5 per cent in Figure 8.2). As the gross profit margins (multiplied by the number of products sold) represents the income from which a retailer has to pay the expenses of running the retail business, allocate funds for business development and pay the shareholders of the company, the prices set are crucial to the success of the business.

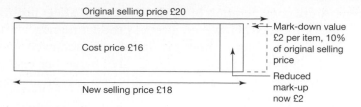

Figure 8.2 **Price mark-down**

Price sensitivity

Price elasticity is a key principle to be observed in the setting of prices. This is the extent to which demand for a product responds to change is price. As a guiding principle, the more discretionary a purchase, the more opportunity for retailers to use price elasticity in their pricing strategy; on the other hand, today's complex shopper does not act as a rational economically driven consumer (see chapter four), and the demand for products is affected by a whole host of variables other than price. It is not the intention of this chapter to explore the variables that influence price sensitivity, a discussion of which can be found elsewhere (for example, Brassington and Petitt 2000: 396), but to point out that demand for products will vary: at the SKU level (for example, a mega-brand versus an own-label variant); at category level (for example, seasonal effects); and at department level (staple product such as foods versus household purchases such as carpets).

Uniform mark-up (cost-orientated method)

At one time it was fairly common practice for retailers to apply a 'uniform mark-up policy' throughout the store, so that every item had the same percentage gross margin. However, whilst simple to administer, this method did not allow the retailer to exploit the opportunity to charge higher margins where the market would stand it or to accept lower margins in the face of competition. It also did not take into consideration the effects of sales volume on overall profits.

Retailers then began to adjust margins according to departments or categories, which generally had the effect of raising margins on less frequently purchased merchandise and lowering margins on volume products. Now, most leading retailers are able to conduct profit margin analysis at the SKU level, so the contribution to profits of every single item within the store is known and prices are set individually for each item.

Demand-led pricing

This approach to pricing considers price from the perspective of the product market (the price which the market is willing to pay). Prices are set according to the demand for the product, the availability of substitutes and the prices that the competition is charging. This allows retailers to react to their trading environment and maximise sales within it, but it may result in retailers selling at a loss. This may be perfectly acceptable if a customer purchases other products along with the loss-making items (the loss leader approach), but of course it is not a sustainable strategy otherwise.

If a retailer is introducing a new product brand or a new product category into its range and is unsure of the likely demand, it makes sense to start with a cost-orientated method, which can then be fine tuned at a later stage when the demand factors are identified.

THE BROADER PICTURE

Pricing decisions for each product in the retailer's outlet are taken within the context of the merchandise assortment plan and within the framework of a broader market positioning strategy. As we saw in chapter seven, it may be the buyer's intention to have similar products at different price levels in the product assortment plan, in order to broaden the appeal of the product range. However, consistency in the pricing level across categories and departments reinforces a positioning strategy in the light of the variety and depth of assortment on offer; therefore a brief reference to the alternative general price level strategies which retailers might use is appropriate in order to provide the context for a more detailed discussion on profitability measures.

Premium pricing

Premium pricing is used in order to obtain maximum profit margins on products by selling at a high level. In exchange for a high price customers will expect some added value in their purchase, such as a high service level or an exceptional or highly convenient selling environment. Taken one stage further, prestige pricing is used for many branded products, whereby the high price reinforces the brand value. Department stores like Harrods in London or Bloomingdale's in New York have worldwide reputations for their premium pricing strategies, which combine with prestigious products and surroundings to maintain an up-market image. However, in consumer markets where increasing numbers of people are value driven in their purchasing decisions, premium-pricing policies are becoming harder to sustain.

BOX 8.1 VIRTUAL PRICE COMPARISONS

The internet is offering the consumer a fast and convenient way to comparison shop. Shopping services such as Yahoo!Shopping, Valuemad and Smart Shop will do the price comparing exercise for customers. This means that on mainstream and branded items which can be compared like for like, the opportunity for retailers to operate a premium pricing strategy is becoming much harder. When the location of the outlet, the shopping environment and the quality of sales service all become irrelevant, then price becomes the primary differentiating factor.

High–low pricing

The objective of a high–low strategy is to sell as much merchandise as possible at 'full price' with a high profit margin for as long a period as possible, and then reduce margins after a time in order to clear out older merchandise to make room for new. Clearly this is an inappropriate strategy for stable products, but it is widely used for seasonal and fashion products. Timing is crucial for this strategy, because retailers who reduce their prices too quickly lose the trust of their customers, who will wait for the next 'sale' and become reluctant to buy anything at full price. Being too cautious about reducing prices, on the other hand, runs the risk that competitors will get to the customer's purse first and the merchandise become outdated and stale. High–low pricing works well with prestige pricing, so that outdated prestige merchandise can be sold off as a bargain in order to keep the ranges looking fresh and innovative.

Every day low pricing (EDLP)

Every day low pricing has a considerable appeal for customers because they feel confident that they are buying at 'fair' and 'good-value' prices, reinforcing a feeling of good sense and judgement in the shopping process. A constant stream of offers and promotions might appeal to the bargain 'junkie', but a time-poor multiple-occupation 'striver' might consider that variable pricing is time consuming to evaluate. The EDLP strategy, where margins and prices are kept constantly low, makes customers feel that the retailer has done the price comparison exercise for them. For staple products this strategy makes good sense and helps a retailer gain customer loyalty. Asda, for example, informs its customers at its checkouts that 'Customers prefer low prices to loyalty points', referring to Mintel's (1998) report on loyalty. However, low margins may result in retailers not being able to afford to invest in other parts of their strategy, such as service provision, which may become a more important differentiating factor. There is also a danger that EDLP may lead to a downward price spiral into discounting in a highly competitive retail environment, which will have a highly detrimental effect on overall profitability.

Discounting

Discounting is a strategy whereby the retailer sells at prices that are 'lower than average' on a permanent basis. It is only sustainable if the retailer has other low cost element(s) within their marketing mix, such as a low rent location, merchandise that is procured on an opportunistic basis, minimal service and a 'basic' store environment. Discounting is a useful strategy for clearing end-of-line merchandise or 'seconds' stock, and is the underpinning of retail phenomena such as factory outlets. Retailers like the Body Shop use factory outlets to sell off discontinued lines, allowing the 'high street' retailers to sell the current ranges without old stock cluttering the store (Hall 1999).

BOX 8.2   WHAT RIP-OFF?

In spite of reports to the contrary in the popular press, it appears that British retailers do not 'rip-off' their customers. In January 2000, the UK government's Competition Commission issued the initial findings of its major report which indicated that there was no evidence that retailers keep prices artificially high, that food prices had actually dropped over the past year, and that customers were generally satisfied.

Nevertheless, the Competition Commission has highlighted a number of more complex pricing issues such as regional pricing and retailer–supplier pricing arrangements. The Competition Act 1998 gives the Office of Fair Trading new powers to investigate businesses that have anti-competitive agreements (for example, with their suppliers) or abuse a dominant market position. In the area of pricing and competition, retailers are under increasing government scrutiny.

(Sources: Cartlidge 2000; Hall 2000)

MEASURING PRODUCT PROFITABILITY

Gross margin

The gross margin generated (see Figure 8.1) is the most basic form of measuring a product's profitability. Because it does not consider the sales volume generated by different products and the effect on overall profit contribution, it is only a starting point in the analysis of retail profit.

Gross margin return on investment

In order to account for the different rates of sales generated by products it makes sense to multiply gross margins by the rate of sales for each product so that the gross profit contribution by each product, each category and each department can be compared. However, rather than considering the sales volume for this calculation, the sales turnover is used. For example, it would not be surprising if a retailer sold a large quantity of sweaters, if a large percentage of floor space was devoted to sweaters and the stock holding was high. Using sales turnover in the GMROI calculation allows the comparison to be made between the gross profit margin generated on a product and the return on the money invested in stocking that product. GMROI can be calculated at different levels of merchandise calculation, for example category, department or SKU, as shown in Table 8.1. The higher the GMROI, the more 'work' that merchandise is doing for the profitability your business.

This simple analysis will indicate to the retailer which products are making the largest contribution to its overall gross profits in relation to the financial investment made in that stock. However, not all products within a retail offer require the same amount of resources in order to sell. Some products require special storage facilities (frozen or chilled foods, for example); some products

Table 8.1 **Illustration of GMROI (gross margin return on investment)**

Product category	Gross margin (%)	Turnover ratio	GMROI (%)
Baked beans	10	12	120
Biscuits	20	6	120
Boxed chocolates	40	3	120

In this example, product categories with different gross margins and different turnover rates result in the same GMROI value.

Product category	Gross margin (%)	Turnover ratio	GMROI (%)
Baked beans	25	12	300
Biscuits	25	6	150
Boxed chocolates	25	3	75

Here, the gross margin is equal for all three product categories, and the resulting GMROI shows considerable variation.

require much larger amounts of space (a toilet roll compared with a jar of honey, for example); other products require a high level of personal service to sell (musical instruments compared with stationery, for example); and with these resources go costs. More refined retail product profitability measures therefore take into account the costs that can be attributed to more areas of product management.

Direct product profitability (DPP)

The concept of DPP emerged in the 1980s and to a certain extent only began to be used in retail profitability analysis when the direct product costs (DPCs) could be accurately calculated using computerised cost analysis programs. These not only include the costs of selling within the store, but they also attribute direct charges to the product right through the supply chain, so that all transportation, warehousing and storage and handling costs are analysed at SKU level. A DPP calculation will also include any additional 'revenue' that a product generates, such as a contribution from suppliers for advertising.

Activity-based costing

Activity-based costing is similar in principle to direct product profitability analysis, but where DPP allocates direct costs to individual products, activity-based costing also includes allocations for indirect costs on an individual product basis. This approach has highlighted areas of significant 'internal spending' which may not be paid back by the resulting merchandise range. For example, buyers' salaries and the costs of running a buying office in the centre of a commercial capital are considerable indirect costs which cannot be changed in the short term. In order to cover such indirect costs, many retailers make a charge at a flat rate to each product sold. In actual fact, a flat rate may not be applicable; for example, developing own-branded merchandise will be costly in terms of buyers' time and effort, compared to selecting products from a branded supplier's range. The costs associated with overseas sourcing may be greater than those associated with using domestic suppliers, and so the view might be taken that the cost of overseas sourcing activities (such as buyers' travel costs, buyers' time on trips and additional input from technologists) should only be charged to imported merchandise. Otherwise areas of significant 'internal spending' may not in the end be paid back by the resulting product range that caused the costs to be incurred.

Clearly, such a detailed approach to cost analysis is beyond the scope of a small retailer, who is less likely to be in a position to alter any of the direct or indirect costs. However, this type of detailed analysis has played an important contribution to cost saving in the supply chain and improvements in space productivity (see chapter nine). These initiatives have allowed retailers to improve their operating profit levels without the need to raise prices. Activity-based costing is the basis of the measurement of efficiency in ECR systems, discussed in chapter three.

Another way to improve profit margins without the need to raise prices is to reduce the buying-in price of a product or, from an alternative point of view, 'squeeze the supply base'. One of the key responsibilities of a buyer is to obtain the very best deals from the suppliers. As discussed in chapter five, the best deals do not often result from concentrating on short term price-orientated battles; but the ability to negotiate well, even within the context of a partnership, is an attribute every retail buyer or product manager should possess.

NEGOTIATION

According to Baily *et al.* (1994), negotiation implies a mutuality of wants, resolved by exchange, and it can be as specific in nature as the design of a pocket on a shirt or as multi-faceted as in the setting up of a supply pro-gramme of pre-prepared meals under a retail brand. Negotiations may take place between two people, each representing one organisation (a buyer and a sales manager, for example), or the negotiation may involve whole teams of people including product developers, product managers, and logistics and marketing managers.

Negotiation is generally regarded as having three stages. The first stage takes place before the two negotiating parties meet and involves a large amount of formal and/or informal preparation, including gathering together relevant information (for example, costing and performance data from previous dealings), setting objectives for the negotiations, and preparing strategies and tactics that might be used, including the roles the various people will play. The second stage is the meeting itself; this will develop from the formalities of welcoming (this can be very important in some cultures); to exploration and debate regarding all the relevant issues; to bargaining; and finally agreement. The third stage takes place after the meeting stage (which may in fact include meeting more than once in order to reach agreement) and involves the implementation of the agreement, such as the modification of a prototype, drawing up a specification (see chapter four), and preparing contract documents. Any of these can be performed by either retailer or supplier, depending on their individual facilities and established procedures, but there must be a signature of acceptance by both parties to the agreement to conclude it. The absolutely final stage of the implementation of negotiations is the supply of the right goods, at the right time and place and with the agreed price on the invoice.

Everything is negotiable

Negotiation is not just about price, but the agreement reached should include an understanding between the retailer and the supplier on what a particular price represents. Negotiation therefore often revolves around alternative product features. For example, a cheaper raw material or a different type of packaging may be a way of getting a price down to the level the buyer wishes to pay without any fundamental change to the product itself. It is, therefore, important in the preparation stage to be clear about those product features that are essential and those that are desirable but not essential. In addition, a buyer should try to be as open-minded as possible during the meeting stage because a supplier may present an unforeseen solution.

In order to be able to evaluate a product's contribution to retail profitability in comparison to others in a range, the cost prices of all products must start on a 'level playing field'. Prices quoted by suppliers to a retailer can be subject to a great deal of variation. There may be a discount for prompt payment or a stepped discount for increasing quantities. Prices may be quoted in different currencies, which may cause price fluctuations, and they may or may not include delivery. Additional services may be included in the price that a retailer would otherwise have to pay for (delivery and installation at a customer's home for example). There may be an allowance for promotional activity or for a particular shelf location. It is very important, therefore, that in any profit comparison exercise between products the cost price is calculated in the same way and the kind of pricing variables listed above taken into account in the individual product profit equation.

THE IMPACT OF MARK-DOWNS

In a retailing situation where the product range is relatively stable, profitable retail management is principally a case of fine-tuning prices in response to the trading environment and monitoring costs. However, as discussed earlier in the chapter, where the sales patterns are subject to fashion and seasonality, it is important to monitor prices with a view to clearing out the old season's goods to make room for the new season's stock arriving. If good buying decisions have been made and the trading environment is buoyant, mark-downs will only be needed to clear broken ranges (odd sizes and colours) and the total mark-down for any particular product line will be low. However, by analysing the total mark-down applied in order to clear stock, other problems may become apparent, as illustrated in Table 8.2.

Table 8.2 **Mark-down patterns**

In these three grids, the numbers indicate the £ value of the mark-downs taken across all styles of women's trousers, broken down into colours and sizes.

(a) Mark-down pattern indicating a healthy trading season

	Size 8	Size 10	Size 12	Size 14	Size 16	Size 18	Size 20	Size 22
Pink					10	10	15	15
Green	40	30	10	10	10	5	10	5
Red	40	40	20	20	10	20	25	25
Neutral	20	15			10	10		10
Navy	30	35	10				10	10
Black	20	20						

(b) Mark-down pattern indicating a generally poor trading season

	Size 8	Size 10	Size 12	Size 14	Size 16	Size 18	Size 20	Size 22
Pink	20	20	30	40	30	40	50	40
Green	80	70	50	50	50	40	50	40
Red	90	80	70	60	60	70	80	80
Neutral	60	50	40	30	40	30	50	40
Navy	50	60	40	40	50	50	60	60
Black	30	30	20	20	30	30	20	30

(c) Mark-down pattern indicating a small number of poor buying decisions in a healthy trading season

	Size 8	Size 10	Size 12	Size 14	Size 16	Size 18	Size 20	Size 22
Pink	80	100	80	100	120	130	130	140
Green	40	30	10	10	20	10	10	10
Red	40	40	20	20	10	20	25	25
Neutral	40	30	40	80	130	150	160	180
Navy	30	35	10				10	
Black	20	20						10

This pattern indicates that:
1 the colour pink has been overbought in this season;
2 certain styles did not sell well in the larger sizes of neutral colours.

A number of retailers have discovered that customers respond better to deep price cuts applied on an occasional basis than to smaller cuts on a frequent or on-going basis (see Box 8.3).

BOX 8.3   THE START OF DISCOUNT CULTURE?

The onslaught of the recession in the UK at the end of the 1980s caught many retailers by surprise. Interest rate rises, negative equity and rising unemployment suddenly put the brakes on discretionary consumer spending. Many retailers of clothing, jewellery, home furnishings and electrical goods were faced with masses of pre-ordered stock flowing into stores and little flowing out! Clothing retailers such as Principles, Dorothy Perkins and Top Shop had little choice but to implement mark-downs. However, rather than slashing prices deeply, the stores opted for a series of incremental discounts in an attempt to claw back as much profit margin as possible. Unfortunately, the rest of the high street was going through similar difficulties and so customers, learning that if they waited further price reductions would come their way, began to be reluctant to pay for anything at full price. The discount culture had begun!

Ten years on it has been estimated by Verdict Research that 'discount' clothing retailers will command over 8 per cent of the clothing market, rising to 14 per cent in 2004, in what is overall a virtually stagnant market sector. Often referred to more courteously as 'value' retailers (although there is no accepted distinction between the two terms) stores such as New Look, T.J. Hughes, Matalan, Primark, Ethel Austin, Peacocks and TK Maxx are eating away at the mid-market share previously dominated by 'variety stores' like Marks & Spencer and BhS, and specialist groups like Arcadia. Many of the store chains such as New Look and Ethel Austin are entering a classic trading-up phase (Brown 1988) as they improve their stores and merchandising techniques. However, in terms of consumer behaviour, discount shopping is now seen to be 'smart' as opposed to an economic necessity.

(Source: Morrell 2000)

LEGAL ISSUES

Since the abolition of the resale price maintenance legislation in 1964, UK retailers have been able to set the prices of most product categories themselves, and gradually the last vestiges of manufacturers' price maintenance are being eroded by either government action (for example, the abolition of the Net Book Agreement) or by consumer pressure (for example, the importation of motor vehicles into the UK from European dealerships). However, multiple retailers themselves have repeatedly been accused of keeping prices artificially high and of putting pressure on suppliers not to deal with competitors (see Box 8.2). In an era in which consumers have the ability to build knowledge of pricing structures and the confidence to tackle retailers on pricing issues, a retailer that does not offer value for money will suffer.

SHRINKAGE

Shrinkage is the term applied to stock that is removed from a retail outlet without any payment being made to the retailer. Selling at full price is to be recommended as part of a profitable product strategy, but having to mark down is better than missing the opportunity to sell the product at all. Losing stock through theft is one of the least controllable aspects of retail management, yet in high crime locations it could be the element that has the most bearing on a branch's profitability. Theft, whether it is external or internal, is the main contributor to retail shrinkage, but the term also encompasses damage to goods, which are then either sold with a mark-down as shop-soiled goods or have to be destroyed. Closed circuit television (CCTV) systems and electronic tagging of goods are among a number of methods used to combat theft, although the method of product presentation itself, for example secure fixturing and open layouts, can help reduce opportunistic thieving (see Box 7.1).

SUMMARY

Although the products and their price tags ultimately determine the income of the retail business, the way in which a retailer accounts for the costs associated with bringing that merchandise to the customer interface can determine how successful individual product items are viewed as profit generators. The marketing objectives and the financial objectives associated with product management often work in conflict, therefore a rigid adherence to financial objectives may be detrimental to the long term health of a retail business. Remembering for how long early internet retailers traded at a loss in order to gain market share in an important growth market helps us to appreciate just how strategic profitable product management can be.

REVIEW QUESTIONS

1 Outline the difference between a uniform mark-up approach and a demand-led approach to retail pricing.
2 Review the alternative pricing strategies that will guide retailers in their individual pricing decisions.
3 Describe the various stages that a retail buyer goes through when negotiating with suppliers.

DISCUSSION QUESTIONS

1 Retailers are increasingly abandoning high–low pricing in favour of EDLP strategies. Suggest reasons for this trend.
2 To what extent do you believe that retailers charge 'rip-off' prices? Provide evidence to back up your opinions.
3 The ability to assess profitability accurately is dependent on the ability to analyse its associated costs. Discuss.

REFERENCES AND FURTHER READING

Bailey, P. Farmer, D., Jessop, D. and Jones, D. (1994) *Purchasing Principles and Management*, 7th edn, Pitman, London.

Brassington, F. and Pettitt, S. (2000) *Principles of Marketing*, Pearson Education, Harlow, Essex.

Brown, S. (1988) 'The wheel of the wheel of retailing', *International Journal of Retailing* **3** (1): 16–37.

Cartlidge, H. (2000) 'Sharking up the industry cartels', *Retail Week*, 25 February.

Hall, J. (1999) 'Body Shop set for Euro outlet stores', *Retail Week*, 29 October.

Hall, J. (2000) 'DTI delay fuels rumour about "rip-off" retreat', *Retail Week*, 25 February.

Levy, M. and Weitz, B.A. (1998) *Retailing Management*, McGraw-Hill, Maidenhead, Berks.

Mintel (1998) *Report on Grocery Shopping Habits* (August), Mintel International Group, London.

Mitchel, A. (1999) 'Lure of discounter will raise price awareness', *Marketing Week*, 9 December.

Morrell, L. (2000) 'Discount chains clean up in emerging price-led market', *Retail Week*, 14 April.

chapter nine

ALLOCATING SPACE TO PRODUCTS

INTRODUCTION

Throughout the discussion on stock planning, the issue of space constraint has come up frequently. Space is an expensive commodity for retailers and so it must be used for maximum return for the retailer. Developments in logistics and stock control systems, such as automatic replenishment, have allowed retailers to improve their productive space by cutting out the need for storage room at the store. However, increasing pressure on retail space, in response to the tightening up of retail planning guidelines, means that for many retailers the opportunity to expand their selling space, either by opening new stores or adding to existing stores, is limited or simply not available; therefore, maintaining or increasing the levels of sales and profits of products sold from existing space has become a priority in retail management.

Sales and profitability per square foot (or square metre) are key indicators of buying and merchandising success, and high levels depend on offering the right range, in a logical layout, with products available and easy for the customer to find. Decisions about how much space to devote to each product line and its location in the store play an important role in the pursuit of merchandising success. This chapter attempts to provide an insight into this process.

Space constraint applies to all retailers, but in non-store retailing the constraints are different. A mail order retailer, for example, has page space and the number of pages in a publication as constraining factors, whilst a TV shopping channel needs to break down the airtime to different products.

However, internet retailing offers great opportunities for adding space without much additional resource input. The main constraint on the amount of space used in a virtual outlet is the customer's attention span. In spite of this additional freedom, the objectives of space allocation are essentially the same no matter which retail format is used.

THE OBJECTIVES OF SPACE ALLOCATION

Space management in retailing is concerned with two key objectives.

- to optimise both short and long term returns on the investment cost of retail space;
- to provide a logical, convenient and inspiring interface between the product range and the customer.

In order to achieve these objectives, space management involves a number of process stages. The first is to determine how to measure retail performance in relation to retail space; this relates to the sophistication of retail performance analysis, considered in the previous chapter. The second stage is to determine the amount of space to be allocated to merchandise at various levels, that is, department level, category level and SKU level. The relationship between stock levels and sales discussed in chapters six and seven is important in this operation. The third stage involves determining the quality of space required by product classifications, categories and items. The strategic roles played by product categories and items discussed in chapter three need to be considered when making these decisions. The retailer also needs to consider the practical requirements of individual products that will have a bearing on their space allocation, thereby applying pragmatic retail management to the theoretical concepts regarding space allocation in relation to performance. Finally, space allocation plans have to be implemented in retail outlets and their effectiveness monitored.

When customers walk into a grocery supermarket, they may be looking for some basic items like bread, milk, corn flakes and so on. Difficulty in locating these products would cause high levels of customer dissatisfaction. Such a scenario is unlikely: first, because the products will be located in a part of the store that the shopper will pass on the normal route around the store (see chapter eleven for a discussion on store layouts); and second, because there will be a large enough number of these products on the shelves to grab the attention of the shopper. In addition, there are likely to be similar, substitutable products nearby, which contribute to the 'clue' to the customer about where the specific product is to be found. On the other hand, for an infrequent purchase such as shoe polish, a customer is more likely to have to search out the product or may need to ask a sales associate for assistance in locating it. When the product is found, it is probable that the amount of display space devoted to shoe polish will be restricted, with a small number of facings (the number of SKUs facing a customer) per product item.

MEASURING RETAIL PERFORMANCE IN RELATION TO SPACE

As discussed in chapter eight, the two principal measures of retail success are sales and profits. However, these measures have previously been directly related to individual products. Sales and profitability can also be measured in relation to the amount of space used to generate those levels of sales and profits. This can then be compared with the level of financial investment in that space. The resulting measures express the productivity of retail space. The following measures of retail space productivity are all commonly used in retailing.

Sales (or profits) per square metre

This is a measure of sales according to the area of floor space taken. Profits per square foot can also be measured. This is an appropriate measure to use when only one level of product is displayed and a variety of fixturing is used, as is typical of clothing retailing (see Figure 9.1).

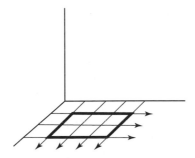

Figure 9.1 **Using floor area measurements**

Sales (or profits) per linear metre

This can provide a more precise measurement, as it measures the income generated by footage of shelf space. This may be a more applicable measure when using a multi-shelved fixture such as a gondola. In order to take account of the height value of shelf space, the area of exposed space rather than the linear metre value might be more appropriate (see Figure 9.2).

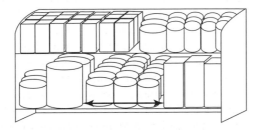

Figure 9.2 **Using linear measurements**

Sales (or profits) per cubic metre

This measure allows for the length, width and depth of the fixture allocation to be taken into consideration; this might be relevant in frozen food retailing, for example (see Figure 9.3).

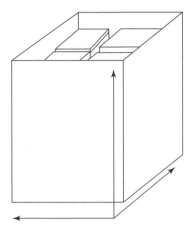

Figure 9.3 **Using cubic measurements**

The productivity of retail space will be dependent on the levels of sales and the profitability of the products located within that space and the value of the space. Product profitability was discussed in chapter eight; however, some consideration should also be given to the value of space.

THE VALUE OF RETAIL SPACE

The financial value of retail space is usually expressed in square metres. Rent and local government rates are usually charged at a rate per square foot or square metre, and although the alternative measures of retail space productivity are useful for retail product management, sales per square metre, otherwise known as sales density, is the measure most commonly used to compare the productivity of different retail outlets. Richer Sounds and Next, for example, are well known for having very high sales densities in their outlets.

It will be apparent to anyone who has worked in a store that, in terms of generating income, the value of space within a retail outlet can vary enormously. Ground level space for example is more valuable than that on other floors because it is more inconvenient to customers to get themselves to a different level. In a multi-level shopping centre, this becomes evident when the rent values of ground level outlets are compared with those of basement or upper levels. Even on the same level, the quality of space varies. It is generally accepted that the value of space reduces from front to back of the store and increases when close to high footfall routes. The following elements of a store's design will therefore influence the value of space:

- entrances;
- lifts and escalators;
- service departments (toilets, cafés);
- destination product areas (for example, a delicatessen counter in a supermarket);
- payment areas.

Where these 'hot spots' are located in any particular store will depend on the physical characteristics of individual outlets, but Figure 9.4 shows the likely hot spots in a typical supermarket layout.

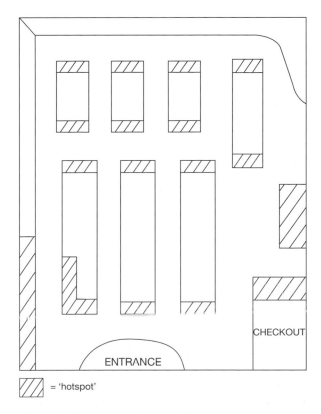

= 'hotspot'

Figure 9.4 **Typical 'hot' spots in a retail store**

Retail management can also manipulate customer flow in an attempt to maximise space productivity by allocating poorer retail space to 'destination' products and services. This is particularly evident in department stores, where specialist products such as furniture and home entertainment as well as hairdressing salons and accounts departments are located on basement or upper floors. Customer flow can also be encouraged by locating high demand items throughout the store layout, with plenty of impulse items located in between. Retailers need to find a balance between maximising sales of high demand products, generating flow around slower selling products (which may have higher profit margins), and providing logic and convenience in the layout for the customer.

Space allocation decisions are taken at department level, category level and SKU level. Vary rarely are these decisions taken without some historical data to inform and influence them, but the two alternative starting points for these decisions are space allocation according to rate of sales and space allocation according to product profitability.

ALLOCATING SPACE ON THE BASIS OF SALES

The guiding principle here is: the more a product sells, the more space it should be given. Retaining a high stock service level will depend on retailers ensuring that they devote enough space to a high demand product, such as milk, to prevent replenishment of that item becoming inefficient and inconvenient to the customer. A fast-selling item, however, may not be one on which retailers make much profit (again milk is a good example), and so they may decide to allocate more space to their profitable lines. In taking this approach, however, retailers are likely to encounter the problem of not devoting enough space to fast-moving lines, so a balance has to be achieved.

Another decision that has to be made is which 'sales' figure to use for the allocation exercise. Alternatives are historical sales figures (for that branch); market share figures; or projected sales figures. The advantages and disadvantages of these methods are outlined in Figure 9.5.

SPACE ELASTICITY

Allocating sales according to a measure of sales assumes that there is a relationship between the amount of space and the rate of sales. This relationship is termed the space elasticity of a product and refers to the extent to which the sales of a product change in response to a change in the amount of space allocated to that product. Research (McGoldrick 1990: 306) suggests that space elasticity is not uniform amongst products or across stores or departmental locations. In particular, the extent to which a product is bought on impulse affects its space elasticity. If our attention is grabbed by a tonnage (high volume) display of a product such as cereal or wine we may succumb to an impulse purchase, but we are unlikely to respond as positively to an increase in display space of a staple store cupboard item such as salt or sugar.

The influence of other products in the retail offer

The sale of one product can be influenced by the sales of other products in a number of ways. Cross-elasticity is the direct relationship between an increase in the sales of product A caused by an increase in sales of product B. For example, if there is a promotion on pasta sauces which increases sales, the rate of sales of pasta is also likely to increase. If brand X has a price

Historical sales data

Advantages

- Easy to access
- Will indicate local preferences and influences

Disadvantages

- Will not allow for the potential of product lines that the store does not carry or for new products
- Does not allow for current and forecasted changes in trading environment
- Sales data may be net of returns, therefore where stores have a high level of returns from other branches, this will distort the sales figure recorded and could undermine the potential sales of product categories (see Box 9.1)

Market share

Advantages

- Easy to access
- High demand products will be well supported, which is likely to appeal to the mass consumer

Disadvantages

- New or emerging products and categories will not be given the space allocation that their potential could warrant
- The product selection may appear mundane or non-specialist, as it is reflecting the mass market rather than being tailored to the individual branch catchment profile
- Local preferences are not catered for
- It may be appropriate to shrink the space of a declining category faster than sales would indicate to prevent the product selection looking outdated

Projected sales

Advantages

- Projected sales are likely to be based on historical sales as far as possible, and will therefore reflect individual branch characteristics
- Incorporates (estimated) sales figures for new products and categories
- Historical figures may have been affected by stock control or quality problems, which can be accounted for in the projected sales figure

Disadvantages

- Actual sales may not meet projected sales, resulting in space being devoted to slow sellers while the faster selling products are underrepresented

Figure 9.5 **Comparing alternative approaches to allocating space according to sales**

BOX 9.1   THE EFFECT OF RETURNS ON SALES FIGURES

Store A is a branch of clothing retailer XYZ in a medium sized town centre. Ten miles away there is a regional shopping centre where branch B is located, and twelve miles in the opposite direction branch store C is located in the heart of a city centre shopping complex. The policy of retailer XYZ is to offer a returns policy in all its stores for product bought in any branch nationwide.

Shoppers from the town where store A is located often take shopping trips to the neighbouring centres where B and C are located, especially if they want to make a major purchase such as a coat or a suit and require a wide choice of retail stores to select from. Unfortunately for store A, any unwanted products usually end up being returned to the local store. This has the effect of distorting the sales figures for store A, upon which space allocation decisions are made. Unfortunately, the retailer's information system does not recognise the difference between a returned garment bought from the original store and one bought from a different store.

In order to counteract this problem, which can be quite widespread, a retailer would need to allocate space on the basis of estimated sales rather than historical sales.

---

reduction, the sales of competing brand Y would decrease. Therefore space allocations of complementary and substitute products may have to be adjusted according to the situation regarding a separate product.

ALLOCATING SPACE ACCORDING TO PRODUCT PROFITABILITY

Allocating space by any of the sales-based methods are likely to result in sales rather than profits being maximised and, if strictly implemented, would not take into account some of the more practical considerations about allocating retail space. Therefore an alternative approach would be to use the profits generated by each product as the basis on which to allocate space. As we saw in chapter eight, product profitability can be calculated in varying degrees of fineness, for example gross margin, GMROI or DPP; but using profit measures as a basis for space allocation will prevent a retail manager from allocating large amounts of best-quality retail space to unprofitable products. It could mean, however, that a retailer was allocating unnecessarily large amounts of space to products that would sell just as well in a smaller space. Profitable lines may not in fact sell very quickly at all, and allocating extra facings or shelves of the product may have very little impact on the sales of the product. In this case the quality of the space becomes important, so the retailer can locate high profit items in locations around the store that are better for selling. Figure 9.6 illustrates the relationship between the sales and profits generated by different products and suggests how space should be allocated accordingly.

Allocating space according to sales and, in particular, product profitability is to work with the interests of the retailer and not the customer in mind

Figure 9.6 **Space allocation alternatives**

(Sanghavi 1988) and therefore may suggest an illogical and confusing presentation of products. Long term profitability relies on customer loyalty, which is dependent (among many other things) upon being satisfied with the presentation and assortment of products. Fine-tuning the allocation of space within a retail outlet therefore requires extensive amounts of high quality data, together with a pragmatic and customer-orientated managerial approach at store level.

PRACTICAL AND CUSTOMER CONSIDERATIONS

Seasonality

Seasonal products need to be allocated more and better space at their peak selling periods. It may be necessary to allocate larger amounts of space to keep pace with customer demand; and allocating the best quality and increased quantities of space in line with seasonal events also has a reminder effect on customers and increases impulse purchases. It also has the more general positive effect of giving the perception of an interesting and relevant product selection overall.

Product characteristics

The characteristics of the product itself may determine its space allocation in terms of both quality and space. Slim diapers are not only convenient for parents: smaller packs are welcomed by the retailers in order to offer more choice within the same space. Heavy and hazardous products (such as large bottles of bleach or bags of charcoal) should not be located on high shelves because of the increased danger and difficulty of handling for customers. Some products have special requirements of the display space that is allocated to them, which adds further complications to space decisions. Chilled or frozen products, for example, not only have to be displayed in dedicated fixtures, but it also makes sense, from a safety and hygiene point of view, to have the products near to the chilled or frozen storage space. Other products may need protection because they are hazardous or fragile or simply expensive.

Customer characteristics

Not all space in a retail outlet is accessible by customers. This might be an advantage, for example for the storage of expensive and fragile goods, but if your target market includes children, then their physical size must be considered in terms of the space allocated to their products. The eye level space will be lower, and if the product is self-selection (pick and mix confectionery, for example) then the reach must be comfortable for the smaller person. In today's market where 'pester power' is a considerable force, the space allocated to cereals, desserts and soft drinks must have the child's viewpoint in mind.

Fixture limitations

When allocating space to products, retail merchandisers must bear in mind the fixturing that is available for the product. Fragile products, for example, need fixturing that is attached to a wall to provide additional stability. A large variation in pack size wastes vertical shelf space and looks untidy. Long garments must be displayed on fixtures that prevent the product trailing on the ground but still enable the customer to see all the product detail. Using flexible fixturing can create additional space, such as dump bins for promoted merchandise, as discussed in chapter eleven.

Category management

When shopping, customers browse through and around fixtures in a way that is similar to how they read a magazine. They will scan the product offer until they find a product category of interest, and then they will focus their attention so that they can choose between the product offerings within that category. The final choice may take some time, with the customer evaluating the product against a list of criteria that are relevant to them, for example price, brand, pack size and flavour/colour variation. It makes sense therefore to allocate space to products that fall into a particular category together so that the customer is faced with a logical offering. This understanding of the way in which people shop has helped retailers to refine category management (see chapter three). Within any one category there will be both competing and complementary products, but by grouping products in this way the shopper is faced with a more logical offering and retailers can fine-tune their sales and profit margins so that the performance of the category is maximised rather than the individual product item.

SPACE ALLOCATION SYSTEMS

Clearly, the factors that contribute to a good or a bad space allocation decision are numerous and often interrelated. Space allocation was therefore an early candidate for computer applications in retailing. Nowadays systems allow retailers to feed in a wealth of relevant data about individual SKUs and, according to the objectives of the retailer, the computer system will suggest the space allocation to use.

The most up-to-date systems allow retailers to use both qualitative and quantitative data as inputs:

- direct product costs, or activity-based costs;
- sales data (forecast or actual);
- space elasticity;
- cross-elasticity;
- size of product;
- size variations;
- complementary products;
- specific display requirements (for example, shelf level);
- size of fixturing.

Along with the increasing sophistication of space allocation systems in terms of the kind of data that can be processed, the outputs of the systems have also improved. Early systems often gave only a numerical output: lists of product codes in the order they were to be placed on the shelves. Today's systems, such as those produced by Gallerai, Intactix and A.C. Nielsen, produce illustrations of photographic quality which give store personnel a clear indication of the ideal allocation and appearance of the products on the shelf. These outputs are referred to as planograms, and the producer of the planogram, or space planner, provides a link between the buying and merchandising section of the retail organisation and the store network.

The planogram helps a retail chain to maintain its corporate identity through the arrangement of products within the outlet whilst maximising space productivity. Some of the latest space planning systems are able to simulate the entire store environment, so that the product manager can view an assortment plan in virtual reality and make any adjustments seen to be necessary. Lectra Systems' 'Visual Merchant', for example, generates three-dimensional store environments, featuring actual fixturing and products, which can be customised according to specific retail product areas.

STORE GRADING

The complexity of space planning is taken a level higher when a retailer has a large variation in store size. Most large retail groups apply a system of store grading which is largely dependent on store size and sales level, but can also take into consideration local catchment characteristics such as population profile, shopping centre profile, competition and so on. For each grade of store, a separate planogram will be produced; but even within the grades, physical constraints may make it necessary for store management to use a certain level of interpretation of the general plan to allow a sensible arrangement for their particular store. With the use of virtual systems, however, it is possible to enter individual store information and produce individual planograms for each store in the group. This might be appropriate for a product range that is relatively stable throughout the year, but for a retailer who reacts to season and fashion changes, once again the task becomes so complex that the use of virtual systems is currently unlikely to be cost-effective. An additional consideration for the retailer is that if store planning is so rigidly enforced from a central planning department, local managers may lose the motivation to take initiatives and apply commercial creativity to their stores. Often, the use of a retail manager's commercial acumen and practical application and interpretation is much more efficient than a new systems update.

BOX 9.2　MICRO-MERCHANDISING

When the pressure is on to maximise the contribution from every inch of retail space, the relationship between that space and the customers who use it needs to be highly integrated. A retailer that is experiencing slow-selling products, high levels of mark-downs and that ends up doing a high number of in-store transfers could be a good candidate for a micro-merchandising strategy. Micro-merchandising concerns the activity of targeting store-specific customer audiences with tailored ranges, in order to meet needs more profitably at the local level. Micro-merchandising combines the variable nature of retail space, in terms of how large the store is and where it is located, with the variable nature of customers, in terms of their purchasing behaviours.

Micro-merchandising relies on using customer information, captured and enabled by loyalty schemes and databases. Customer information is then layered over store information so that the real personality of the store emerges. For example, the size of a retail outlet in Sheffield's busy Meadowhall centre may equate in terms of size and turnover to one located in the elegant and affluent Bath city centre, but the personality of the two stores may be quite different in terms of consumer preferences and purchasing habits.

Therefore it is the store's personality traits that determine the core product ranges, and not the size; the size of the outlet determines the width and depth of the merchandise type that would appeal to the local customers. Stores are empowered with the merchandise that allows them to drive local market opportunities, and local suppliers can also be involved in the process of providing tailored product for individual store needs.

(Source: Scull 2000; Ziliani 1999)

Trial and error

For many small retailers the cost of a computerised space planning system is prohibitive, and so many rely on basic sales and profit margin analysis combined with trial and error in space allocation decision-making. This approach is likely to be sufficient, and the matrix shown in Figure 9.6 may provide a basic analysis on which to start making space decisions.

SUMMARY

A great deal of space management is carried out in order to achieve relatively short term retail objectives, such as maximising the benefits of a product or departmental promotion, meeting seasonal sales figures, or improving branch profitability. However, the long term strategic objectives of the retailer provide the framework within which these decisions are taken. Space allocations must be in line with the overall positioning strategy of the retailer; the variety and depth of assortment and the stock availability service level should not be compromised by the need for short term productivity gains. In addition, the arrangement of products around the store needs to be considered in the light of the contribution that product items, brands and categories make to the positioning statement. It may be necessary to over-represent new products or to allocate extra space to growing or seasonal categories in order to reinforce an innovative positioning strategy. The local customer profile may also lead to exceptional space allocations in an effort to meet individuals' requirements more closely. However, the retailer's space is the extent of its empire, and every inch of that space must be used to its maximum effect even if, as we shall see in the next two chapters, some space is designed to be devoid of products. The measurement of that effect, however, must be appropriate in terms of the overall aims for that space.

MALTMANS: A MINI CASE STUDY EXERCISE

Maltmans is a value retailer. Its stores are located on out/edge of town retail parks or stand-alone sites, with an average sales area of 7,000 square metres. They are usually on one floor only. Maltmans sells clothing for all the family and a range of home furnishings. The business is split into a number of departments: ladies' outerwear, children's wear, men's wear, ladies' lingerie/sleepwear; ladies' accessories and shoes; soft furnishings; home accessories (kitchenware, gifts, bathroom accessories).

Maltmans is opening a new stand-alone store located on the ring road of a major city. The store is essentially featureless, with automatic doors at the front and service space (stock rooms, staff rooms and so on) at the back of the store. The location of the changing room facility has not yet been decided. The dimensions of the store are shown on the store plan in Figure 9.7.

Task: To develop a layout plan for the new Maltmans store. You have to decide where the departments should be located within the store and how much space should be allocated to each department.

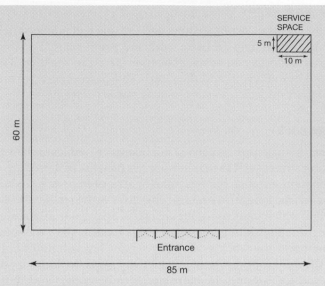

Figure 9.7 **Maltmans' store plan**

The sales figures in Table 9.1 are derived from a store that is similar in size and catchment area characteristics. The figures are from the current (autumn) season's sales.

Table 9.1 **Maltmans' departmental performance**

Department	Weekly sales (£)
Ladies' outerwear	34,500
Children's wear	27,000
Men's wear	25,500
Ladies' lingerie and sleepwear	15,000
Ladies' accessories and shoes	13,500
Soft furnishings	18,000
Home accessories	16,500
Total	150,000

When designing your plan, the following guidelines should be considered.

• Maltmans usually locate a bank of tills at the front of the store. For security reasons, customers have to walk through the payment area to exit the store.
• A typical Maltmans store layout takes the form of a 'race track' around the store, with free flow areas in between.
• Being a family orientated store, it is important that prams and buggies can be moved easily within the store.

- Maltmans allocate department space on the basis of estimated sales. For example, if the sales estimate for ladies' outerwear is 30 per cent of the total store's takings, it should be allocated 30 per cent of the selling area.
- When deciding how to break up the space, remember that each department should be given the opportunity to be seen from the main walkway (race track).
- Wall space is useful for display purposes. Maltmans makes use of movable partitioning around the store to create more wall space, but it is carefully planned so that visibility between departments is kept at a high level and additional security problems are not created.
- Links between merchandise areas should be carefully considered.

To facilitate your task the following information is given: the total selling area within the store is 5,000 square metres. This does not include the space taken by the till area (15 sq m), the space taken by the proposed changing rooms (15 sq m), the space taken by the walkway (20 sq m) and the service space (50 sq m).

Additional task: Using the historical figures for the previous season's Christmas selling period given in Table 9.2, identify the departments that will need to undergo a seasonal expansion. Create a new plan for the Christmas selling period which gives the seasonal departments the additional space and impact they warrant.

Table 9.2 **Maltmans' Christmas sales**

Department	Weekly sales (£)
Ladies' outerwear	31,875
Children's wear	22,500
Men's wear	33,750
Ladies' lingerie and sleepwear	22,500
Ladies' accessories and shoes	18,750
Soft furnishings	13,125
Home accessories	45,000
Total	187,500

REVIEW QUESTIONS

1 Identify the steps that retail product managers need to follow in order to achieve their space allocation objectives.
2 On a matrix, identify the alternative space allocation decisions available to retailers, following an analysis of both sales and profitability of individual items within a range.
3 Review the benefits of computerised space management systems.
4 Identify the practical considerations that retailers should make when drawing up their space allocation plans.

DISCUSSION QUESTIONS

1 To what extent would an independent retailer benefit from a sophisticated space allocation system?
2 There is often a conflict between allocating space in order to achieve short term productivity targets and the strategic management of retail space. Discuss.
3 Discuss the benefits of taking a micro-merchandising approach to space management.

REFERENCES AND FURTHER READING

Corstjens, J. and Corstjens, M. (1995) *Store Wars: The Battle for Mindspace and Shelfspace*, John Wiley, Chichester, Sussex.

Dreze, X., Hock, S.J. and Purk, M.E. (1994) 'Shelf management and space elasticity', *Journal of Retailing* **70** (4): 301–26.

McGoldrick, P.J. (1990) *Retail Marketing*, McGraw-Hill, Maidenhead, Berks.

Sanghavi, N. (1988) 'Space management in shop: a new initiative', *Retail and Distribution Management* **16** (1): 14–18.

Scull, J. (2000) 'Getting down to the nitty gritty of range-planning', *Retail Week*, 12 May.

Ziliani, C. (1999) 'Retail micromarketing: strategic advance or gimmick?', in *Proceedings of the 10th International Conference on Research in the Distributive Trades*, Institute for Retail Studies, University of Stirling, August.

chapter
ten

STORE DESIGN

INTRODUCTION

Whilst sales analysis, stock planning and profitability are all integral parts of what the product management function means to retailers in the twenty-first century, a retailer should never lose sight of the fact that, for customers, primary concerns when choosing a retailer are: the price of the products; the service that they receive, which may or may not include employee contact; and what the outlet looks like. Customers are not concerned with profitability, unless they happen to be shareholders, nor are they concerned with how much training a sales assistant has received. What is important to them is whether they believe that a product represents value and their own personal encounter with the outlet. In fact, a shopper may make the decision not to enter a store based purely on its appearance, without having any experience of the products, prices and services they might encounter once they are inside. The management of the physical product and its relationship with the physical elements within the store, or the designed element within a non-store outlet, is as important as any other part of the product management process. If the product range and the outlet work in harmony, the retailer's positioning strategy is reinforced; but if they work in conflict, the positioning will be unclear to customers, who will become confused and disappointed.

The term store design can be used broadly to encompass the total physical attributes found in a shop-based retail outlet; but in this book a distinction has been made between the aspects of the store that contribute to the general retail environment and atmosphere, whilst those physical elements which are in direct contact with the product, such as the fixtures and displays, are referred to as visual merchandising and are discussed in a separate chapter. The design of the store space itself is discussed in this chapter including: the interior decoration of the store; the materials used; the use of space and atmospherics to create effects; and the use of lighting, signage and colour. This chapter also considers the relationship between store design and the retailer as a corporation, and the relationship between a store design and its location. Most of this chapter is unashamedly a store-based discussion; however, the notion that retail identity and brand image are used by customers to evaluate retailers is of concern to store and non-store retailers alike.

THE INTERIOR DECORATION OF A STORE

When a store owner or manager buys or rents a retail outlet, he or she is essentially faced with an empty shell, like a flat that a young person may have just moved into. There may be some interior decoration, but it could be tatty or not appropriate to the new business. There may be some structural work that is necessary to make the store operational, for example the shop windows may need to be enlarged or, if it is a clothing outlet, changing rooms may need to be built, or a lift may need to be installed if the store has more than one floor. The architectural features of a store must be considered very carefully, as they may be subject to planning restrictions or could be creatively incorporated into a design to provide originality and distinctiveness.

The interior of a building is essentially a collection of materials and colours. In a retail store materials have to be sturdy in order to withstand customer traffic, and colours have to be chosen so that they do not detract from the merchandise but still blend into the overall design.

BOX 10.1 STORE CEILINGS

Ceilings in stores were ignored for some time. If customers looked upwards, they would often be met with a very dreary sight comprising faded or grubby tiling interspersed with panels of uninteresting diffused lighting. Thanks to innovative retail designs things are improving, and now this expanse is viewed as an architectural opportunity which may feature a wide range of upward and downward lighting effects, murals, painted skies, sculptures, cornices and even 'flying' mannequins. A variety of materials are being used in a range of imaginative ways, and sometimes features like heating pipes and lighting tracking are left for design effect.

MATERIALS

Retail outlets are public places to a large extent, and therefore they need to send messages out to the general public which will be received and understood by the type of customer a retailer wishes to attract. That section of the public may be large, for example it may be more important for a superstore not to put off any particular customer group rather than specifically to try to attract a particular type. On the other hand target customers may be more narrowly defined, in which case the interior decoration of the store will go a long way towards making these customers feel that it is a store for them. Miss Selfridge, the young fashion retailer, for example, has incorporated fake animal skin into their store interior, giving the store a lively and humorous atmosphere. Figure 10.1 lists a range of materials commonly used in retail outlets.

Flooring
Carpet
Polished wood (dark, light, stained)
Unpolished wood
Terracotta tiles
Linoleum
Marble or stone tiles
Textured rubber/plastics

Walls and partitioning
Painted plaster, paint effects
Opaque glass, coloured glass
Wood panelling (dark, light, stained)
Slatted wood
Textile
Textured rubber/plastics
Ceramic tiles
Illuminated panelling

Trims
Chrome
Stainless steel
Metals – polished, matt, brushed
Galvanised metal, e.g. aluminium
Textile
Coloured acrylic

Figure 10.1 **Materials used in retail outlets**

Decisions regarding the type of material to be used depend on:

- *the type of product being sold* For food retailing the materials should be easy to clean, such as ceramic and marble tiling. In a jewellery store, plush carpet flooring may help to create a luxurious and intimate atmosphere.
- *the cost involved* Some materials are very expensive and, whilst investing in good quality materials is often worthwhile for mainstream retailing, a discount store would send confused messages if the interior decoration

looked too expensive. Something robust and basic, such as textured plastic, is a more suitable choice.

* *the store traffic*   A busy store, such as a supermarket or a DIY superstore where customers are likely to be visiting in their work boots, needs to use material that will withstand wear and tear. Even though a substantial entrance mat is essential in any store, the flooring must not become slippery when damp, and it must be easy to clean. For easy maintenance, department stores incorporate wood block or tiling in the main walkways and restrict the use of carpets to the departmental display area (see race track layout in chapter 11).

* *fashion*   Stores selling fashion orientated merchandise must keep up with fashions in interior decoration in order to maintain a modern image. The problem is that the more fashion orientated the look of the store, the faster it is likely to look out of date, therefore fashion retailers have to accept that frequent refurbishments will be part of the retail strategy. That being the case, these retailers are able to be more experimental with materials and not so concerned with longevity. Miss Selfridges and Top Shop both target the teenage to mid twenty-year-old consumer, and expect to refurbish their stores every 2–4 years.

* *environmental and safety concerns*   Materials should be in keeping with a retailer's desired image. If a retailer professes to be concerned with environmental issues, then natural materials (from sustainable sources) are more likely to be in tune with the overall store design. Retailers also have to conform to health and safety regulations. For example, glass has become very popular in retail architecture, but of course it has to be of a type that will not be dangerous to the public.

ATMOSPHERICS

Retail stores, like homes, have different atmospheres and auras. This formation of a subliminal message is an important part of the store design. There are many things that blend together to create an atmosphere, and atmospherics are cues that act on the subconscious through the senses to create a state of mind in the customer. Figure 10.2 gives some examples of atmospheric cues: the more favourable the state of mind, the longer a customer is likely to remain in the store, and thus is more likely to make a purchase.

The use of colour in both store and corporate design is an interesting and complex subject. Apart from a colour's ability to be warm (reds, pinks, oranges) or cool (blues, greens and white), colours have both cultural and societal meanings and associations which may make them more or less appropriate for use in a retail outlet.

Although some retailers have embraced a colour into their corporate design and carried this through into the store design successfully, many retailers restrict the use of colour in the store to trims and signage, using neutral colours and materials for much of the store interior. Many materials left in their natural state are neutral. Light-coloured wood for example was used

Sense	Cue	Example
Vision	Colour	Red and orange used to create warmth
Vision	Material	Galvanised metal to create 'industrial' impression
Hearing	Music	Mozart piano concertos to encourage browsing
Smell	Aroma	Bread in supermarkets to create a 'homely' feeling
Touch	Texture	Glass and ceramic to create clean, hygienic impression
Touch	Temperature	Constant temperature to relax customers
Vision/smell	Colour/aroma	Fresh fruit, vegetables and flowers at the front of the store to give a lively sense of freshness

Figure 10.2 **Retail atmospherics**

extensively in the early 1990s to create a neutral minimalist look in many fashion stores. Neutral shades (black, white, creams, browns and greys) are useful in store designs because there is no danger of the merchandise clashing or having to compete with the store's decoration, yet they contrast well with a highlight colour used for corporate communications (see Figure 10.3). Towards the end of the 1990s many retailers began to use white tiling and opaque glass in large areas of the store in order to create a clean, modern and versatile backdrop for colourful merchandise.

Retailer	Colours	Used for
Body Shop	Green	Fixtures, labelling, store fascia, bags, corporate communications
Boots the Chemist	Blue/white	Fascia, packaging, uniforms, bags
Next	Black and Cream	Fixtures, bags, fascia

Figure 10.3 **Retailers' use of corporate colours**

LIGHTING

A great contributor to the overall atmosphere in store is the lighting used. The overall level of ambient light needs to be such that customers can see the merchandise clearly and the store looks bright and inviting. However, lighting can be used to create interest in the store design itself, for example by using banks of up-lighters or down-lighters, and the space in the store

---

BOX 10.2 RETAIL AROMATHERAPY

Scents evoke atmospheres, and if the product cannot provide this service for the retailer then a wide selection of natural essential oils and artificial concentrates can. For example, the smell of pine can be used to evoke a Christmas seasonal atmosphere, and the waft of freshly mown grass takes our mind outdoors, whilst we shop indoors for sports and leisure goods. Other oils are less specific, but evoke feelings of relaxation or calm. It has even been known for chocolate retailers to reproduce artificially the alluring smell of their goods, because the packaging prevents enough of it escaping!

---

can be moulded by using a combination of wall lights and spot lights. Lighting is an integral part of any off-shelf display and enormously enhances the dramatic effect, with product areas being accentuated by suspended lighting and pin spots.

Lighting can also affect the colour of merchandise. This can be used positively to highlight products; for example a blue light might be used to create a cool and hygienic mood in a toiletries department, whereas orange lighting enhances the colour of bread. However, lighting can create problems when it comes to colour matching, and so buyers should ensure that they use both store lighting and natural lighting when approving colour matches in the product development process.

Although fixtures, fittings, display props and mannequins will be dealt with specifically in the next chapter, their contribution to the overall design of the store must not be overlooked. The materials used in the fixtures should complement those used in the interior decor, and the styling of fixtures should be in keeping with the architectural design of the store, so that all the physical features work in harmony and deliver a consistent message to the customer.

SIGNAGE

Much of the communication process within a store relies on visual cues rather than the written word. However, there may be messages for customers that are so important that they have to be spelt out. The location of merchandise or service departments in large stores is important information without which a customer could become disorientated and frustrated. Information about a retailer's policy, for example on returned goods or perhaps more general product information, is also important to communicate, and the type of signage used in terms of size, lettering and colours all have to be incorporated into the overall store design. Generally a retailer has to strive for a balance between giving customers the information they require and preventing the store looking too cluttered. Illuminated signage, either by spot lighting or by using lit-up panels means that smaller signage is not necessarily less noticeable than large. The signage used in the store, like any other aspect of the design, should complement rather than compete with the merchandise.

STORE DESIGN AND THE CORPORATE IMAGE

Retailing is a very visible industry. We are able to become intimate with retail businesses in a way that is not feasible with manufacturing businesses. This interface between the business and the customer is what gives retailers their advantage as well as many of their problems. Many of the largest retailers around the world have become part of everyday life to many people and the relationship between stores and individuals is something that retailers are keen to strengthen in pursuit of customer loyalty. Maintaining a favourable corporate image is therefore vitally important in competitive retail sectors.

Retailers work very hard to keep their image favourable in the mind of the consumer; and although, as we shall see later in this chapter, the formation of an image incorporates many more components than purely physical ones, the store and its environment plays a big part in the formation and maintenance of a corporate image. Retailers that do not update their stores on a regular basis run the risk of appearing out of touch with the customer, and if a refurbishment programme is left for too long, the change required to modernise the store may be so extensive that the retailer runs the risk of alienating the customers who are left.

THE EXTERIOR DESIGN

The exterior of the shop must communicate to the potential customer what that retailer stands for. The main external features of a retail outlet are the fascia, the window display and the entrance. The fascia is the most visible part of a retail brand. It is the name of the retailer, but it is also the logo, the graphics and the colours that are incorporated into whatever appears over a shops entrance. The fascia may incorporate exterior lighting to highlight the name, and it may incorporate a company logo or character, such as children's wear retailer Adam's apple, or Colonel Sanders in the Kentucky Fried Chicken fascia. Whatever the fascia includes, it becomes a key feature of the retail identity, which is then locked into the overall impression that a customer builds up about a store. Figure 10.4 compares and contrasts some internationally famous fascia designs.

Retailer	Graphics	Colours
Ikea	Chunky	Blue and yellow
Toys 'R' Us	Fun	Multi-primary
Laura Ashley	Classic	Green and cream
Muji	Bold	Silver

Figure 10.4 **Fascia design components**

The store entrance

The ways in which customers gain access to stores have to satisfy both functional and aesthetic criteria. The opening to a store must be accessible to all customers, including those using wheelchairs and buggies, and it has to be secured when the shop is closed. A very wide opening may be very welcoming for customers, but this type of entrance is problematic from a store security point of view, it does not offer much protection from the weather, and it does not allow the retailer to construct window displays. A number of alternative store entrance types are illustrated in Figures 10.5–10.8.

The open entrance is inviting and accessible, and breaks down the barrier between the store and its exterior. However, open entrances can feel anonymous and do not help to establish a retailer's identity (Din 2000). One way round this is to use a semi-open entrance, where accessibility is still good, but a window display can be created. Open entrances are often found in enclosed shopping centres, where the shop is protected from the outside elements.

Figure 10.5 **The open entrance**

Figure 10.6 **The semi-open entrance, using pivoting doors**

The funnel, recessed or lobby entrance increases the proportion of window display space and invites shoppers into the retail space without the commitment of stepping over the threshold. At the other extreme, a standard doorway gives a more exclusive feel to the retailer, and the window display stands out to communicate the retailer's offer. A problem with the standard entrance is access, which may be overcome by using an automatic door.

Figure 10.7 **The funnel or lobby entrance**

Figure 10.8 **The standard door entrance**

Awnings or canopies, which originated in order to shade merchandise in store windows, are now often used to give emphasis to a store entrance.

The contribution that window displays make to the external design of the store has traditionally been a very important one. Window displays as part of the visual merchandising function will be explored in chapter eleven; nevertheless, there are some retailers who do not use window displays at all. In this case the retailer relies on its name and reputation (communicated by the fascia) to draw customers into the store, as opposed to the visual product offer. Many retailers who use the superstore or category killer format do not use window displays. It is therefore very important for this type of retailer to use a store brand name that gives an indication of the type of product that is on offer. Some retail names leave no doubt: Texstyle World, Carpetwise, PC World, Toys 'R' Us, Petworld and so on, whilst others provide a product association, for example Staples or Homebase. Retailers who do not use brands that are linked to the product offer have to rely on their reputation and other communication tools to interest the customer base. Ikea, for example, issues a full product catalogue in a wide catchment area around their stores to familiarise consumers with its product offer, and Comet uses regular newspaper advertising to remind customers what its product range includes.

LOCATION

The actual location of a store often has a strong bearing on the store design in general, and in particular may impinge on a design strategy quite significantly. Whether it is a greenfield site (building a store from scratch) or whether it is a conversion from a different use, or even if it previously housed a retail business, a retail site will be subject to planning and building regulations. For new stores, it will be necessary to consider the material to be used and whether to incorporate local architectural features, the design may need to be constrained in terms of height, and the surrounding area may need to be landscaped. For conversions, architectural features, both internally as well as externally, may need to be preserved, yet the building may also require a programme of modernisation. All these challenges inevitably add to the cost of refurbishment, but compliance may be a small price to pay for a site in the best location. In purpose-built shopping centres there may be certain store design restrictions; therefore the needs of the centre to create a cohesive look whilst promoting the individual retail identities is a fine balance and subject to negotiation between centre management and tenant.

The location of a store must be appropriate to the retail business: to reach the target customer it is important for a store to be in a street that reflects its image. Oxford Street may be the busiest street in the UK, but for a company like Whistles designer clothes St Christopher's Place, a pedestrianised lane tucked away just around the corner, offers the kind of environment that attracts a more discerning shopper, with its café bars and outdoor seating, ornate street lamps and flower baskets.

STORE IMAGE

In this chapter, we have alluded several times to the concept that a retail store has an 'image'. Over the years, 'image' has been used as a qualitative, all-encompassing evaluative tool for retailers. The concept was referred to in 1958 by Martineau as 'the way in which the store is defined in the shopper's mind'. In today's retail environment, where consumers have an enormous choice of outlets for products and an extensive range of products within the outlet, where the actual product being offered is generally of comparable standard to many other retailers products, the image that a store conveys may be a key determining factor in the decision to choose one retailer over another. According to Barr and Field (1997: 11) image is 'multi-sensory, multi-dimensional and subject to fading without reinforcement'; image building, they say, is intended to provide value added benefits to shoppers: a place where they feel comfortable, that is in tune with their lifestyle, stocks the items that reflect their taste and requirements in what they wish to eat, wear, give to others and furnish their homes with. The reinforcement of a retail brand, what it stands for and how it is adapted to multi-channel retailing is the focus of many current retail strategies.

Sometimes retailers become aware that their brand image is not as good as it was. This may be because a close competitor has undertaken a change in strategy (for example, a store refurbishment or a change in pricing strategy). It may also be because a retailer has not paid enough attention to its customer's needs. Becoming familiar with retailers is often in the customers' interest: they are able to do their shopping more efficiently, they can go to a store that caters for their taste without having to search around, or they know which retailers will be offering products that are within their price range. However, customers will not be satisfied if that retailer becomes complacent. Customers' tastes change, their lifestyles change and a retailer has a choice of changing with their existing customers or changing to attract new customers to replace the ones who naturally move on. The process of knowing, as a retailer, who your customer is and what they want from you sounds like a straightforward operation, yet it is probably the hardest thing for retailers to get right. Listening to the customer requires input from all layers of the organisation, as discussed in chapter four, and listening to what customers say about a store's image is one of the starting points in this process.

THE RETAIL BRAND

The retail brand, like a product brand, can be extended to offer customers something more than the core product or, in the case of the retailer, the core product range. Understanding what is a core range and what is not may be a matter for research or judgement, but a number of retailers have been able to introduce successfully more and more product categories without experiencing any detriment to sales of existing product ranges. The superstore grocery retailers have extended product ranges of both manufacturer and own-label merchandise into many non-food areas; many clothing retailers have moved into accessories, toiletries and gifts; and variety stores are moving into coffee shops and restaurants. Din (2000) considers that retail design has an important role to play in this brand stretching process, because in the long term design adds value to the retailer by increasing brand awareness, confirming brand values and developing new markets.

LIFESTYLE RETAILING

The trend towards offering extended product ranges that are focused on a particular customer type is called lifestyle retailing, and it has been the basis of many exciting retail developments throughout history. In chapter one a table presented a list of retailers who were classified as generalist or specialist. A lifestyle retailer can be either generalist or specialist. A generalist lifestyle retailer would offer a wide variety of product categories, with a shallow but very specific orientation to the products (for example see Mini case study 6). The specialist lifestyle retailer might offer both depth and variety but targeted to very specific lifestyle needs. The key feature of lifestyle retailing is a real understanding of how far a lifestyle can extend, and formulating a product offer that reflects the approach to life and the likely choices such a consumer would make.

PLANNING RETAIL DESIGNS

Planning a retail design is a risky operation. The interplay between walls, floors, ceilings, lighting, colours, materials and fixtures is a challenging enough process. However, these are the static elements of the retail design. The template must also incorporate two further important yet changing elements: the merchandise and the customers. Think of the difference between a store on a quiet morning just a few moments after opening time and a store during its peak selling periods or during an end of season sale, and the impression can be very different. Virtual store plans and computerised visualisations are increasingly becoming an indispensable tool in the pre-installation phase of store refurbishments. Some of the latest models incorporate into the simulated store lighting, fixtures, merchandise stacks, hanging merchandise, colours and even human forms. This allows store designers and visual merchandisers to assess the interplay between the store design elements, the visual merchandising elements and the live elements of a working store. Computer-aided store design systems can provide the following additional benefits to retailers:

- store designs can be linked to retail productivity and space allocation schemes (discussed in chapter nine);
- store designs can link product and the architectural space to create an holistic and consistent image;
- a new store fit can be demonstrated to staff, who can do a virtual walk-through of the store as part of their pre-opening training. This is particularly useful if the new store design is a major departure from previous ones.

FLAGSHIP STORES

Flagship stores are those stores regarded as the pinnacle in the retail chain. They are usually large and located in high footfall, prestigious locations. They offer a full range of merchandise, with an emphasis on the more expensive, high quality and high fashion lines. The role of the flagship store is essentially about retail brand building and reinforcement rather than profitability. The media coverage that flagship stores attract adds to the communications process. When entering new international markets, retailers often begin with a flagship store incorporating the latest store design, to test the reaction to the retail concept. Shops of 'high design' lead the way in retailing, 'along the "avenue" of every major global city' (Glass, in Barr and Field 1997: 8).

THE STRATEGIC ROLE OF STORE DESIGN

There are many aspects of the retailing world that are threatening store-based retailers. Many consumers feel time pressurised, therefore if they do go out to shop, they want and expect a highly favourable experience. Shopping centres are increasingly filled with an international collection of retail businesses, and whilst many UK retailers are searching for opportunities for overseas expansion, the domestic retail market becomes ever more competitive. Shoppers are being offered products from a diversity of marketing channels, giving the consumer the opportunity to shop in all kinds of locations, at all times of day. The shop-based retailer must therefore work extremely hard to make sure that consumers remain interested in visiting the store. The store, the service received and the product selection must be 'right'. Customers have so much choice: they will not give a retailer a second chance.

In order to keep the consumer of the new millennium feeling interested in store-based shopping, retailers have to make 'functional service spaces into places that feed the popular spirit' (Williamson 1999). By creating a store environment that delights and enthuses the customer, retailers are able to transcend the pulling power of manufacturers' brands and the store space provides them with an enormous advantage over the non-store channels. Consumers play out rituals when they shop, such as making lists, searching out and trying on, making choices and carrying the bag. Store-based retailers need to continue to raise the level of enjoyment of store-based shopping so that customers do not desert them for other forms of shopping or other leisure pursuits. The shopping trip must be worthy of recall and repetition. When the Bluewater shopping centre opened in East London in March 1999, 200 of the 300 stores opened with a new store-branding concept. This highlights the importance that retailers are putting on fresh approaches to store environments as part of their strategic direction.

Levy and Weitz (1998) compared the store environment to a theatre where the walls and floor represent the stage; the lighting, fixtures and signage represent the set; and the merchandise is the show. But Williamson (1999) went one stage further, suggesting that shopping is the living act in an event, and the customer is the star in his or her own 'self-created, brand assisted drama'.

SUMMARY

Retail environments must satisfy the operational objectives of minimising costs, allowing flexibility and providing the right kind of space for merchandise. In this respect the practical aspects of store design, such as the materials used, the lighting and the signage, as well as the size and location of the store, all have to be blended into a spatial totality. However, retail design is also very much concerned with communicating the right messages to the target customer, reinforcing the retail brand values and encouraging consumers to experience the store and the products within. A store atmosphere adds emotional feelings, heightening the shopping experience, to create the enthusiasm and the loyalty that retailers so badly need.

MINI CASE STUDY 6   MUJI

Muji is the shortened form of the original name of a unique Japanese company – Mujirushi Ryohin, which means 'No Brand Goods'. Muji started up in 1980 as a supplier to Seiyu supermarkets. In response to the excessive premiums being charged for branded products, a range of well designed, high quality products was developed to sell as a private label within the supermarket store. The idea was well received, more products were developed and in 1983 Muji opened its own store in Tokyo and expanded its trading in dedicated areas to department stores in addition to the supermarket outlets. Over time Muji has developed a wider product range and opened more stores, so that it can now be considered one of the most important international lifestyle retailers, trading as a separate entity from the supermarket that once owned the brand.

Muji's product range is an exemplar of the wide variety lifestyle concept. Very little depth in the product choice is offered, yet the coverage of product items housed in a typical 'high street sized store' is unbelievably extensive: stationery, clothes, furniture, home accessories, toiletries and food products are all on offer. People who like Muji do not need choice; the products are 'the ones the customer wants'. For example, Muji sells two types of bicycle, of similar design, but one is a mountain bike and one is a road bike. They also sell two chairs, both designed specifically for a function: one is a dining chair and one is a casual chair. However, Muji sells a range of stationery as wide as Staples, the category killer, but the Muji approach is one product, one brand and one choice.

The strength of the Muji concept emanates from the principles on which the company operates, stated in their company catalogue:

- good value for money;
- simple and functional design;
- basic and understated colour;
- complete lifestyle range.

These values are translated into a product development strategy that covers the sourcing of low cost, basic and industrial materials for use in products that aim to enhance the natural properties of the raw materials. They also pay attention to the processes used to create the products, emphasising efficiency, waste elimination, high quality manufacture and minimum environmental impact. Where possible Muji reduces prices in order to pass on cost and efficiency improvements to customers.

The resulting offer is a range made up of simple, stylish, durable and adaptable products that evolve with customers' lifestyles and living patterns. The store environment works in harmony with the product range. Bold signage, neutral colours and industrial materials create a basic functional theme, yet an understated sense of style is added by using the Japanese lettering in the logo and an effective combination of spot and pendant lighting to highlight the products.

(Source: Muji product brochure 1999)

REVIEW QUESTIONS

1 Review the physical elements that contribute to a designed retail environment, indicating the variety of materials that can be used.
2 Identify the different types of retail atmospherics. Using your own experience, describe different atmospheric approaches used by retailers in different product sectors.
3 Examine the contribution that the following make to a store's design:

- lighting;
- signage;
- architectural base;
- exterior.

4 Outline the benefits of using technology in the planning of store designs.

DISCUSSION QUESTIONS

1 The store environment blends tangible features with intangible auras in order to create an appeal to the customer. Discuss.
2 Make a critical analysis of a store design of your choice.
3 Discuss the notion that the role of store design in a retail brand reinforcement strategy increases as more people turn to alternative shopping methods.

REFERENCES AND FURTHER READING

Barker, J., Levy, M. and Grewel, D. (1992) 'An experimental approach to making retail store environmental decisions', *Journal of Retailing* **68** (4): 445–60.

Barr, V. and Field, K. (1997) *Stores: Retail Display and Design*, PBC International, New York.

Bellizzi, J.A., Crowley, A.E. and Hasty, R.W. (1993) 'The effects of color in store design', *Journal of Retailing* **50** (1): 21–45.

Din, R. (2000), *New Retail*, Conran Octopus, London.

Doyle, S. and Broadbridge, A. (1999) 'Differentiation by design: the importance of design in retailers' repositioning and differentiation', *International Journal of Retail and Distribution Management* **27** (2): 72–82.

Kotler, P. (1973) 'Atmospherics as a marketing tool', *Journal of Retailing* **49** (4): 48–64.

Levy, M. and Weitz, B.A. (1998) *Retailing Management*, McGraw-Hill, Maidenhead, Berks.

Martineau, P. (1958) 'The personality of the retail store', *Harvard Business Review* **36** (1): 47–55.

McGoldrick, P.J. and Pieros, C.P. (1998) 'Atmospherics, pleasure and arousal: the influence of response moderators', *Journal of Marketing Management* **14**: 173–97.

Mintel (1999) 'Retail store design', *Retail Intelligence*, August.

Smith, P. and Burns, D.J. (1996) 'Atmospherics and retail environment', *Journal of Retailing* **24** (1): 7–14.

Williamson, S. (1999) 'Spaces into places', *Retail Week*, 21 May.

chapter eleven

VISUAL MERCHANDISING

INTRODUCTION

The relationship between a retailer's product positioning strategy and the branded store environment was explored in the previous chapter; however, the store environment has to fulfil operational objectives for the retailer in order to support buying and merchandising activities. The product has to be presented on fixturing that is appropriate for the merchandise, and the merchandise itself should be displayed in a way that enthrals customers. After all the product management work that has gone into planning the ranges, selecting the products, liasing with suppliers and getting the physical product through the supply chain, the product is now handed over to store managers, who provide the best opportunity for the product to sell. This chapter concentrates on the direct relationship between the physical product and the store elements that contribute to the product presentation process. The concept of visual merchandising provides a useful framework for the discussion of this interface, as the product range make its entrance into customer space.

VISUAL MERCHANDISING

Visual merchandising is a commonly used term for the aspect of product management that is concerned with presenting the product within the store to its best advantage. Visual merchandising has often been used as a synonym for display in retailing, but in today's retail industry the term incorporates a much wider brief. In the words of the editor of *VM Insight* trade magazine (Hall 1999): 'it is about taking the product and using it to let the entire retail environment speak'. Visual merchandising combines a commercial approach with a design approach within the store environment, to support product management objectives and to maximise the efforts of the buying teams. Visual merchandising also contributes to the strategic aims of the retailer sending out clear messages to consumers about what they can expect from the retailer, and that the brand values of the retailer reflect the shopping experience values of the customer.

Visual merchandising plays a much greater part in the product management process in some retail sectors than others. Fashion and home furnishings have always devoted considerable resources to display, but even in a grocery superstore elements of visual merchandising can be found, and indeed some grocery retailers have used visual merchandising as a way of providing interest to the customer and of differentiating themselves from their competitors (see Box11.1).

BOX 11.1   REGIONAL SUPERMARKETS WITH A DIFFERENCE

The grocery supermarket sectors of most European retail markets are highly concentrated. In the UK, the grocery sector is dominated by retail giants Tesco, J. Sainsbury, Asda and Safeways. Below this 'premier league' of operators, a number of smaller, regional chains are managing to survive. One such retailer is Morrisons. Founded in 1899 by William Morrison, the father of the current chairman, the company has survived until recently as a regional grocery supermarket chain, with the majority of its stores covering the North of England. Morrisons' stores offer a wide product range in both foods and non-food items, half of which are sold under the Morrisons brand. The stores are supported by modern retail operations and a central buying organisation.

In fast-moving consumer goods retailing, differentiation is not easily achieved however, Morrisons have chosen to use visual merchandising as a route to making its stores a little different to the other grocery stores that it competes with in the region. The careful attention to store design begins with the architectural detail of the stores; each is visually different and complementary to local architectural styles and materials. For example, the Sheffield store is housed in disused Yorkshire stone army barracks, which makes for a sturdy and impressive backdrop to the store.

Inside, Morrisons have adopted a 'market street' concept, where a number of stall-type service counters, complete with striped awnings and street signs, hark back to the time of the traditional specialist shops, including a butcher, a fishmonger and a baker. The signage and canopies help to create the atmosphere in this part of the store, where customers are encouraged to interact with store personnel and gain the individual attention often lacking in the supermarket shopping experience. Other themed areas include modern food combinations such as American donuts and popcorn, curry selections and salad bars, whilst the fresh produce area returns to the traditional theme, with fruit and vegetables displayed on old-fashioned wooden carts.

Responsibility for visual merchandising within the retail structure

Responsibility for this part of product management at board level varies. Lea Greenwood (1998) found that visual merchandising was under the remit of directors of visual merchandising, corporate communications or promotions. In some retail organisations a team of brand managers co-ordinates the visual merchandising effort with other promotional activities, so that it becomes part of the marketing activities. In fact elements of visual merchandising (particularly the use of point of sale material and photographic imagery) are sometimes sloppily referred to as 'in-store advertising'. The structure beneath the director is sometimes unclear, but a visual merchandise manager supported by area teams is a format frequently used in multiple retailers. In smaller retail companies, somebody based in the store may be partly or wholly responsible for visual merchandising. Visual merchandising at the implementation level is a creative activity and usually attracts people with a design training or background, although specific training for this aspect of retailing is becoming more common. (see Box 11.2).

BOX 11.2   A NEW QUALIFICATION IN VISUAL MERCHANDISING

A less than inspiring shopping experience within the stores has been suggested as one of the contributing factors to the downfall of Marks & Spencer plc in the late 1990s. However, the company has been taking steps to address this problem. Along with John Lewis Partnership, Marks & Spencer has been a key instigator in the development of the UK's National Vocational Qualification in visual merchandising which was launched towards the end of 1998. One of the difficulties associated with visual merchandising is that it requires creativity and commercial acumen, combined with specific skills which traditionally have been picked up during a kind of informal apprenticeship. The theoretical framework of visual merchandising can be provided by college courses, but in-work training allows for a wider appreciation of the role, from the need to comply with health and safety regulations, to gaining an understanding of how visual merchandising plans link to buying and merchandising strategies. As the need to create better store environments increases, formal recognition of the qualifications of those who work at store level is a positive move for the retail industry.

(Source: Young 2000)

Visual merchandising as a support for a positioning strategy

In a retail environment that is increasingly saturated, competitive and subject to international competition, visual merchandising is a way of communicating and differentiating the retail offer. It must be an integral part of any strategy in which a retailer attempts to position or re-position the retail offer in the mind of the consumer. It is apparent, then, that visual merchandising is frequently used by multiple retailers to strengthen the retail brand, but a highly centralised and inflexible approach to visual merchandising may not be appropriate in all circumstances. Figure 11.1 considers centralised and decentralised approaches to visual merchandising.

Local approach
- Can adapt to local market product preferences
- Can incorporate local themes into displays
- Can adapt to local competition

Centralised approach
- Controls retail brand communication
- Promotes a stronger identity nationally and internationally
- Can co-ordinate corporate communication themes and messages with the visual merchandising effort (for example, by using images from media advertising in displays)

Figure 11.1 **Visual merchandising: local and centralised approaches**

THE SCOPE OF VISUAL MERCHANDISING

The discussion above has promoted the idea that visual merchandising encompasses a wide range of activities, but has not detailed what specific activities are included in the visual merchandise process. Across all retail sectors, visual merchandising may include all or some of the elements outlines in Figure 11.2.

- Choice of fixtures and fittings to be used
- Method of product presentation
- Construction of 'off-shelf' displays
- Choice of store layout (to encourage complementary purchases)
- Use of point of sale material (to encourage impulse purchases)
- Construction of window displays

Figure 11.2 **The scope of visual merchandising**

FIXTURES AND FITTINGS

The way products need to be presented and displayed within the store will largely determine the choice of fixturing. The principle types of fixtures are illustrated in Figures 11.3–11.7.

Gondolas

The term gondola refers to a system of shelving which offers stacked merchandise to the customer in a longitudinal presentation (Figure 11.3).

The gondola is used in the 'grid format' where consumers move along aisles between gondolas, which offer merchandise on both sides. The end of the gondola is a particularly effective in attracting customers to products as they slow down to turn the corner to view merchandise on the other side.

Figure 11.3 **The gondola**

Rounders

As the name suggests the rounder fixture offers merchandise in a circular presentation (Figure 11.4). The merchandise might be hung on a series of prongs, as in the case of belts or bubble packed products, or the rounder may be a more solid structure, showing the variety available in a merchandise type. Gap uses this type of fixturing to show all the colours available in basic tops or sweaters

Four-ways

Four-way fixtures offer the retailer flexibility when a degree of co-ordination is needed. The fixture offers a combination of front facing merchandise presentation, with the space efficiency of side hanging (Figure 11.5).

Shelving

Wall space is useful for incorporating the general display of merchandise within the overall interior design of the store (Figure 11.6). Levi's, for example, used a system of wooden wall shelving which allowed a large quantity of merchandise to be stacked from floor to ceiling, whilst offering

Figure 11.4 **A rounder fixture**

Figure 11.5 **A four-way fixture**

interest by showing all the alternative shades of denim. However, as this type of shelving arrangement became popular with other casual-wear retailers, Levi's introduced a new 'wavy' shelf design in its flagship store (*VM Insights* April 2000) in a move to retain their innovative image.

Figure 11.6 **Shelving**

Bins, baskets and tables

Bins and baskets are normally used to house large quantities of merchandise. They are effective for small items and for heaps of promotional merchandise. They may be filled with one type of product, or the customer may be invited to rummage through a variety of products retailing at a particular price point. Promotional merchandise can also be stacked on tables, which provide flexibility in terms of space allocation and display area. However, tables can also be used in a more elegant display of product, as shown in Figure 11.7.

The increased use of self-service in retailing has meant that the use of drawers and cabinets has decreased, but they may still be used for very functional merchandise that does not really need displaying or in instances where merchandise needs protection. For example, traditional hardware stores that sell screws and nails by weight, rather than pre-packaged, keep this type of

Small baskets for small
merchandise

Large bins for promotional
merchandise

Table

Figure 11.7 **Bins, baskets and tables**

merchandise in drawers. Watches and jewellery are often housed in glass
cabinets in order to prevent damage and theft.

Many retailers have their own customised fixturing and their own
customised terminology. Marks & Spencer have a basic unit of fixturing called
the 'Luton gondola' named after a prototype successfully trailed in the Luton
store. Fixturing should have a degree of co-ordination throughout the store
so that they can be considered in 'families', using the same type of materials,
whether it is chrome, wood, acrylic or melanin, and the same set of design
features. In all retail circumstances the fixturing should complement and not
compete with the merchandise, although the fixturing may be used to
reinforce the retail brand image. Fixturing also needs to be flexible, so that
an ever-evolving product range can be successfully accommodated. Many
modern systems are modular, which enables a great number of alternative
combinations to be built.

Figure 11.8 **A movable hanging fixture**

PRODUCT PRESENTATION

The way in which products are presented as routine will depend on the type of fixture available (see above) but essentially can include:

- vertical stacking, for example, for magazines or CDs;
- horizontal stacking, for example, for tinned foods or folded garments;
- hanging – on hangers or hooks;
- hanging – mounted on card or bubble packed.

Merchandise presentation is largely determined by product category or end use of product, but in some instances other product characteristics may bear a relation to the presentation method. Colour, for example, is often used effectively, and many clothing and home furnishings retailers incorporate a corporate colour palette into the buying plan so that different product categories can be presented together.

Retailers may group merchandise together according to price levels or even sizes. Many variety stores use a system of price lining where merchandise is selected to fit into key price points, for example, men's ties at £7.99, £9.99, £15.99 and £19.99. Women's clothing retailers may use sizing groups such as petites, regular and 'plus'; and charity shops generally use product, sizing, then colour to provide some logic in their disparate merchandise offer. There may also be a case of grouping products according to levels of technical involvement; for example, PC World houses software and accessories at the front of the store and the full PC systems are positioned at the back of the store. The customer is faced with gradually increasing product complexity as he or she moves through the store.

Product presentation can instigate a number of issues for other members of the product management team. Fixturing may determine the size variation a retailer offers, for example a small convenience store may not find it practical to stock family size cereal packets as they require such tall shelves; it would be preferable in this type of retailer to offer a smaller pack size and another product item in the same available space. The method of presentation may also determine the packaging or 'get-up' of the product; for example, a folded shirt is likely to need board and pins or a paper sash around it to keep it looking neat, but all these add to the cost of the item. Small items, such as stationery products, are much more manageable when bubble packed or mounted on card and hung on a wall fixture. It may be necessary to attach an illustration of the product in use if it has little 'hanger appeal'; for example, a swimsuit tends to look like a crumpled rag on the hanger, and most uncooked pre-prepared meals look unappetising and rely on the photograph on the package to encourage purchase.

New approaches to point of purchase presentation methods have been part of the orientation towards category management in the management of customer demand. Dedicated product fixturing can provide clarity and logic to the product presentation, whilst incorporating suggested complementary and impulse purchases in the arrangement.

STORE LAYOUT

Visual merchandising also encompasses the design of a store layout. A store layout will be heavily influenced by the assortment and variety on offer (see chapter one) and will be constrained by the size and structure of the shop itself. The layout used will also determine or be dependent on the type of fixturing used. There are a number of different approaches to store layout, although they are all designed with the intention of moving customers to every areas in the store in order to expose them to the full range of products.

A common store layout has fixtures positioned in the form of a grid (Figure 11.9). This method maximises the use that can be made of the available space and provides a logical organisation of the products on offer. However, it is rather mechanical in its approach, and rows of gondola type fixtures with aisles between them can lack interest. A grid layout, by the nature of the large fixturing used, is also relatively inflexible.

An alternative approach is to place the fixtures in a more random pattern. This type of layout is appropriate when variety in the fixturing is needed and when the shopping process involves browsing rather than a more systematic product selection process. Referred to as a free form or a free flow layout, this kind of arrangement can successfully incorporate a mix of small gondolas, hanging rails and shelving units. Although the free form layout generally offers more opportunity to create interest than the grid layout, a unending mass of fixtures set out in a random fashion can look chaotic and for large expanses of retail space, such as in a department store, some attempt must be made to break up the space and create pockets of interest for the customer. According to Din (2000), the product areas in a free form layout should not be too large or too deep, to prevent customers from feeling trapped (see Figure 11.10).

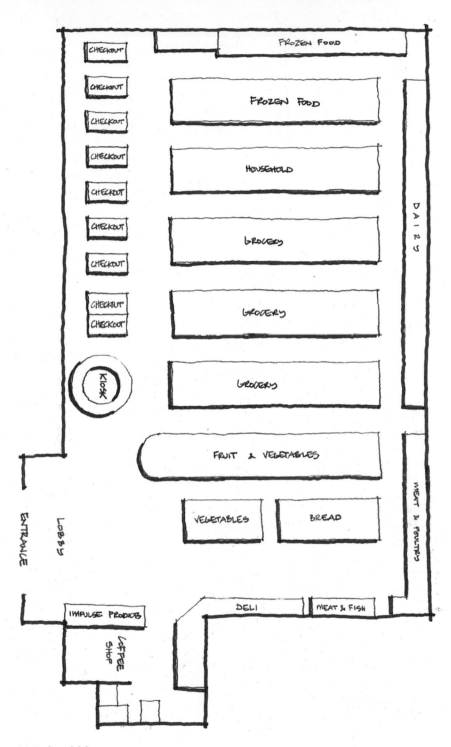

Figure 11.9 **A grid layout**

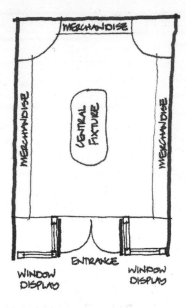

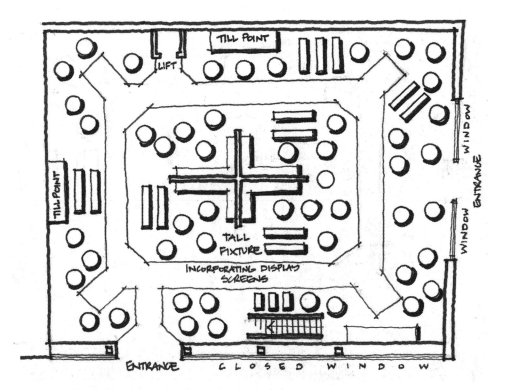

Figure 11.10 **Free form layouts**

Where the merchandise range is limited or in situations where a high level of personal selling is desirable or necessary, a 'boutique' layout could be used. This layout surrounds the customer with merchandise, most of which is displayed in or on wall fixturing, with one or two other central fixtures offering interest or, perhaps, housing the till. In larger stores a definite walkway or 'race track' is incorporated into the layout, guiding the customer between the main classifications of merchandise, which are often set out in free form or short grid fixturing.

Modern layouts are generally more airy, with voids replacing walls and glass replacing solid partitioning. 'Decompression zones' are used to give shoppers time to relax and refocus their attention, for example at the front of the store or near escalators. Vertical access and visibility is also becoming increasingly important as a means of encouraging customers to multi-level retail space, as the amount of available ground floor space decreases in prime shopping centre locations.

Complementary products

Within the overall store layout, decisions concerning which categories of merchandise should be place next to one another need to be determined. This is where the principles of space allocation and store layout are inter-twined. A store layout must provide a logic to the customer, whilst helping the retailer to achieve its own objectives in terms of exposing the store visitor to as much of the product range as possible and to increase the value of the transaction of each customer. This is done by getting customers to buy additional items that might be linked to the intended purchase or by encouraging them to 'trade up' by buying a higher value item than they had originally intended to buy, or they may be tempted to buy a completely unplanned purchase in a moment of impulse.

Although the achievement of this kind of retailer objective might be viewed as a manipulation of customers, more and more shopping trips are made with only a vague plan or 'list'. Introducing product suggestions on the shelf, or by virtue of the store layout, could be viewed as a provision of retail service – making the shopping experience easier and more convenient for the time-pressured customer. In supermarkets customers find dips displayed alongside Nacho chips and salad dressings alongside pre-prepared salads. In a department store accessories will be located in their own department for customers who have a specific purchase in mind and alongside larger items like suits or coats in order to encourage impulse buying.

DISPLAYS

Displays can normally be broken down into three different types: on-shelf displays, off-shelf displays and window displays. On shelf displays are the 'normal' displays around the store that show all the different variations of product on offer in some kind of logical sequence. The various presentation methods used in on-shelf display were discussed in the section concerning product presentation earlier in the chapter.

Off-shelf displays

These displays are designed to have additional impact by showing the product as it might be used, or perhaps alongside other products to suggest complementary purchases. Displays can also be considered as visual features that create interest or excitement within the store. They might be placed on walls, within alcoves or at the end of a fixture such as a gondola. Whilst on-shelf displays have to combine functionality with aesthetic sensibility, many off-shelf artistic displays are not used in the routine selling process and therefore can be constructed to make a significant visual impact. They are often very artistically arranged and only changed by the visual merchandise team. They may incorporate 'props', which are not part of the product range for sale, or they might be based on a body form or mannequin (see Box 11.3).

BOX 11.3 BODY FORMS

Products that we wear can look entirely different with and without a body in them. Retailer used a wide range of body forms in clothing displays, from headless torsos for tops and bum-forms for jeans, to stylised figures and lifelike mannequins for full outfits. Body forms can be a much more important part of a store design that a glorified coat hanger. Customers relate strongly to body forms because of their human imagery and so the choice of mannequin is a crucial decision in order to send the right kind of messages to the target customer. Body forms are an expensive part of the visual merchandising tool kit, and so ideally should have lasting appeal. Using the features of role models, such as supermodel Jodie Kidd or pop celebrity Liam Gallagher, is an effective way of communicating with potential customers.

In contrast, off-shelf displays are also used for promotional purposes and may well incorporate a fixture such as a dump bin, which offers the functional purpose of housing an increased quantity of the promotional item with the visual impact of a tonnage display (see Figure 11.13).

In 1981, Rosenbloom described a number of different display types, including open, theme, lifestyle, co-ordinated and classification dominance displays. Nowadays, most on-shelf displays can be regarded as open displays since the customer is encouraged to inspect, and handle products unaided in most retail situations. However, many of the other display classifications are still seen regularly in retailing, most commonly for off-shelf, artistic displays.

The themed display can be used for a local event, such as a theatre production or a film release, and is commonly used for seasonal purchases. Display props can be worked into the product theme, as shown in Figure 11.11.

Lifestyle displays offer the opportunity to incorporate a wide variety of products. For example, a display based on the theme of a barbeque could involve garden furniture – the barbeque itself, outdoor tables and loungers;

Figure 11.11 **A themed display**

kitchenware products – utensils, plastic crockery and tumblers, informal cutlery; essentials such as charcoal and matches; food produce such as marinades and sauces; accessories such as outdoor lighting and candles; and books on the subject of barbeque building or barbeque cookery.

The 'classification dominance' display allows a retailer to show that it has a very deep assortment of merchandise within a classification or category. The photograph in Figure 11.12 shows how Salami sausages are displayed to show the extensive range on offer.

At the opposite end of the scale a display can be very eye-catching if the same product is used in a quantity that is much larger than normal. Referred to by Levy and Weitz (1998: 560) as tonnage merchandising, this type of display is often used for in-store promotions (Figure 11.13).

The co-ordinated display often uses a colour theme to connect the products being grouped together. It is quite common for lifestyle displays to be colour co-ordinated in order to create additional impact. Texstyle World, a UK-based soft furnishings category killer, uses colour themes in both on-shelf and off-shelf displays to arrange its merchandise, rather than grouping by product category. Other co-ordinating themes could be texture, style or brand. Co-ordination can also be based around the end use of product, sometimes referred to as idea orientated displays. DIY retailers like B&Q use 'projects' to co-ordinate a seemingly diverse range of products that will be used during a specific DIY task, and even have demonstrations of projects in-store to get customers started. Similarly, grouping products into meal ideas can stimulate unplanned purchases of components for a new menu. Figure 11.14 shows a colour co-ordinated window display.

Figure 11.12 **A classification dominance display**

Figure 11.13 **Tonnage merchandising**

Figure 11.14 **A colour co-ordinated window display**

Product focus displays reflect the trend for spacious retail interiors. A single product or a small group of products are displayed in isolation, leaving the product and its juxtaposition with the space around it to create a visual impact. This type of display is most frequently used for products with prestige value because of the resource implication associated with a higher customer space to merchandise space ratio.

The principles of design

Although the principles of design relate as much to the overall design of the store as to a display within, it is perhaps appropriate to consider them in relation to product displays. According to Diamond and Diamond (1999), a visual merchandiser generally employs more than one of the following principles in a display:

- balance, whether symmetrical or asymmetrical;
- emphasis, including the use of size, repetition or contrast;
- proportion and scale;
- rhythm, including continuity, progression and alternation;
- harmony.

Window displays

Window displays have a particularly important role to play in communicating to the potential customer what the retailer stands for in terms of product and shopping environment. Window displays make customers aware of the type of merchandise being sold, and hopefully will attract the interest of target customers. In fact the window displays of retailers such as Selfridges, Harvey Nichols and Bloomingdale's are so novel and exciting that they have become visitor attractions in themselves. Window displays can be open, allowing the customer to see past the merchandise and into the shop. Alternatively, windows may be backed by partial or complete boarding, which allows the retailer to build promotional photography into the display or create dramatic effects (see Figure 11.15). Some window displays have even incorporated moving features, for example the flagship store of young fashion retailer Top Shop at Oxford Circus in London surprised customers with animated legs and arms in its Christmas 1999 party season window display.

Some retailers do not use window displays at all. This is commonly the case in superstores and retail warehouses, where the retailer's name either must be so well known that the general public will know what that retailer represents, for example J. Sainsbury (grocery) or Curry's (electrical), or leaves little doubt in the customer's mind about what the retailer is selling (Toys 'R' Us, PC World, Shoe Express).

SUMMARY

The role of visual merchandising within retail product management cannot be separated from any of the more 'scientific' aspects of retail product management, because of its crucial role in creating and supporting the retail brand's position. Getting the product right in all its attributes, ensuring it arrives in the store at the right time and in quantities that are appropriate to customer demand, are only worthwhile objectives if customers notice the product when they walk into the store. Visual merchandising highlights and draws attention to merchandise and has the ability to set the 'tone' of the retail brand (Din 2000). The consumer is being offered products from an increasing variety of distribution channels such as the specialist catalogue, the internet and even the vending machine. Only stores can offer customers a social experience with actual products in real space, and if they do not use

Figure 11.15 **Window displays: open and closed**

this key asset to their competitive advantage, the drift of customers away to alternative shopping formats will gather pace. Effective product management brings the buying arena and the selling arena together in a seamless product strategy.

REVIEW QUESTIONS

1 Compare a centralised approach to visual merchandising with a local approach.

2 Outline the various aspects of retailing management that would fall under the heading 'visual merchandising'.

3 Review the different methods of product presentation, and discuss how they impact upon the choice of fixturing and store layout.

4 Make a distinction between on- and off-shelf displays, indicating how the latter provides more opportunity for artistic creativity.

DISCUSSION QUESTIONS AND LEARNING ACTIVITIES

1 For a retailer of your choice, make a critical appraisal of the fixtures that are used in the store. In particular, comment on the variety and flexibility in the fixturing and the extent to which the fixtures are complementary in terms of design and material.

2 Describe the use of different store layouts in the following retail sectors:
- beauty and healthcare;
- electrical/electronic;
- grocery.

3 Discuss the relationship between visual merchandising and the reinforcement of a retail brand.

4 Use your local shopping centre to find examples that illustrate the various types of display. Also, indicate how the principles of design have been used in the display.

REFERENCES AND FURTHER READING

Barr, V. and Field, K. (1997) *Stores: Retail Display and Design*, PBC International, New York.

Buttle, F. (1994) 'Jaeger ladies (case 22)', in P.J. McGoldrick (ed.) *Cases in Retail Management*, Pitman, London, pp. 259–77.

Diamond, J. and Diamond, E. (1999) *Contemporary Visual Merchandising*, Prentice-Hall, Englewood Cliffs, NJ.

Din, R. (2000) *New Retail*, Conran Octopus, London.

Hall, J. (1999) Editorial, *VM Insights*, April.

Lea-Greenwood, G. (1998) 'Visual merchandising: a neglected area in UK fashion marketing?', *International Journal of Retail and Distribution Management* 26 (8): 324–9.

Levy, M. and Weitz, B.A. (1998) *Retailing Management*, McGraw-Hill, Maidenhead, Berks.

Peglar, M.M. (1997) *Merchandising and Display*, 4th edn, Fairchild, New York.

Rosenbloom, B. (1981) *Retail Marketing*, Random House, New York.

Young, J. (2000) 'We don't need no education', *VM Plus*, Spring.

chapter twelve

PRODUCT MANAGEMENT IN NON-STORE RETAILING

INTRODUCTION

The principles of buying and merchandising have so far in this book been predominantly discussed within the context of store retailing. The author makes no apology for this fact, given that store retailing is still the main channel for the majority of retail sales, accounting for more than 80 per cent in the UK (estimate based on various sources). However, a significant and increasing proportion of goods are being sold to consumers through distribution channels that do not include a store, and so an appreciation of the additional challenges in the product management process faced by non-store retailers is essential.

NON-STORE RETAIL FORMATS

Non-store retailers make ranges of products available to potential consumers in a number of different ways. Some retailers take the product directly to the customer, for example in the 'party plan' method of retailing made so famous by the lingerie retailer Ann Summers, where a group of potential customers are invited into a friend's home in order to inspect a range of merchandise. However, the majority of non-store retailers offer their products via some form of product representation, whether on paper or screen-based visual display. Figure 12.1 outlines the main non-store formats used in retailing.

Format	Retailers
The general catalogue	GUS, Littlewoods, Grattans, La Redoute, Sears Roebuck
The specialist catalogue	Innovations, Land's End
TV retailing	'Shop' Channel, QVC, Home Shopping Network, Teletext
Interactive TV	Open, iSec (Telewest)
Internet retailing via PC, mobile phone or TV monitor	Amazon.com, Zoom.com, Yahoo!Shopping

Figure 12.1 **Principal non-store retail formats**

HOME SHOPPING

Non-store retailing has a long history. Catalogues and mail ordering are as old as retail stores and were originally devised in order to offer customers who lived in remote areas the opportunity to acquire the kind of products their urban counterparts were able to buy in their local towns and cities. They also offered a service to people who disliked shopping in stores, especially for more personal items such as clothes.

In the postwar period, catalogue retailing, often administered through an 'agent', entered a period of steady growth, because the mail order companies offered low income families a credit facility that most store retailers would not allow. The biannual tome is still a feature in many homes, but the agency business has declined as disposable income has risen and credit facilities have become more widely available.

Whilst generalist catalogue sales have stagnated, more specialist mail order businesses have thrived. Many of the larger catalogue retailers launched more targeted catalogue offerings as a defensive strategy against more narrowly focused mail order retailers such as Land's End and N. Brown, and high street retailers started to enter the home shopping market with their own store catalogues in the early 1990s as retail trends predicted a convenience shopping boom. The large mail order retailers now generally accept that agency business will increasingly be replaced by one-to-one marketing activities.

Through the 1990s home shopping became a strategic option for many previously store-based retailers in a diverse range of product sectors. Consumer trends (see chapter 4) towards the cash-rich, time-poor consumer seemed to favour an increase in home shopping, and many of the store-based retail giants entered this market, for example Tesco and Marks & Spencer, initially with specialised range catalogues such as school wear, home furnishings and gifts. However, as the century drew to a close, the internet as a non-store retail format began to take over the interest of the retail industry as the probable home shopping format of the future, using either PC, digital TV or mobile phone access.

PRODUCT MANAGEMENT IMPLICATIONS

In order to begin exploring the challenges of non-store product management, it is perhaps useful to be explicit about the principal differences between store and non-store retailing; and in order to make meaningful generalisations, the direct selling methods (party plan, pyramid selling, door-to-door selling and telesales) are not included in the comparison shown in Figure 12.2.

Store retailing	Non-store retailing
Product presentation	
Real, tangible	Represented by image
Selling environment	
Use of store environment to enhance	Difficult to create atmosphere, although website better than printed media
Pricing	
Flexible and highly visible, but time consuming to make comparisons	Easy to compare prices between competitive non-store retail offers. Not always possible to administer price changes immediately (especially print-based media)
Customer service	
Direct, personal	Detached, impersonal; product information (especially comparison price) is often easy to access
Convenience	
May be low, depending on individual circumstances	High (in principle)
Product delivery	
Usually immediate	Not immediate; arranged, if product cannot be posted

Figure 12.2 **Store and non-store retailing: a comparison**

PRODUCT PRESENTATION

Non-store retailers have a real challenge when it comes to product presentation. If a product is largely standardised and its tangible features wholly understood, for example a CD or a book, then the presentation of the product is less problematic. If the benefits of a product are mainly functional rather than aesthetic, then again a photographic image and a wealth of product performance detail is likely to be sufficient. However, for goods where the aesthetics and the sensory elements of the product are important, for example, fresh food, clothing and cosmetics, then a two-dimensional image may not adequately represent its benefits. Representing the product in use may help, for example showing clothing modelled or home furnishings in room settings, but problems concerning the match between customers' own self-image and that of the photographic image can arise. Some mail order companies are adopting magazine type layouts, to offer a more lifestyle approach to product presentation and to transfer media familiarity to shopping formats.

Internet sites are considered by Din (2000) to be visually lacking in stimulation, with too much written text and essentially offering the customer little more than the pages of a catalogue. The product offer is often presented on websites in a list type of format, and can be organised according to retail categorisation rather than being consumer orientated. For example, Tesco have used the term 'dry goods' on their website, which is a trade term for packaged goods like sugar and flour and not a term that would necessarily be understood by customers (Packshaw 2000). However, unlike static pages, the internet does allow some moving imagery to be lodged in the website, such as a fashion show or a live product demonstration. In addition, the opportunity to deal directly with internet customers offers the possibility of tailoring the website image to individual customers. Home shopping retailer Land's End, for example, has experimented with displaying merchandise in a variety of ways, according to the demographics of the on-line customer (Wills 1999).

Internet shopping via the mobile phone clearly offers market opportunities, given the popularity of the handset as a communication medium with its convenience, easy access and low cost. However, product presentation on a mobile handset is challenging: transmission bandwidth can make screen information slow to receive and limited in scope. Mobile shopping requires a handset that incorporates a mini-web browser (the Wireless Application Protocol or WAP), which is accessed via the phone keypad, and in itself presents difficulties with site navigation. The web pages written for a PC (in hypertext mark-up language, HTML) may continue to be too complex for mobiles, which have to be written in wireless mark-up language (WML), and so compatibility and consistency between the two media becomes an issue. However, in the spring of 2000, mobile phone retailer Carphone Warehouse was preparing to pre-install a shopping and information portal in every WAP phone sold, confident in the viability of the mobile as a means of trading information-based service products, such as travel and entertainment tickets. An indication of the potential for this method of shopping is the willingness of grocery retailer Waitrose to become involved in WapWorld, the mobile phone portal company founded by Sir Bob Geldof[1] (Hall 2000).

Interactive TV offers much more flexibility in product presentation, in particular through links from TV programming and interactive advertisements to websites. The first interactive TV advertisement in the UK aired by Open, for example, was for 'Chicken Tonight' cooking sauces, which linked the advertisement to recipes, related product and vouchers. Although this is an interesting development, it raises a complex issue concerning the blurring of the distinction between programming and advertising and the freedom of viewers to 'surf away' from other advertisements and programming, which is an issue of concern for the Independent Television Commission (Clements 2000).

THE SELLING ENVIRONMENT

Creating an atmosphere within the brick walls that represent the store is not easy (see chapter 10), but creating an atmosphere on the flat and static page of a catalogue or on a website is even more difficult. The principles behind a store design and a non-store format design are, however, essentially the same. The layout must be logical and easy to browse around, products should be easy to locate within the sub-sections of the format, there should be links between complementary merchandise, and there should be consistency between the merchandise and the retailer's brand image. For example, internet retailer BagsOfTime.com offers a wide range of impulse and emergency products, with a one-hour delivery promise within London. The website is easy to navigate, and despite a wide range of goods on offer, which includes shirts, sandwiches, toiletry items and a large selection of gifts, there is a consistent image across the site. When the on-line customer reaches the pay point, they are presented with a list of further impulse items, in a way completely comparable to the impulse items presented at a retail store checkout (Retail Week 2000a).

PRICING

Home shopping retailers have the potential to offer goods at competitive prices because they do not have the expense of running a portfolio of stores. However, in traditional mail order retailing, much of this saving is offset by the need to finance the high stock holding level that is necessary to guarantee good service, as well as the funding of long customer credit terms. In theory, an internet retailer can reduce these two costs: payment is usually taken at the point of product dispatch (if not earlier) and arrangements could be made for direct delivery from a supplier. However, skimping on infrastructure seems to be one of the commonest reasons for internet retailing failure (as discussed later on in this chapter), and so virtual retailing at very pared down prices becomes a risky business. Nevertheless, price comparison is very easy to make between alternative internet offers, with shopping portals such as Yahoo!Shopping and Shopsmart offering to undertake this process in an extremely convenient manner for the shopper, free of charge. It is difficult to justify a premium pricing policy without the benefit of the store environment as an arena for adding value to the shopping process.

One further issue with home shopping media is pricing flexibility. Catalogues have a comparatively long lead-time, and price changes have to be communicated separately once the catalogue has been issued. Store retailing offers much more immediacy in terms of price changes, and discounted items can be visibly promoted in a much more effective way, for example by moving the goods to the front of the store. Internet retailing, again in theory, offers price flexibility, as an immediate medium, but promoting offers is more complex, requiring flexibility in the web page design. One of the most complex issues regarding pricing is consistency when a retailer is using more than one shopping channel (see later section on multi-channel retailing). Next, the UK clothing specialist, for example, does not discount products in its stores outside the strictly controlled end of season sales periods in order to protect the integrity of its catalogue, which offers a high proportion of products that are identical to the range found in the stores.

SERVICE

Both customer service and stock service are important when carrying out a retail transaction. Dealing with live people in real time is one aspect of store shopping that eventually may be its salvation. Information about the product, its applications and uses, demonstrations and trials are available on demand within a shop. Also the stock position is immediately apparent and if a product variant is not in stock, the position can be established immediately and/or alternatives offered. Therefore the store arena offers the opportunity as a stage for delivering an excellent standard of customer service. In addition, the quality of the service is relatively easy to measure in this environment. Poor quality service can be detected through visible signs of customer dissatisfaction or via customer complaints. It is much more difficult and in many cases impossible to evaluate levels and frequencies of poor customer service with an impersonal medium.

Customer service through non-store channels is not only different, but provides more opportunities for service implementation. A customer has to make a contact, for example by telephone or email, in order to find out any information about the product that is not immediately apparent. The stock position may be communicated, but this information has to be accurate and therefore continually to be updated. If the communication is via email the customer has to wait for a response. Following transactions the customer waits for the product to be delivered whereas in store retailing the customer (usually) departs with the product. Again the delivery promise must be rigidly adhered to in order to prevent customer dissatisfaction. The infrastructure that supports the product communication is absolutely vital to the success of any non-store retailer. One of the most frequent causes of internet shopping dissatisfaction ('cyber-shopping rage') is poor response times to enquiries and poor order fulfilment, and in such cases all the convenience advantage of the shopping format for the customer is lost. Some internet retailers who have become aware of these problems have taken steps to prevent customer loss by incorporating service orientation in the website design, for example by including email contact points and 'phone-me' options. Some sites also allow customers to access real-time stock availability and delivery information, so there is no need for them to wait for an order acknowledgement or delivery arrangement.

One feature of home shopping that is attractive to consumers is the ease with which goods can be returned. Catalogue retailers accept that around one-third of customer purchases will be returned, and in some departments, such as clothing and footwear, this proportion can be considerably higher, as the customer will order two or more sizes to try, only ever intending to purchase one. Reducing the amount of returns is a way of improving retail productivity, whether store or non-store based, but internet retailers have to accept that returns are a necessary evil of home shopping, and make adequate provision for this service, clearly setting out the returns policy for the customer. One of many problems cited in the demise of on-line clothing retailer Boo.com was an indiscriminate returns policy and an inadequate infrastructure to deal with returned goods. Again, multi-channel retailers have to consider how flexible their various outlets will be in terms of offering a multi-channel service, as well as a multi-channel selling strategy. Nordstrom, the highly service orientated US department store, allows catalogue returns to be taken back to the store, but many retailers are not able to offer this flexibility.

CONVENIENCE

One of the most oft-quoted sayings in the retail industry is the following: 'There are three factors for success in retailing; these are location, location and location' (anon.). Perhaps the most pleasant and convenient location for a consumer is at home. Traffic jams, weather and crowds can be avoided, prices can quickly be compared between outlets, and heavy and bulky shopping is delivered rather than having to be carried and loaded. In addition the consumer gains privacy and personal efficiency as they browse through non-store outlets that are geared to their individual needs. In a convenience orientated society, home shopping clearly purports to offer a set of tangible benefits. However, home shopping is only convenient if it delivers its promised service; if it does not, then it is highly inconvenient and risks high levels of customer frustration. The infrastructure behind the non-store outlet must therefore not only support the product offer but also the stated or assumed service offer.

ORDER FULFILMENT AND DELIVERY

In theory, the advantage of a product representation to sell from rather than 'live' stock is that the retailer can effectively operate a stock-free order fulfilment system (see chapter 6). Only when customer orders roll in are products ordered from the suppliers. If the supplier holds stock and the product is not subject to seasonal trends and potential obsolescence, then this type of order fulfilment system would be possible. However, in the case of seasonal goods and retail branded items, suppliers are unlikely to hold stock without some form of order commitment from the retailer, in which case the buying processes and operations are similar to store retailers, except for determining order quantities.

Determining order quantities in non-store retailing

As indicated above, non-store retailers will wish to commit themselves to as little stock investment as possible. They do not have the need for stock to fill stores, but may need a level of safety stock in order to guarantee a fast delivery service. For seasonal and fashion goods, however, it is much more difficult to forecast and respond to peaks in demand (as discussed in chapter 6) and so the larger fashion catalogue retailers use a 'preview' catalogue in order to test market the new season's products. Previous customers of the retailer are sent a catalogue early in the season, offering a discount for early ordering and a longer delivery time. This allows the retailer to anticipate the season's demand based on the level of orders placed from the preview catalogue. Repeat orders are then placed with suppliers accordingly so that their production can be geared up to produce the best sellers for the season and keep the mail order retailer in stock throughout the selling period. If a product does not sell at all in the preview catalogue, there may be an opportunity to delete the offending article from the main catalogue or modify it in some way to improve its appeal. Likewise, multiple channel retailers like Next can cherry-pick the best-selling lines from the catalogue for the new season's ranges in the stores. Internet retailing also offers the scope to pre-test new products or product variations; however, a consideration is how closely the profile of the overall target matches that of the current internet-using consumer. In many circumstances these may be very different customer groups.

Delivery

The product categories that have seen early adoption of internet retailing (such as books, CDs and services) all have the characteristic of being easy to distribute, either physically through the post or digitally downloaded. Catalogue retailers are already set up with an organisational structure that understands rapid order fulfilment, delivery and returns of bulkier products, and they have a customer base that is more likely to be at home during 'normal' working hours to receive the goods. Internet retailers must appreciate that the bulk of their clientele are people who are working long and irregular hours. Weekend or evenings are the periods in which deliveries are going to be acceptable to these customers, and these present increased operational costs. It is predicted that this may be less of a problem for inter-active TV retailers, who are more likely to be selling to high-volume TV watchers from the 'cash-poor, time-rich' section of the population (Wills 1999).

Non-store retail infrastructure

The illustrations in Figures 12.3 show how the infrastructure of non-store retailers compares with that of a store retailer. The apparent simplicity of the internet retailer in itself is what bodes ill for retailers in general, as it is

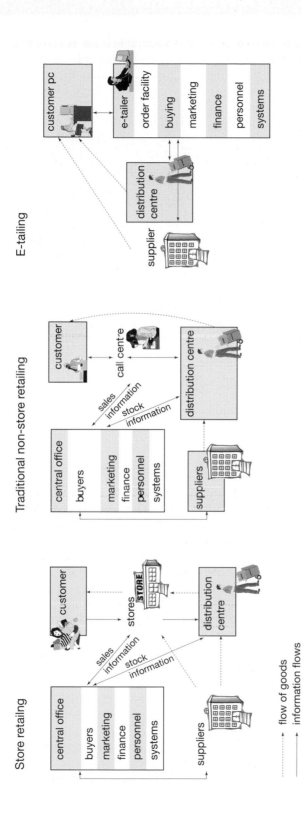

Store retailing

central office
buyers
marketing
finance
personnel
systems

suppliers

customer

stores

STORE

distribution
centre

sales
information

stock
information

Traditional non-store retailing

central office
buyers
marketing
finance
personnel
systems

suppliers

customer

call centre

distribution centre

sales
information

stock
information

E-tailing

customer pc

e-tailer
order facility
buying
marketing
finance
personnel
systems

distribution
centre

supplier

----➤ flow of goods
⟶ information flows

Figure 12.3 **Retail infrastructure: store-based, traditional non-store and 'e-tail'**

as easy for a consumer to reach a producer's website as a retailer's. This opportunity has not passed manufacturers by; for example, in the US a group of high-profile branded goods manufacturers, including Proctor & Gamble, launched Consumer Direct Co-operative in order to test the viability of direct delivery to consumers (Fernie 1999). In the end it is the seller who presents the best brand identity and most accessible method of product acquisition that will win the customer's purse. For the time being, retailers still have the advantage of being able to offer a product range that is understood and convenient for consumers to choose from, like Tesco Direct's on-line grocery shopping service. Consumers need simplification, speed and choice which retailers, rather than branded goods suppliers, are able to offer, no matter how exciting and well designed a branded good's website might be (Rivett 2000). However, the internet does offer specialist producers fast and inexpensive access to a potentially huge market of interested individuals. Obvious contenders for specialist retailing are themed shopping sites that tie into themed TV channels, for example a virtual sports club merchandise superstore linked to a sports channel. Likewise, a themed programme, such as one about home improvements, can be linked to relevant retail offers such as B & Q or Homebase via interactive TV. However, the technology and distribution support must offer superior benefits to the consumer than simply going to the shops. Internet retailers must also remember that they are essentially linked to a global market offering extensive opportunities, and so the organisation must be able to support the 'front-line' selling page and cope with the complexities of international retailing (see chapter thirteen).

MULTI-CHANNEL RETAILING

As this text goes to press, retailing via the internet is being rapidly adopted using both PC and the more affordable and accessible TV as a shopping 'route'. Consumers are getting used to the time flexibility that virtual shopping allows. Retailer businesses are viewing the multiple channel approach to distribution as a strategic necessity rather than a novelty, and are seeing the potential for product development and diversification without the need to acquire more store space.

As well as the retail infrastructure mentioned earlier, retailers must consider their branded identity. The new routes to consumers must reinforce the image that has been built up over years of hard work within the framework of the traditional retail format.

Maintaining this image may require considerable investment in new product management skills. According to Ody (2000) 'clicks and mortar' retailers are able to accrue the benefits of cross-marketing that 'pure-play dot.com' retailers are unable to access. These would include better (more experienced) stock management, greater buying power, the opportunity to advertise in order to gain site awareness, and a better opportunity to track customer shopping habits by means of existing and new customer links. The importance of order fulfilment and delivery service in the support operations for a home shop 'front page' activity was highlighted earlier; whilst traditional catalogue retailers look most vulnerable to internet retail offers, they also possess assets and specialist management skills that new internet company start-ups are most keen to acquire. They have distribution centres, logistics networks and established supply channels; they also have experience in sales forecasting and responding to unpredicted demand, and supply market knowledge. Merging the skills of an innovative internet-based retail business and an established retail distribution organisation is an available and fast route to multi-channel retailing. Ahold, the Netherlands-based international grocery retailer, for example, acquired the US grocery company peapod.com in 2000 in pursuit of rapid development of a multi-channel retail strategy.

One of the most inhibiting factors in the process of multi-channel retail development is cost allocation. In chapter 8, we examined the various ways in which product profitability can be approached. A new, and potentially important, retail format involves many start-up costs which seriously distort the finely tuned profit calculation used, for example in activity-based costing. Cross-channel shopping behaviour compounds the complexity of sales and profit analysis because one medium may be used for the all important information search part of the purchase process, whilst an alternative medium may be used for the actual transaction. For example, consumers may conduct a considerable web-surf for product information, but prefer to see the product in the store before the final purchase. Other customers may prefer to browse in shops, spending time talking to sales assistants and using facilities to trial products but, rather than carry the goods home, order them via an interactive TV internet service. Knowing how consumers shop and how this can be profitably managed takes efficient consumer response to another level. Next, for example achieves its highest transaction values from customers who use a combination of internet and the Next Directory, selecting from the catalogues and ordering on-line (*Retail Week*, 31 March 2000).

Another cost involved with multi-channel retailing is sales cannibalisation. In all the complexity of multi-channel shopping, a retailer may not be gaining any more customers, in a similar way that opening more and more stores may just be providing more convenient outlets to existing customers. However, from a strategic viewpoint, cannibalisation is market share being protected, rather than market share being lost to retailers who offer more convenient product offers (Butler 1999). Other multi-channel operational complexities include how loyalty schemes transfer across channels, and how a comparable service is offered across all formats, such as in the case of a returns policy, discussed earlier in this chapter. Multi-channel retailers have to appreciate that, from a consumer's viewpoint, the retail brand applies to all the alternative shopping formats and the internal structuring and financial reporting is of no interest to them. For example, an on-line purchase either adds to or detracts from the retail brand value built up by a store-based retail operation, whilst an uninviting store environment is unlikely to encourage customers to visit a website of the same retail fascia.

BOX 12.1   PRODUCT AND SERVICE EXTENSION COMBINED

W.H. Smith, as a book, music and stationery retailer, has been seen as a business that is vulnerable to non-store retail competition. However, it is not only developing an on-line shopping service of its own, but is also using its stores as a base from which to offer extended product ranges to customers using the internet. Outlets like their Leeds City railway station store are encouraging customers to use the internet to search on a virtual catalogue, which offers well over one million titles.

Being a small store, it can only carry 3,500 titles on site, and so the internet allows them to offer a much better stock service. Customers who are not familiar with the technology are given an introduction to the internet within the store, and email is made available to customers who wish to use the store's PC. Those customers who have their own PC are encouraged to take home a free W.H. Smith online CD-Rom. Internet book orders can either be delivered to the customer's home or be picked up from the store.

(Source: Clements 2000)

In spite of the various difficulties, multi-channel retailing as a strategic development offers some really important marketing opportunities. Retail brand positioning and reinforcement was a central theme of earlier chapters of this book when considering the relationship between product ranges and the selling environment. Making the retail brand more visible and more accessible to more customers will reinforce recognition and loyalty. Multi-channel retailing allows consumers more choice and flexibility so that the process of shopping can be blended into their busy and changing lifestyles (see Box 12. 1). However, a multi-channel retailing strategy does not always develop in the 'brick to clicks' direction. Some retailers who have established successful internet-based operations are realising that the more traditional retail formats can be used very effectively as a means of reinforcing their position in an increasingly competitive virtual market place. Gateway 2000, for example, started selling computers on the internet, but later started a store portfolio development. The famous internet book retailer Amazon is also looking at stores as a means of extending its retail brand.

SUMMARY

New methods of retailing emerge and shopping processes evolve, but the product management issues associated with retail operations which do not enable customers to interact with the 'real' product will not disappear. Shoppers will adapt to the product offers made available to them in various forms but it is the extent to which consumers accept the various home shopping methods available that will determine the market size, not the number of retailers subscribing to the new technologies. The developments in non-store retailing are as vital to traditionally store-based retailers as they are to those who have never relied on the physical presence of a product to help in the purchase process; and in the meantime, the role of the store is evolving from the point at which goods are distributed to consumers to an arena where a branded retail identity is reinforced, through a blend of product presentation, information provision, access to retail services, and in-store interest and entertainment.

NOTE

1 Bob Geldof was previously a rock musician and was knighted for his work as the organiser of Live Aid, which took place in 1985.

REVIEW QUESTIONS

1 Review the developments in home shopping, highlighting the benefits and drawbacks of this retailing format for consumers.
2 Identify the main challenges in non-store retail product management, and suggest the steps that retailers might take to overcome these.
3 Conduct a SWOT (strengths, weakness, opportunities and threats) analysis on internet retailing within a product sector of your choice.

DISCUSSION QUESTIONS

1 Identify retailers that already successfully use multi-channel retailing, and make a critical analysis of their product offer across the different channels that they use.
2 Suggest retailers that you feel could benefit from alternative retailing methods, and the formats you feel are appropriate for them. Justify your recommendations.
3 The shopping medium may change, but the principles of retail product management remain the same. Discuss.
4 One of the future trends in retailing is predicted to be a series of 'clicks and mortar' joint ventures, mergers and acquisitions. Discuss the reasons for this trend, and give some examples of companies which have joined forces to create multi-channel retail organisations.

REFERENCES AND FURTHER READING

Butler, S. (1999) 'The high street heads for home', *Draper's Record Focus*, February.
Clarke Hill, C.M., Ward, P. and Toogood, A. (1999) 'Internet retailing: designing the transactional interface', *Proceedings of the 10th International Conference on Research in the Distributive Trades*, Institute for Retail Studies, University of Stirling.
Clements, A. (2000) 'Clicks and mortar and customer service', *Retail Week*, 4 February.
Din, R. (2000) *New Retail*, Conran Octopus, London.
Fernie, J. (ed.) (1999) *The Future of UK Retailing*, Financial Times Retail and Consumer Reports, London.
Hall, J. (2000) 'Pioneers get mobile to woo channel hopping shoppers', *Retail Week*, 18 February.

Markham, J.E. (1998) *The Future of Shopping: Traditional Patterns and Net Effects*, Macmillan, Basingstoke, Hants.

Ody, P. (2000) 'Channel-hopping is the key', *Retail Week*, 5 May.

Packshaw, H. (2000) 'Rational balancing act', *Retail Week*, 26 May.

Retail Week (2000a) 'Charge-free site's a gift' [unattributed article], 26 May.

Retail Week (2000b) 'Next customer spend more online' [unattributed article], 31 March.

Reynolds, J. (1999) 'Who will dominate European e-commerce? Threats and opportunities for European Retailers', *Proceedings of the 10th International Conference on Research in the Distributive Trades*, Institute for Retail Studies, University of Stirling.

Rivett, D. (2000) 'Brands at the mercy of the killer portals', *Retail Week*, 12 May.

Wills, J. (1999) *Merchandising and Buying Strategies: New Roles for a Global Operation*, Financial Times Retail and Consumer Reports, London.

chapter thirteen

INTERNATIONAL ASPECTS OF RETAIL PRODUCT MANAGEMENT

INTRODUCTION

Very few large retailers can ignore the opportunities afforded by an international approach to their business. As domestic markets become saturated and increasingly competitive, the attractions of serving emerging new markets become greater. In addition, competitive pressure to provide the best value in the product offer to the customer forces buyers to look further than their own domestic supply base for product sources.

For the product management team there are a number of important issues concerning international retailing, and these are explored in this chapter. The first issue is the extent to which the product range should remain the same as outlets are opened in an increasing number of different places, with all their geographic and cultural diversity. The second issue is the extent to which the retailer becomes involved in international sourcing; and the third issue is how an increasingly international retailing operation organises itself for product management.

INTERNATIONAL RETAILING AS A STRATEGY

For many retailers an international strategy has been central to their success; for companies like Woolworth's and Safeway, and more recently Ikea, Ahold, Tesco and Wal-Mart amongst many others, international operations have been a logical way to grow. Other retailers such as Next and Marks & Spencer have taken a more cautious approach and have met with varied success. The various entry and growth strategies have been well documented in other texts and sources (for example, Alexander 1997; McGoldrick and Davies 1995), and so the discussion of internationalisation in this text is tailored to those specific retail operations that are concerned with product management.

PRODUCT RANGE: STANDARDISE OR ADAPT?

As a retailer opens more and more outlets in an increasingly diversified set of locations, it would seem logical to tailor the product range to the needs of the population. However, one of the attractions of an international market is to take a current successful retail format to a new set of customers who have similar characteristics and needs. Many retailers with a highly differentiated product range have had considerable international success without any great change to the retail identity or product range, for example Body Shop, Ikea and (initially) Laura Ashley.

Salmon and Tordjman (1989) suggested that retailers either use a global strategy or a multinational strategy for international operations. A global strategy is one that takes a successful retail formula from a domestic retail market and reproduces it around the world, whereas a multinational strategy involves setting up retail outlets that are owned or partially owned by the domestic retailer but are adapted to the local market. A global strategy is said to concentrate on market similarities whereas a multinational strategy takes into consideration the differences. In fact most successful international retailers' companies combine these two strategies to a greater or lesser extent. Adhering to a global strategy makes a retailer unable to react to local market opportunities and threats, so that once the novelty value of the new retail format has worn off, the formula becomes tired and vulnerable to local competition. The Spanish clothing retailer Zara, for example, has successfully adopted a product management strategy that allows it to adapt the product range within an operationally global business. They have a very fast turnaround of new products, with rapid replenishment and swift and deep markdowns of unsuccessful products. Once the bulk orders for a successful product have sold out, the original product is not repeated but the successful design features are incorporated into a new product. The replenishment and the allocation of the new product are made according to the sales of similar products sold previously in the individual outlets. Local preferences on colour and local needs for different size ratios are also taken into consideration in the product allocation, and the stores are encouraged to speak to the company's product developers about popular designs in their region (Wills 1999).

A multinational strategy generally takes longer and involves more invest-ment from the parent company. A considerable amount of market research is required, followed by a programme of planning and implementation that may require new skills and approaches throughout the organisation. Scale economies may be difficult to achieve, given the diversity of marketing techniques and the tailoring of products to individual market needs. However, the opportunities for the transfer of knowledge and experience are much greater with a multinational strategy and the opportunities for international learning are also increased through the process of adaptation.

Treadgold (1990–1) and Dawson (1994) developed the idea of a continuum of international retailing strategies, ranging from intensely global (no adaptation) to completely multinational (highly customised), with what were termed transnational companies in between. The transnational approach, which combines global operational efficiency while responding to national needs, opportunities and constraints, is the basis of the strategies of many successful international retailers. Even an essentially global retailer like Ikea has had to adapt 20 per cent of its product range for the US market; for example, European bed linen does not fit US beds (*The Economist* 1994).

THE INFLUENCES ON DIFFERENT PRODUCT STRATEGIES

The differences in consumer behaviour in terms of product choice, brand preference, consumer economics, spending patterns and shopping methods, whilst challenging in a domestic market, become a myriad of changeable variables on an international scale. Some products, such as food, have a deep cultural relevance and localised interpretations, and so these products are more difficult to ascribe to a global strategy. US consumers, for example, generally have more storage space than their European counterparts and so are more inclined to buy groceries in bulk or large pack sizes. On the other hand, if the target market is a narrow segment of the worldwide population, then the customer characteristics and product preferences may be more homogeneous. Luxury goods traditionally have developed a universal appeal to the upper income brackets. Brands such as Dunhill, Hermes, Gucci and Ralph Lauren have all 'travelled well'. With the increased globalisation of communications, the notion of 'international youth' has offered significant opportunities for retail brand globalisation, as shown by Gap, Levi's and DKNY.

UNAVOIDABLE ADAPTATIONS

Whilst the adaptation of the product range to a new geographic market is a matter of strategic judgement, there are some product modifications which are completely unavoidable. For example, product information in a dozen languages on one label may be necessary but can render the information unreadable, and so the packaging or labelling design may need to be reformulated. Packaging and labelling requirements may also vary from country to country, and different climates may require alternative approaches to storage. Technical compatibility is often an issue in the electronics market. Likewise there is no escaping the additional documentation and administration that international trading brings, or the barriers to trade that may be insurmountable, such as quotas or trade embargoes.

Retail pricing in the international market is a very complex issue with different currencies and exchange rates, import duties and taxes all having a bearing on the final pricing decision. In addition, a retailer needs to consider the different costs involved in retailing internationally, especially the distribution costs. In many cases an international retailer will have a higher market positioning in non-domestic markets in order to cover the additional costs. Marks & Spencer, for example, have a much more up-market product positioning in their East Asian markets, where the clothes are considered to be 'designer wear', compared to the middle market position they occupy on home ground.

ORGANISATION FOR PRODUCT MANAGEMENT

A retailer has the choice of adopting a centralised approach to its international activities or a decentralised approach. Earlier in this text the benefits of a centralised buying organisation were presented and some of the drawbacks given (see chapter two). This discussion can be expanded to explore the issue on a global scale. A centralised approach has the advantage of retaining the significant economies of scale afforded by having a specialised team handling all sourcing operations from one base. However, one of the problems with simply extending the current roles to handling international outlets along with domestic ones is that the non-domestic outlets may not be given the attention they deserve. Reasons for poor performance may not be explored and product opportunities may not be optimised, because the domestic business (which will normally be larger at the start of international operations) takes priority.

Ultimately the organisation that is adopted should reflect the product strategy being used. Where a high degree of standardisation is retained in the product range, with little adaptation to local markets, a centralised structure is more appropriate; but where a retailer adopts a strategy of adaptation, then a decentralised product management structure is more appropriate. A retailer may start its international expansion using the existing buying organisation, and then as the international operations grow and adaptations begin to appear necessary a separate or decentralised structure may emerge. Body Shop, for example, introduced a decentralised structure in 1999, in order to gear its operations more closely to different international markets, in terms of both product development and sourcing. The company split its international markets into four regions: UK, Europe, the Americas and Asia, and put a management team in place for each region. In this way it can identify and respond to product market opportunities more quickly and efficiently, rather than having everything managed from a UK base (Wills 1999).

Where the entry strategy for a new geographical market is by means of acquisition, it makes sense to retain the existing buying organisation, at least until the opportunities for consolidation can be fully explored. Local sources and existing relationships with suppliers may offer benefits that outweigh the efficiencies of increased buying power. The extent of synergy will depend on the similarities in the product range. Kingfisher, for example, has undertaken an aggressive international growth strategy by means of acquisition, predominantly in the European market. Whilst it has retained separate management teams for the store fascias in the different locations, the teams are working together to exchange best practice and achieve joint buying economies in some areas (Kingfisher Group, *Annual Report*, 1999).

LOCAL SOURCING

Local sourcing can help an international retailer in a number of ways. Local sources are in touch with local tastes and preferences and may already be integrated into the retailer's own supply chain, as in the case of an international acquisition for example. Supporting local industries can have a positive effect on the local economy and can help a retailer to develop a positive image with local customers. In some cases, the host country may even insist that a retailer purchase local supplies as a prerequisite for trading. Toys 'R' Us, for example, tends to purchase around one-third of its product range from local suppliers, which helps them to integrate into the new economy (Berman *et al.* 1996).

GLOBAL SOURCING

Operating outlets 'abroad' is the most common interpretation of international retailing; nevertheless importing goods from other countries is often the first step a retailer takes towards being an international player. Whilst many retailers never get beyond this step, there can be no doubt that an international outlook and transfer of expertise on a global scale has contributed to the growth in international retailing activities.

Improvements in technology, transport and logistics, and communication have made global sourcing a viable option for more retailers, whilst consumer demand and competitive pressure has pushed retail buyers to all corners of the earth to find producers for a wide and consistent selection of keenly priced goods. We are gradually losing the notion of seasonal produce; to the supermarket operator, the more months in which customers can be offered premium products such as fresh strawberries the better.

The manufacture of labour intensive products is part and parcel of a nation's industrialisation and economic development, and as a new region enters the frame as the lowest cost producer, international buyers change their travelling routes. Training shoes, for example, are now sourced from Vietnam, having moved from Hong Kong to China and to Korea previously.

As consumers travel more, both for leisure and on business, their knowledge and experience of 'foreign' products widens. In addition, the influence of more confident ethnic communities becomes more widespread, and so markets in developed countries have become keenly international in their tastes. At the same time, consumers are deepening their interest in their own cultural heritage, and so product diversity is an ever-increasing trend in retailing, in spite of the dangers posed by the need for product rationalisation in order to achieve efficiency (see chapter three).

Lui and McGoldrick (1995) note that international sourcing is different to importing. Often retailers sell imported goods without trading internationally, by purchasing goods from agents or distributors, and in many cases even large retailers prefer to deal with a domestic supplier who imports from its own global network of factories. However, as retailers become increasingly international in terms of outlet operation, it makes sense for them to develop supply and distribution networks that reduce the time products have to spend in costly transit. The retail industry is consolidating on a global basis, giving rise to an international league of mass-market retailers; and so global scale competition will force international trading to become central to a competitive worldwide operation. In its bid to become a player in this field Tesco has established buying teams around world, adding India, Thailand and Europe to its established operations in Hong Kong. This network of buyers are to source in particular non-food ranges for both the domestic stores and its increasing number of international outlets, which in 2000 covered central Europe, Ireland and the Far East (Riera 2000).

Although not the only consideration, the fact that products can be bought in at lower cost prices means that retailers will continue to source from abroad. Improvements in product quality, communications and customer service (such as product development and sampling) have made the overseas buying trip ever more viable. International logistics have decreased lead times and improved the reliability of delivery, so many of the traditional problems associated with global sourcing have diminished. Global sourcing requires a global set of selection criteria, but to operate efficiently the activities that it entails should be costed. What might appear to be an excellent profit margin could quickly diminish if additional time spent controlling quality and chasing deliveries were taken into account. Box 13.1 describes how information technology applications have helped US retailer Petsmart to source efficiently on a global scale. In selecting suppliers from a global supply base, retail product managers may use some or all of the following strategies:

- limit the percentage of internationally sourced goods, using domestic suppliers for specific product or service requirements (for example, to repeat fast-selling merchandise);
- spread the risk by sourcing from a number of different countries and different manufacturers;
- limit buying to certain geographical regions to keep sourcing travel costs under control, possibly sourcing other regions through agents.

Locating sources around the world is another challenge for the retail buyer. As in domestic supplier selection, trade journals, directories, web pages, trade

---

BOX 13.1   PETSMART

Petsmart, the US based category killer retailer, sources products around the world from its buying office in Phoenix, Arizona. Suppliers are based in the US, Asia and Europe, and range from small-scale specialists to multinational producers. The internet has given Petsmart the opportunity to create a standardised sourcing system, allowing all suppliers to be linked into a single buying network. The information technology solution, supplied by SourcingLink.net, provided a tailored retail-supplier procurement system that allows buyers to build up contact information, gather product source information, and then place and track orders with suppliers. The system is capable of producing digital imagery to help with product development at suppliers across the globe. Benefits from using such systems include a reduction in buyer's travelling time and costs, improved and cheaper communications with suppliers, and more product innovations at a reduced time to market.

(Source: Ody 2000)

---

conventions and trade associations are useful points of information. Retailers will want reassurance that the supplier is experienced in international trade, is financially sound and has an established network of raw material suppliers and transporters. Some retailers, usually the larger groups, have buying offices located in the global supply markets. Otto Versand, for example, has a network of offices in Europe and the Far East through which buyers from all their mail order companies can source products. Smaller retailers may be able to tap into global markets by becoming affiliated to an international buying office organisation. The buying office may undertake a number of tasks, including the identification and recommendation of suppliers according to the retailer's needs, obtaining samples and price quotations, organising buying fairs, contract negotiation, collating orders, arranging payments, progress chasing and overseeing shipments.

Increasingly, e-commerce trading networks are becoming a feature of the global supply market. GlobalNetXchange, for example, is a joint venture between Sears Roebuck (US), Carrefour (France), J. Sainsbury (UK), Kroger (US) and Metro (Germany); whilst Worldwide Retail Exchange has eleven large retail groups including Tesco, Marks & Spencer, Kingfisher (all UK), Casino (France), Ahold (Netherlands) and Kmart (US). The benefits that are likely to accrue to retailers from electronic trading are principally concerned with lower order processing costs and obtaining price transparency, but they also allow retailers to compare suppliers easily on a global scale; whilst entering new supply markets cautiously on the back of a larger organisation or an experienced partner. Order processing is also much faster, which will help retailers and their suppliers, whilst other opportunities for suppliers include the means by which excess product can be sold off quickly and easily, and providing a route to large retail buyers that can be made available to smaller, remote suppliers (Clements 2000a).

ETHICAL SOURCING

One of the difficulties associated with global sourcing is that the distance away from the supply source makes it more difficult for buyers to assess suppliers. A buyer may be placing orders with a sourcing agent or with a trading company that uses a network of manufacturing units, and so it is often difficult to establish exactly how and where the products are actually manufactured. Buyers may be unaware that their products are being made in factories where the working conditions fall short of what would be considered satisfactory. Of course, different countries have different laws and regulations concerning working hours, age limitations and working conditions, but the international trading community has a collective social responsibility to ensure that international trade does not result in the exploitation and abuse of humankind.

Retailers have recently been under increasing pressure by both consumers and human rights organisations to be more concerned about the way they conduct trade. As consumers become increasingly knowledgeable, experienced and sophisticated, the more concern they have about what goes into the products they buy and the way they are produced. Many large international retailers have borne the brunt of unwelcome publicity concerning the production of their goods, including Gap, Eddie Bauer, Toys 'R' Us, Sears, Nike and Wal-Mart (Lavin 1999). In response to this ethical concern, retailers have introduced codes of conduct, backed up by supplier development and monitoring procedures. The Ethical Trading Initiative is an example of this kind of retailer response (see Box 13.2).

In a similar vein, there has been a growing interest in 'fair trade'. According to FINE, a network of organisations promoting fair trade in Europe, fair trade is defined as 'an alternative approach to conventional international trade. It is a trading partnership that aims at sustainable development for excluded and disadvantaged producers' (Fair Trade Fact Sheet 2000). The move towards trade rather than aid is a hopeful sign for developing countries in an international society that provides low levels of aid and investment in these areas. Affiliated to FINE is the Fairtrade Foundation, a trading organisation which endorses products that are produced by suppliers in need of investment and support. The Co-operative retailers in the UK, for example, consider Fairtrade tea and coffee to be profitable and innovative additions to their beverage range; but one of the complications with the Fairtrade brand goods is that they only apply to products that are produced in parts of the world where suppliers need assistance; the label is not applicable to all types of produce, and so branding consistency is not achievable. Fair trade has been at the heart of Body Shop's supply policies for a number of years, where sustainable trading relationships have been established with thirty-six supplier groups in twenty-one countries through its growing Community Trade Programme (Clements 2000b).

BOX 13.2   THE ETHICAL TRADING INITIATIVE

The Ethical Trading Initiative (ETI) was launched in 1998, with the backing of Christian Aid, an official aid and development agency of forty British churches. It was formed as a result of co-operation among campaigning groups, trade unions, major retailers, manufacturers and the British government, with the view to enabling third world workers to get a decent deal for producing the foods that we shop for in our supermarkets. One of the first grocery multiples to get involved was J. Sainsbury, which presented its ethical policy to the press in 1996, and by 1999 Asda, CWS, Somerfield and Tesco were all members of the ETI.

To become a member a company must agree to a set of commitments. This includes adopting a 'base code' of labour practice that incorporates relevant internationally agreed labour standards. They then work with suppliers to move towards these standards. The ETI believes that a retailer should not have to choose between trade and ethics, and provides a forum at which the overlap between these interests can increase. Although a majority of leading UK retailers have expressed an interest and many have become members of the ETI, the success of this initiative will be dependent on how quickly the code of practice is implemented by the retailers, how well it is adopted by suppliers, and how rigidly it is enforced. This calls for extra resources to be invested by the retailer. The extent of consumer pressure will influence the level of investment retailers are prepared to make and the speed of adoption of the new practices.

Full implementation of the Ethical Trading Initiative would mean that consumers could shop in their supermarkets in the knowledge that what they buy comes from suppliers who offer working conditions which meet internationally accepted standards.

SUMMARY

International activities are no longer an 'add on' in a retail strategy; the vision of the globe as the market, both in terms of demand for the retail offer and supply of products to sell in the retail outlet, is one that is taken by an increasing numbers of retailers. International consolidation is taking industry leaders out of domestic markets and putting them into an international premier league. The opportunities for international retail expansion are becoming increasingly attractive as established markets tighten up and new markets open. However, product management is fundamental to the formulation of an appropriate strategy for the individual retailer, and the extent to which ranges and sources remain the same or are adapted will depend on the retail formats used and the product sector being developed. A global approach to product sourcing can help a retailer to maintain an innovative and price competitive product offer. However, planning and control and measuring the results remain the crux of product management on an international scale, and must increasingly incorporate ethical issues.

REVIEW QUESTIONS

1 Outline the differences between a global product strategy, a multinational product strategy and a transnational product strategy, and discuss how the retail product sector might determine which strategy is used.
2 Examine the reasons why an international retailer might adopt a decentralised international buying organisation.
3 Suggest reasons for the increasingly global approach to product sourcing by retailers.
4 Explain what is meant by the terms 'fair trade' and 'ethical trading', in the context of international retailing.

DISCUSSION QUESTIONS

1 Discuss the additional selection criteria that it might be necessary to consider when assessing non-domestic suppliers.
2 To what extent do you think that developments in e-commerce will benefit the global supply market?
3 Discuss the reasons why retailers are under increasing pressure to ensure that the products they are supplied with are the result of fair and ethical trading. From your own research, provide some examples of unfavourable publicity for retailers concerning this topic.

REFERENCES AND FURTHER READING

Alexander, N. (1997) *International Retailing*, Blackwell, Oxford.
Berman, B., Evans, J.R., Berman, L.N. and Berman, G.L. (1996) 'Toys 'R' Us Inc.: analysis of a global strategy', *Proceedings of the 4th International Conference of the European Association for Education and Research in Commercial Distribution*, ESCP, Paris, 4–5 July.
Clements, A. (2000a) 'Chains hope to net the benefit', *Retail Week*, 14 April.
Clements, A. (2000b) 'A fair chance for the Third World', *Retail Week*, 10 March.
Dawson, J. (1994) 'Internationalisation of retailing operations', *Journal of Marketing Management* **10**: 267–82.
The Economist (1994) 'Furnishing the world', Management Brief, 19 November,
Fair Trade Fact Sheet (2000) <http://www.tradcraft.co.uk> (accessed 2 April 2000).
Lavin, M. (1999), 'Press accounts of sweatshop atrocities: the potential for consumer negative evaluation of retailers', *Proceedings of the 10th International Conference on Research in the Distributive Trades, Institute for Retail Studies*, University of Stirling, 26–28 August.
Lui, H. and McGoldrick, P.J. (1995) 'International sourcing: patterns and trends', in P.J. McGoldrick and G. Davies, *'International Retailing: Trends and Strategies'*, Pitman, London, ch. 5.
McGoldrick, P.J. and Davies, G. (1995), *International Retailing: Trends and Strategies*, Pitman, London.
Ody, P. (2000) 'Smarter sourcing of supplies', *Retail Week*, 5 May.
Riera, J. (2000) 'Tesco sourcing teams to drive down global costs', *Retail Week*, 17 March.
Salmon, W.J. and Tordjman, A. (1989) 'The internationalisation of retailing', *International Journal of Retailing* **4** (2): 3–16.

Treadgold, A. (1990–1) 'The emerging internationalisation of retailing: present status and future challenges', *Irish Marketing Review* **5** (2): 11–27.

Wills, J. (1999) *Merchandising and Buying Strategies: New Roles for a Global Operation*, Financial Times Retail and Consumer Reports, London.

appendix one

A CASE STUDY OF BUYING OPERATIONS AT BOOTS THE CHEMIST

INTRODUCTION

Managing the product range of a retail business is a surprisingly complex task. Product concepts must be developed in line with rapidly changing market opportunities; the product and its packaging have to be designed; suppliers need to be found who can produce an item to the required quality standard; marketing communication support must be organised for the product launch; and once on sale, the performance of the product must be monitored and its position in the range be under constant review. In today's fast-moving and competitive industry, retailers like Boots have to ensure that every product in the store is earning its place within the total product offer.

COMPANY BACKGROUND

In 1997 Boots the Chemist generated a sales turnover of just over £3,300 million from its 1,258 outlets (see Table A1.1). Originally a specialist retailer in the pharmacy sector trading in toiletries, cosmetics, healthcare and pharmaceuticals, Boots now had an extensive product range including gifts, music, photographic supplies and processing, and electrical appliances; the range is so diverse that it is now classified as a variety store in the mixed retailer sector. During the early 1990s, Boots was faced with increased competition from discount retailers in the sector, whose price orientated offer seemed appealing to consumers in the economic recession. However, since 1993, sales have grown by 24 per cent, and the company continues to have a very high customer flow, with one in three people visiting a Boots store every week. This enables Boots to maintain a healthy profit performance (see Table A1.1).

Table A.1.1 **Boots the Chemist: sales and profit performance (£ millions)**

	1995	1996	1997
Sales	2,943.8	3,107.6	3,313.5
Operating profit	349.7	384.8	426.5

STORE PROFILE

Boots has a wide range of store formats. Traditionally situated on high streets of large and small towns, with the size of the store roughly in line with the size of the town, recent store investment has included EOT (edge of town) locations and Boots now has eight large EOT stores. It is also opening stores in airport terminals, motorway stations and hospital sites. Internationally, Boots is not yet a major player, but a chain of stores (currently six) is being developed in the Republic of Ireland and test stores have been opened in Thailand and The Netherlands.

BOOTS' PRODUCT OFFER

The business is split into three main divisions for sales reporting:

* healthcare, dispensing, baby consumables and dietary food;
* beauty (includes toiletries);
* leisure (includes gifts, clothing, photographic processing/supply and food).

The leisure division accounts for around 20 per cent of Boots' sales, while each of the other two divisions account for around half of the balance. The traditional emphasis on high quality pharmaceutical and healthcare products has earned Boots the reputation of being a trustworthy retailer with a high ethical standing. This does, however, have implications for the introduction of other products, with a risk of being criticised for being hypo-critical by selling chocolate, sugary soft drinks and so on.

Boots has a wide range of own-label products which is constantly being updated and developed in response to market opportunities, aided by its vertical integration with Boots Contract Manufacturing and close relationships with other major suppliers. In addition, Boots branded ranges, such as the well known and trusted No. 7 (cosmetics), Soltan (suncream) and Shapers (slimming foods) are market leaders in their respective product sectors. Like many other leading UK retailers, Boots has recently launched a customer loyalty scheme – the Advantage Card – which will enable the company to build a customer database and refine its marketing activities.

MERCHANDISE AND MARKETING

Located at company headquarters in Nottingham, the merchandise and marketing (M/M) operation of Boots is centralised, as are the other operational areas: store development, information systems, finance and logistics. The organisational structure of M/M is led by product area, with teams headed up by a director of merchandise and marketing. The leisure product area includes the following merchandise categories: gifts, kitchen and home, children's clothing, 'photo' and 'lunchtime food'. These are lead by a category general manager (CGM) who is responsible for strategic merchandise planning, including buying, supply chain management and marketing. The CGMs are supported by a team of category managers who in turn lead a team of product managers who are concerned with the finer detail of a concise product range. Within the general merchandise area of 'lunchtime food', for example, there are three category managers responsible for coffee shop (in twenty stores), lunchtime (sandwiches and so on) and snacks. Product managers then support the category managers; for example, in the snacking category there is a product manager for drinks/savoury snacks and one for sweet snacks. The merchandise and marketing teams are given technical support by the product quality and development department which works on a project basis for them. The corporate brand is managed by a separate marketing department, which liases with the category management teams to ensure that all products and their presentation conform to the corporate brand image and standard.

Product reviews occur between one and three times a year depending on the seasonality of the product. These are accompanied by a distribution review, when decisions are made on which product ranges will go to each store, depending on the store format. Product category business reviews, which involve the whole of the category team, take place formally on an annual basis, although supplier approaches may prompt an informal review more frequently. Likewise, product market strategy is formally reviewed annually, but may be instigated on an 'as needed' basis. Sales are reported to the product managers at different levels, as shown in Table A.1.2.

Table A.1.2 **Levels of sales reporting within a Boots' product category**

Level	Examples of sales report
Concept group	All lunchtime and snack products
Product Group	All sandwiches
Merchandise group	Boots sandwiches, Shapers sandwiches

For each product item, or stock keeping unit, Boots' information system is able to output an 'economic profitability figure', which is a DPP (direct product profit) calculation incorporating a charge for capital employed.

THE LUNCHTIME AND SNACKS DEPARTMENT

Table A.1.3 shows the different product groups within the lunchtime category or concept group. The department does not include any dietary food products, although slimming options (for example, Shapers sandwiches, desserts and so on) are included.

Table A.1.3 **Breakdown of product groups within lunchtime/snacks department**

Sub-category	Product group
Lunchtime	Sandwiches
	Rolls/pastries
	Salads
	Desserts
Snacks	Drinks
	Sweet snacks
	Savoury snacks

Source: Boots unpublished departmental data, 1997

The location of the department in a 'typical' Boots store can be seen in Figure A.1.1.

The sweet snack product market

The majority of products sold under the heading 'sweet snack' can be classified as 'countlines'. Originating from the term 'counter line', which was an item traditionally served on the counter in a retail store (a presentation method still found in many CTNs – confectionery, tobacco and newspapers – and independents), a countline is considered to be a confectionery product which is consumed 'all in one go' and therefore includes the vast array of chocolate bars (Mars, Twix, Lion Bar and so on) and small ready-packed sugar confectionery (Opal Fruits, Polos, Chewits, for example). The product market is dominated by major brands like Cadburys, Mars and Nestlé, whose products are sold through an extensive and fragmented distribution network of approximately 200,000 outlets, which includes larger players like Woolworth's and the CTN multiples, as well as the many convenience stores and small independent retailers. Some retailers have managed to gain market share by producing own-label countlines, notably Marks & Spencer, and

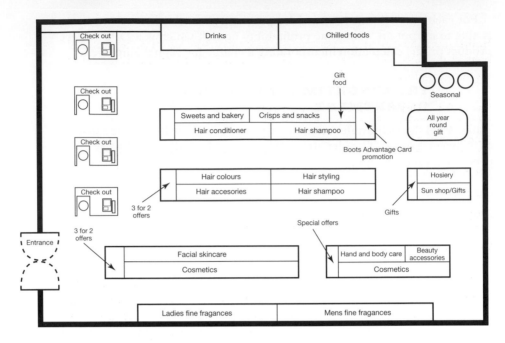

Figure A.1.1 **Boots the Chemist: store layout**

some of the supermarket chains have produced their own versions of some popular lines such as KitKat.

Purchasing motivations for the product are impulse driven, with an estimated 80 per cent of purchases made for snacking (source: Boots' commissioned market research); consequently advertising and on-pack promotional activity are important for driving sales. New product development is also required to maintain consumer interest; for example, some caramel variants of existing products (such as Wispa Gold) are selling faster than the original product. Consumers expect countline products to be of high quality, tasty and satisfying, and consider them an indulgence or a treat. Countlines have wide appeal to consumers of all ages and socio-economic groupings. They benefit from the trend towards 'grazing' or snacking replacing the formal mealtime, and countlines are frequently bought as a 'dessert' in the sandwich lunch.

Although something of a contradiction in terms, there has been an attempt to produce healthy or diet countline confectionery in response to the growing awareness of health issues (dental care, cholesterol levels, weight gain and so on). These products tend to appeal to young, female consumers from the higher social grades. Whilst there is a proportion of the population committed to calorie counting products, many consumers doubt the feasibility of 'healthy' confectionery in terms of delivering sufficient taste satisfaction compared to the 'unhealthy' countline product.

Boots' sweet snack offering

Boots' confectionery offer includes boxed chocolates, seasonal items, family bags and countlines. The countline offer can be broken down into three sections, as shown in Table A.1.4.

Table A.1.4 **Boots' sweet snack products**

Product range	Sales (%)
Boots own-label	8
Shapers range	19
Proprietary brand range	73

Source: Boots unpublished departmental data 1997

Within the own-label section there are essentially two types of confectionery. The first is a small range of premium bars: luxury products with an emphasis on self-indulgence. The second type is the reduced fat and reduced sugar range, which is not positioned as diet products for the calorie counter, but rather as a 'less unhealthy' version of traditional confectionery. In contrast, the confectionery products sold under Boots own-brand name 'Shapers' are directly positioned as diet products for the serious slimmer, with a tape measure incorporated into the packaging design and the calorific value emphasised on the packaging to aid the conscientious calorie counter. 'Shapers' branded products make a significant contribution to the lunchtime food offer at Boots; the range includes sandwiches, drinks, desserts and savoury snacks as well as the sweet snacks. The proprietary brand range includes representations from all the leading confectioners, as well as the well established branded 'slimming' bars Lo and Halo.

The Boots Light Range

Boots launched the Light Range in the early 1990s in response to the increasingly health concerned consumer. The range consisted of seven confectionery products, listed in Table A.1.5 in order of GMROI (gross margin return on investment) performance.

The Light Range launch was initially successful. The point of sale support to encourage trial worked well and public relations activity resulted in considerable interest from various magazines. After a while, however, sales levelled out and it began to emerge that trial of the products was not followed by repeat purchase. After two years of trading, Boots decided to conduct a market research survey, both inside and outside Boots' stores, to establish the reason for the poor take-up of the products, the findings of which are summarised below:

Table A.1.5 **Products in Boots' Light Range**

Product name

Light Mild Mints
Light Nougat Crisp Bar
Light Soft Mints
Light Praline Bar
Light Peanut Bar
Light Lemon Sweets
Light Fudge Caramel

Source: Boots unpublished departmental data, 1996

1 Half of Boots customers and a third of consumers interviewed on the street were aware of the brand Boots Light, although many had no idea what was in the range. The main association was with chocolate bars.

2 Boots Light products were not bought for a second time because:

- the product failed to deliver on taste, substantiality and satisfaction;
- the size of the bar was considered small compared to equivalent countline products;
- product quality was considered to be poor;
- the products did not evoke the kind of emotions generated by conventional confectionery products.

3 Healthy/diet snacks and confectionery are generally bought on a regular basis, are primarily for self-consumption, and are bought as alternatives to other healthy/diet products, rather than as an alternative to standard snacks and confectionery.

4 Motives for buying healthy snacks and confectionery include general health concerns and sugar/dental concerns, as well as calorie counting and weight considerations.

5 Low calorie was considered a main specific benefit of healthy/diet confectionery products, but the word 'light' tended to have a specific meaning for certain product categories:

- for crisps and snacks – low fat;
- for chocolate bars – low sugar or low fat;
- for sweets – low sugar.

Men tended to associate 'light' with low fat, whereas women interpreted 'light' more often as low calorie.

6 Light brand customers do not differentiate between low fat and low calorie, therefore a low fat message is likely to be interpreted as low calorie.

7 The majority of customers who buy Light products also buy Shapers products, but less than one in three Shapers buyers have tried the Boots Light range, indicating that there could be a market for 'light' confectionery products beyond the Shapers customer. The research finding also highlighted the brand loyalty of Shapers customers.

THE SITUATION

In February 1996, Linda Kingston, a graduate in retail marketing, who had recently been promoted from assistant product manager for hair care to product manager for sweets and bakery, was asked to attend a briefing by the category general manager for the lunchtime area, Stephen Panns. Also attending the meeting was Rowena Smith, category manager for snacks.

Stephen began the briefing by stating concerns that the Boots Light Range had not been performing very well for some time. In fact, the snack range as a whole did not generate the volume of sales that might be expected from a busy retailer such as Boots.

Linda sighed inwardly; she had spoken before to Stephen about improving the space allocation of snacks in the past, and in particular about placing countline products at the CPU (cash point unit), but the 'ethical problems', as he put it, prevented any contemplation of change in that direction. The problem was that pharmacy guidelines state that ordinary confectionery must not be displayed around the till area, so as not to encourage tooth decay. The guidelines do not specify what 'ordinary' is, but it would certainly include the bulk of proprietary brand confectionery.

The Light Range, Stephen continued, has never really been a strong performer. Sales peaked 18 months after launch at £4 million per annum, and the most recent figures show the whole range only turning over £1 million per annum. This can be contrasted with Halo and Lo, which generate a combined turnover of £16 million. Again, Linda felt despondent. The taste seemed to be the major concern; she had been briefed about the various difficulties involved with the development of reduced fat confectionery. Chocolate itself is particularly difficult, so anything based on 100 per cent chocolate, whether solid (like Yorkie) or textured (like Aero) had to be ruled out. Wafer also is a high fat component, so a reduced fat version of something like KitKat or Time Out would not be possible, and caramel is similarly tricky. The easiest ingredients in which the fat or sugar content could be reduced seemed to be biscuit, crispies or fudge type centres.

Another significant weakness was the packaging. Linda felt it was outdated and gave the impression that the items in the 'Light' range were niche products, solely aimed at the slimmers' market. The prices were relatively high, being about 5 pence above a comparable 'unhealthy' product, but this was necessary because of the higher raw material costs and Linda did not see the prices as a problem; Boots' market research had indicated that customers were prepared to pay a premium for a specific product benefit such as low fat.

At a recent business review with Mars, Stephen continued, there seemed to be a lot of excitement about a new low fat chocolate-covered bar that was being developed, not specifically formulated as a low calorie bar but with half the fat content of comparable countline products. Stephen, Rowena and Linda were all convinced that there was an opportunity to sell reduced fat and low sugar confectionery within Boots beyond the calorie counting market. The challenge, however, was to come up with a serious and attractive product proposition. Linda was asked to reconsider the Light Range and report back to Stephen and Rowena in two weeks' time. Whilst she felt that this was a hefty challenge, Linda felt encouraged by the motivation of her colleagues to address the situation in an open-minded and flexible manner. She also began to think about the success that her previous department had experienced with a range of own-label versions of leading brand shampoos.

Back at her desk, Linda made a mental list of the suppliers who might be useful in any product development work that might be required should the range be updated or even replaced by something new. It would be her decision who would be used to develop prototypes and it was likely that it would be her decision which supplier would get the business. Rowena would help if it were a difficult choice. Stephen would want to do a taste test on the final perfected sample before it went into production, but he invariably accepts the findings of the taste panel. In general, he only gets really involved if the consideration is of strategic importance to Boots.

There were a number of key issues that would influence the choice of supplier. Price was obviously an important issue, but getting the product right in the first place was the overriding factor. Some suppliers were so difficult to deal with; they seem to find it impossible to understand, or perhaps more accurately to react to the feedback she gave on samples produced. Some of the suppliers she knew were somewhat restricted in their machinery, so that they could not get the appearance, or shape of the product she required, whilst other suppliers simply would not meet Boots' quality standard requirements, for example that all machinery should have metal detectors to identify any harmful foreign bodies. Mars, of course, would be the first choice as a supply partner, but they would not entertain making confectionery under a retailer's brand name. The one thing Linda was quite sure of was that none of her own-label suppliers were making reduced fat and low sugar confectionery at the moment, so few of them were any good at product innovation; but at least that meant that Boots had the opportunity to establish themselves in what was believed to be an important emerging market. At least she would not be relying on the suppliers for any packaging redesign input. If that was necessary it would all be handled by Boots own design agencies, working to a design brief that she would write. Linda picked up the phone and dialled the first supplier on her list . . .

ACKNOWLEDGEMENT

The author would like to extend her thanks to the lunchtime and snacks merchandise and marketing team for their very helpful input in the preparation of this case study. This case study was originally published in *Contemporary Cases in Retail Management* (2000), eds Oldfield *et al.*, pp. 104–12. Reproduced by permission of Macmillan Press Ltd.

QUESTIONS

1 Discuss why you think the product team are convinced that there is a market for reduced fat and low sugar confectionery, beyond the calorie counters. Identify trends and situational factors that will influence the sales estimate of this product range.

2 Identify the product criteria that will be important in the redevelopment and selection of this range. Present a list of criteria upon which suppliers in the sweet snack product area are assessed. (It may help to distinguish between own-label and proprietary brand suppliers.)

3 Outline the organisational structure of the 'buying centre' at Boots the Chemist, and describe how the performance of product ranges is monitored. Use organisational charts and diagrams to aid your discussion.

4 Present a product proposal which includes marketing and store support for the reconsidered range. Each product within the range should be detailed and justified.

5 Develop a design brief for the packaging of this product. This should address the design objectives and the design constraints and include creative ideas (colours, images, words and lettering and so on) that you feel are appropriate.

appendix two

A CASE STUDY OF THE OLYMPIC MUSEUM SHOP

THE MUSEUM

On 23 June 1993, the dream of Mr Juan Antonio Samaranch, President of the International Olympic Committee (IOC), came true when the Olympic Museum opened its doors to the public. The goal of the museum was to be something more than just a building containing Olympic memorabilia: it had to be a place where visitors could immerse themselves in the Olympic atmosphere. That goal has been achieved.

The Olympic Museum is located in the heart of Lausanne (Switzerland) next to Lac Léman (Lake Geneva). The building, of contemporary architecture, is surrounded by wonderful gardens, which are complemented with many attractive statues. This combination of elements provides the visitor with an atmosphere of serenity but at the same time is very stimulating.

The museum takes one back through the history of the Olympics all the way to ancient Olympic Greece, whose values are encouraged as much today as they were then. This philosophy has been summarised by Père Henri Dion, friend of Pierre de Coubertin, the founder of the modern Olympics, in this quotation: 'In order to discover the best of oneself, one must set a goal higher than ever thought possible. *Altius, citius, fortius.*'

The visitor encounters room after room of sporting memorabilia. There are the champions' awards including laurel wreathes, the interactive information points, objects from both the Summer and Winter Olympic Games, the collection of Olympic stamps and coins, Olympic videos and other miscellaneous items. In 1995, this modern and dynamic museum was given the European Museum of the Year Award. This is an acknowledgement of the museum's world-class status.

SHOP DEVELOPMENT

As with most major museums, shops with souvenirs are part of the visit. The Olympic Museum is no exception, and included in the building's design was space for a museum shop where the visitor could browse through its items. We all know that when we experience something very pleasurable, we like to bring something back home that will later remind us of that experience.

Keeping this in mind, the museum's directors realised immediately that their know-how did not include the issues relating to retail management. Therefore, in order to fill the 130 m² of selling space, they contracted some well-known sporting goods retailers of Lausanne to manage the shop. Between the IOC and the local partners the duties were divided: the search for products; wholesale purchasing; recruiting and training of salespeople; bookkeeping; stock management; sales management and so on.

Very soon a collection of products relating to the Olympics was developed. These products were organised in six departments:

1 gadgets, pins, watches and the like;
2 clothes and accessories;
3 stationery;
4 games, puzzles and confectionery;
5 posters;
6 stamps and coins.

From the very beginning it was clear that a specific computer program would be needed to manage the shop's retail operations (total sales, unit sales, total promotion sales, unit promotion sales, value of the inventory, costs, selling prices, gross sales, net sales, profit margins and so on), not only for all the items as a whole, but also for each specific item. Because of this, each item is coded and can be easily identified. This system of tracking the inventory and cost control allows for the constant monitoring of the facts and figures of the business.

THE SHOP'S CUSTOMER BASE

After a period of preparation, the shop opened to the public and started to fulfil its customers' wishes of taking home a souvenir of the visit to the museum. The types of people who visit the museum could be classified in the following categories:

1 sports enthusiasts;
2 tourists coming from post- or pre-Olympic sites;
3 students from the surrounding area (maximum travel time three hours by car or bus);
4 adults who come with organised daily tours;
5 Lausanne residents.

However, due to their proximity, the Lausanne residents tend to visit the museum more frequently and use the shop to buy gifts. This is because many of the other types of visitors live far from the museum and repeat visits are unlikely. Adults who come individually comprise the segment with the highest buying power, and it is estimated that they account for 76 per cent of the visitors. The rest are divided up as follows: 11 per cent are groups of students, and the remaining 13 per cent are senior citizens and children. In general, most of the visitors come in the summer. Approximately 13 per cent of the annual visitors come in July, making this the busiest month.

The number of visitors to the museum in the years 1993–5 was as follows:

1993 (six months)	108,838
1994	200,005 (it was the ninth most visited museum in Switzerland)
1995 (until 10.12.95)	158,219 (the goal for 1995 was to reach 215,000)

THE SHOP'S EXPANSION

In the middle of 1995, it was decided to expand the selling area by 40 m². With this expansion, the marketing director of the Olympic Museum realised the need for a European expert on retailing who could give a professional opinion about the shop's operations.

As the visitors of the museum increased so did the sales, but the figures were not very encouraging. Up until the middle of 1995 the shop's average sale per customer was only SFr45, and the average sale calculated on the basis of total visitors to the museum was only SFr5.9 (from 23 June 1994 to 3 October 1995). In the last quarter of 1995 the average sale per visitor increased slightly to SFr9 on weekdays and SFr8 at weekends. As an additional reference, in 1990 the average sale per visitor to the Tower of London's shop was £1 (£1 = SFr2). Taking into account the type of customers who visited the Olympic Museum, their buying power and their enthusiasm for the Olympics, the average sale per visitor should have been higher.

After visiting the Olympic Museum, the newly hired retailing expert was as impressed as the majority of the visitors. He entered the shop, observed the environment carefully for a long period of time, paid close attention to the buying behaviour of the customers and finally decided to interview the customers as they left the shop. The conclusions from the interviews with the customers and museum visitors plus the quantitative results of a previous survey conducted a few months earlier were the following:

- the general impression of the Olympic Museum was very favourable (76 per cent);
- 42 per cent of the visitors decided to go to the museum on the recommendation of family and friends;
- 82 per cent stated that the interactive computer terminals were easy to use;
- 76 per cent would like to return to the museum;
- the shop's merchandise was generally perceived as being of good quality;
- the maintenance and organisation of the shop was considered very good;
- the most common complaint was that the prices of the merchandise were too high;
- there was a lack of merchandise in the medium price range;
- there was practically nothing for children;
- there was a great variety of clothes, but a shortage of other exclusive products;
- there was no sale merchandise of promotional items;
- one visitor said he would like the shop to be 'more fun and have more personality'.

THE SHOP'S MERCHANDISE BASE

The assortment of products in the shop is organised in six different departments. Their percentages are measured in shelf space, sales in units, sales in volume and contribution margins; these are shown in Table A.2.1.

Table A.2.1 **The Olympic Museum shop: relative contributions of product departments (%)**

	Shelf space	Sales in unit	Sales in volume	Contribution margin
Gadgets, pins, watches	7.90	26.70	35.95	30.67
Clothes, accessories	56.33	16.08	43.39	49.18
Stationery	29.76	45.30	16.01	14.47
Games and puzzles	3.39	1.12	1.88	1.90
Art reproduction	1.49	0.01	0.84	0.84
Stamps and coins	1.14	10.78	1.93	2.94

There are twelve categories of products that make up almost 90 per cent of the shop's sales in SKUs:

Postcards   33%
Stamps   11%
T-shirts   10.5%

Key rings and similar products	7%
Books	6%
Pens and Pencils	6%
Watches	4%
Pins and insignias	3%
Posters	3%
Caps	2%
Sweatshirts and pullovers	1%
Umbrellas	1%

The current situation for these twelve categories is shown in Table A.2.2.

Table A.2.2 **The Olympic Museum shop: contributions by product category (%)**

	Shelf space	Sales in unit	Sales in volume	Contribution margin
Postcards	9.21	32.85	1.74	1.68
Stamps	1.13	10.72	1.33	1.88
T-shirts	22.57	10.48	19.50	22.73
Keyrings	0.45	7.18	4.19	3.84
Books	15.80	5.84	7.30	6.55
Pens and pencils	0.14	5.79	1.56	1.47
Watches	1.81	4.36	21.35	15.70
Pins	0.68	3.49	2.99	3.15
Posters	1.35	3.07	3.40	3.94
Caps	1.81	1.69	3.19	3.75
Sweatshirts	5.42	1.33	7.46	8.30
Umbrellas	0.23	0.67	1.85	2.30
Total	60.60	87.47	75.86	75.29

Here are some examples of prices in the shop: the average price per miscellaneous gadget is SFr23, but we must consider that the most commonly sold gadgets have a psychological threshold of SFr10. The average prices of the various products in this department are as follows: SFr3.5 for the pins, SFr10 for the key rings, SFr5 for the pens and pencils, SFr84 for the watches (Swatch watches SFr100) and umbrellas at SFr48. As for clothing, the average price is SFr32 for T-shirts, SFr96 for sweatshirts and SFr32 for caps. The star products are the T-shirts.

THE SHOP'S DESIGN AND LAYOUT

The museum shop's interior design and layout reflects the trends of most European clothing shops from the early 1990s. The displays and fixtures are basically modular with two types of materials predominating: chrome metal and glass. The fixtures can be converted into freestanding units, which can create small square islands, as well as shelves along the wall. These islands can have a maximum height of 120 cm. The shop is 130 m² distributed approximately as shown in Figure A.2.1.

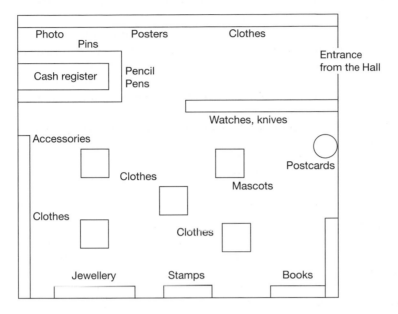

Figure A.2.1 **The Olympic Museum shop: current layout**

The shop has a dark marble floor and a ceiling made from different materials depending on the area. There is a false square cell ceiling with hidden halogen spotlights. There are also sections where the ceiling is made of a metallic material and the light fixtures are visible, exceeding 700 lux when the light is measured 1 metre from the floor. Moreover, the light comes from various sources, with the fixtures focused at different angles illuminating the areas unevenly.

The presentation of the merchandise is that of fashion boutiques, with the garments carefully hung on the fixtures, leaving plenty of space among the merchandise. The facings are not repeated even when the product is small, and the price and product characteristics are not shown on the shelf space. These data are reserved for tags that are stuck to the products or hung on their labels.

The system for arranging the products is not very clear to the visitor. For instance, T-shirts may be displayed in several different areas of the shop. They can form part of an Olympic theme, some are in the winter section, others in the summer section, and some may even be grouped with display T-shirts from a specific supplier. In general, T-shirts are arranged by size, with the larger sizes on the bottom rack and the smaller sizes on the top. However, there are no signs or graphics to indicate this. The agendas, posters and postcards have their own displays, which are positioned so that the customers can easily see them. Some merchandise, such as home accessories and miscellaneous gadgets, are displayed close to floor level.

Outside the shop there is a mailbox. Next to this are two mannequins dressed elegantly with the clothes bearing the Olympic Museum logo. They are also outfitted with accessories such as purses and caps. The prices are not displayed on this merchandise.

The counter for the cash register is white and stands 120 cm high. It is located directly in front of the shop's entrance and is the first thing the visitor sees upon entering. A multitude of gadgets are also displayed on the counter.

Because the shop has practically no graphics or signs to distinguish different sections, the customer is forced to wander through the shop, browsing among the products. Therefore, the type of sales practised here can be classified as assisted sales. The visitors are free to circulate through the shop and have access to the majority of the merchandise. As mentioned above, all the merchandise has tags indicating the price and internal shop codes. For example, visitors interested in T-shirts can choose the colour they prefer, take a garment from the rack or the shelf and examine the tag for size, material and other information. If it is what they want, they can take the garment straight the cash register and pay for it, but if it is not, they can continue looking or else ask for assistance. There are several friendly salespeople to help customers. They speak several languages, which facilitates their dealings with customers from all five continents.

The gross margin for the shop's products is 50 per cent or more, and the sales space will be extended to 166 m², with the layout as shown in Figure A.2.2. In conclusion, increasing the sales space of the shop by about 40 m² is more than just a simple matter of expansion. The plan is to use this sales space as an opportunity to move in a new and different direction to improve

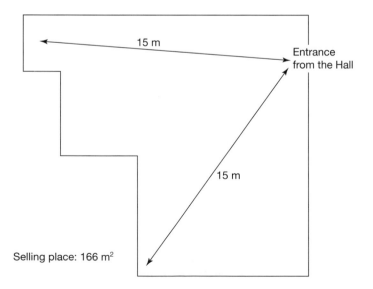

Figure A.2.2 **The Olympic Museum shop: layout showing sales space**

the shop's productivity and personality as opposed to simply acquiring more space for the same operations as before.

ACKNOWLEDGEMENT

The Olympic Museum shop case study, by Lluís Martínez-Ribes and María Dolores De Juan Vigaray, was originally published in *European Cases in Retailing* (1999), eds M. Dupuis and J. Dawson, pp. 263–72. Reproduced by permission of Blackwell Publishers.

QUESTIONS

1 The directors of the Olympic Museum would like to know how to increase the shop performance since the shop should be an important source of income. What do you suggest? In particular, consider the product assortment, space allocation and point of sale information.
2 Given the floor plan of the new shop, what might be an appropriate layout of departments and categories?
3 In order to address the issue of giving the shop more personality, collect some ideas for a new shop design. Consider the type of materials to be used, architectural features, lighting, fixturing and graphics. Present your ideas in a format that you feel is suitable; for example, you might like to put together a collage or a story board, or you might choose to use a report format, or a combination of these.

appendix three

A CASE STUDY OF NEW LOOK

INTRODUCTION

In 1969 a young entrepreneur opened a shop in Somerset selling a broad range of women's fashions at very keen prices. The store quickly became successful and other outlets followed, so that by 1995 Tom Singh's company New Look had 250 stores spread across the high streets of the UK. The philosophy behind the retail business was quite simple: to make fashions accessible to the mass market by introducing the 'new look' quickly and at prices that a high percentage of the population would consider very affordable.

THE RETAIL CONCEPT

The stores are somewhat basic in appearance; they have a strong fascia identity, using a bold monochrome typeface and a facial motif. The inside of the stores are functional in design, but they have a bright appearance, with white floor tiles and ceilings together with illuminated wall sections to add light in the depths of the store. Use of point of sale material and in-store graphics is maintained at a high level, drawing the shoppers attention to discounted merchandise, promotional offers and key price-pointed items. Stock densities are also high, and the clothes are either merchandised by theme (for example, matching tailored garments together) or by product item (for example, tops together), according to the space available and the individual store layout.

The company grew on the high streets of town centres in the UK and gave the clothes shopper additional choice in an already well provided retail sector. Since its inception, the company has maintained that it is not fashion forward, but it does follow trends, translating catwalk ideas into commercial garments with newness offered by means of a styling detail, a fabric design or a new silhouette, whether it is the line or fit of a jacket or the length or width of a trouser leg. A wide selection of new styles is trialled on a weekly basis. Those that sell are re-ordered and promoted; those that do not are quickly marked down to a low price to get them out of the store. The company therefore succeeds in maintaining a high sales turnover with a very lean stock level in the supply chain. The formula is appealing to customers, as they find a blend of key looks at reasonable prices with a selection of heavily discounted 'bargains' in store:

> The essence of the New Look brand is the way we trade our stores. What makes them different is the weekly arrival of new fashion at affordable prices. Since 10 per cent of stock is new lines introduced each week, and slow moving stock is discounted and removed, we arrive at a stock mix which is predominately 'the new' or 'the successes'. Pricing is significantly below competitors for garments of comparable value. Not only that, the discounts which keep stock turning produce real value for our customers, and support our strong promotional theme. This formula demands an active approach to managing the product, but keeps stores interesting and alive – a New Look each week – and ensures that stock is totally cleared each season.
>
> (Company Report, 1999)

In 1998, New Look was successfully floated on the London stock market, allowing Tom Singh to realise the personal fortune that he had built up as principal shareholder of New Look plc. The company had grown to a size that needed additional resources to ensure a smooth and successful transition from a medium sized, entrepreneurial business to a serious contender for retail greatness. Mr Singh relinquished his chief executive status to the highly respected Jim Hodkinson, previously managing director of B&Q, and other directors were recruited to strengthen the management team. Tom Singh remains in overall charge of the company's buying and merchandising operations.

The company has enjoyed a period of impressive and steady growth through the mid-1990s, as shown in Table A.3.1, taken from the 1999 company report. However, some retail industry observers are questioning whether this pattern can be sustained. Having increased the number of stores by means of organic growth and some low-key acquisitions, New Look now has more stores than Arcadia's Dorothy Perkins chain and have near to complete national coverage. This number of stores has allowed the company to obtain the usual set of scale economies and a strong bargaining stance with suppliers in an otherwise relatively stagnated sector of the retail industry.

THE PRODUCT RANGE

The product range that New Look offer is firmly rooted in the fickle, competitive, yet lucrative women's wear market, selling both formal and

Table A.3.1 **New Look: financial results, 1995–9**

	1995	1996	1997	1998	1999
Turnover (£m)	123.7	184.5	242.2	317.8	366.9
Operating profit (£m)	16.0	23.2	33.0	39.2	45.4
Number of stores	249	326	388	440	480

Source: New Look Company Report, 1999

casual clothes from skimpy tops to coats. However, the core range has been extended in a number of ways, for example, by the inclusion of swimwear as a seasonal item. In 1997, New Look introduced a lingerie range into 250 stores and a footwear range into 150 stores. Both these trials have been considered successful enough to roll out to all but 10 per cent of the stores, where space constraints make the additional ranges unfeasible. In particular, the footwear range was well received, as many of the specialist footwear chains continue to disappear from the UK high street.

In 1998 New Look experimented with a range of 'lifestyle' products. These are a range of non-clothing items which are increasingly incorporating an element of fashion orientation: picture frames, mirrors, candles and other novelty items. These products are merchandised with other well performing products such as hair accessories, jewellery, and more traditional accessories, such as toiletries, bags, scarves and hats. Clearly, additional ranges such as these require additional selling space. In 1998, non-clothing products accounted for 13 per cent of the company's total sales, yet in larger stores, where the full range of products can be effectively displayed, non-clothing sales were nearly 20 per cent of the total sales contribution. Rival chain Internacionale has already found this product category to be so successful that it has over twenty Au Naturale standalone 'lifestyle' stores (*Drapers Record*, 10 July 1999).

BUSINESS DEVELOPMENT

New Look has traditionally located in smaller town centres, where the site costs have been low and the typical store size has been around 1,700 ft^2. New Look is increasingly concentrating its property search towards larger store locations. Regional shopping centres, some major town centres and even retail parks are all being considered for alternative New Look sites. Among the forty-three stores opened in 1998 three were in high profile shopping centre destinations: Trafford Centre, Bluewater and Cribbs Causeway. The company is planning to add another 15 per cent retail space throughout 1999 (New Look Company Report, 1999). In the near future, New Look will relocate within the Lakeside (Thurrock) Shopping Centre to a new 12,000 ft^2 unit, the largest in the chain's portfolio. This large store will offer enough space for the company to introduce a new store format which includes a more spacious layout with more emphasis on product categories, including lifestyle products. It will also include a 1,000 ft^2 boutique area for accessories (on similar lines to the haven for young teens, Claire's Accessories), which will feature its own store fascia and window, but will be linked to the main store (*Drapers Record* 14 November 1999).

Another successful venture for the company was the 915 range, launched in 1995 to appeal to the notoriously difficult-to-please pre-teen and young-teen market. There are now eight standalone stores and the company sees significant potential for the concept due to a combination of favourable demographic factors and a lack of competition. New Look stands to do well if it can keep this brand/image conscious, fashion fad oriented customer happy. Footwear was added to the 915 offer in 1999.

As more product ranges are added to the stores, there is a danger that they will appear crowded and cluttered. The company is therefore trying out new store layouts and merchandising techniques in order to improve 'shopability and reachability of stock'. Fitting rooms have also been improved with better lighting, the addition of a stool and extra hanging hooks. After testing these changes in the Poole store, the response has been positive, both from a customer focus group reaction and sales turnover (Hall 1999).

Although most of the company resources have been devoted to expansion in the home market, New Look has been taking quiet steps towards an international presence, although until now success has been mixed. Early in 1999, a decision was taken to close the three stores trading in Germany, but the twenty-nine French stores are expected to contribute profits in 1999–2000. Meanwhile, the company is seeking retail locations in the Republic of Ireland to add to its presence in Northern Ireland, where twelve stores were opened between 1997 and 1999 (*Retail Week*, 29 October 99).

COMPANY OPERATIONS

New Look's company headquarters are located in Weymouth in the South-West of England, where the company has its historical roots. It is here that a company run on low cost efficiency has blossomed into a blue-chip retail chain. 700 employees headed up by a young but experienced management team staff the head office. Jim Hodkinson brings 35 years of retail experience and is widely credited as being the man who built the B&Q business from a one-store operation to the DIY giant it is today; and whilst fashion retailing has additional challenges in terms of stock control, his general approach to efficiency in the supply chain through the use of state of the art logistical systems seems to fit well with the New Look organisation. He is also a strong advocate of ethical sourcing, an unusual credential in a retail sector 'where very few fashion retailers have made any significant moves towards tackling this moral minefield' (Whitehead 1998). Stephen Sunnucks was appointed managing director retail in May 1998, having worked with Marks & Spencer plc, J. Sainsbury plc and Arcadia, and in February 1999, Rose Foster joined the company as retail operations director from Next (Hall 1999).

The company's distribution facilities are also located in Weymouth and have been expanded as the company has grown. The weekly throughput is 1.5 million SKUs delivered to stores on the basis of a minimum of three times per week. New Look uses an integrated primary distribution system whereby the vehicles that deliver stock to the stores through the night then continue on to suppliers, ports or airports to collect orders and carry them back to Weymouth. Obtaining efficiency with such a system relies on powerful information systems, but it gives the company additional negotiating strength with suppliers; 95 per cent of the product intake is collected in this way, and it allows the company to have control over product shipments in a finely tuned quick response merchandise management system (Whitehead 1998; New Look Company Report 1999).

Point of sales systems are also highly efficient, enabling the company to collect and analyse sales data through the night, ready for timely decisions on range management when the merchandisers arrive at work the next morning:

> Product decisions change as the season progresses – in a wait-and-see approach, aimed at matching product volumes to customer demand. We test a wide selection of product in stores, then scale up production accordingly, buying in a way that takes risk out of what is often seen as a risk business. Far from committing our buying resources at the outset, we hold them open as long as possible, so we spend against hard data, rather than hunch.
>
> (New Look Company Report 1999)

New Look is one of a number of retailers who have recently adopted an internet-based tracking system called retail.com. This allows suppliers to access virtual product information with minimum investment in information technology. All that is required is a PC and internet access; the systems transfer product development information and order status between retailer and supplier. This helps to reduce the time it takes for suppliers to get down the critical path of product development, and allows tracking of shipments through the supply chain. Additional services are planned for the system, including a seasonal trading system which allows for information on consumer demand to be matched and collated on-line with the product availability from suppliers, helping to reduce the risk of overstocking due to unseasonal weather (*Retail Week*, 19 November 1999).

New Look's supply base has recently been cut back from 200 to 150 in order to build ever-closer relationships with those who are best able to meet the stringent New Look criteria of competitive prices, high product quality and speedy response to new ideas and changing sales patterns (New Look Company Report 1999). Around half the suppliers are located in the UK, whilst the others are scattered around the globe. Increasingly New Look favours suppliers in and around Europe (for example, Morocco and Ukraine are preferred to the Far East for low cost items) because of their geographical proximity, short lead times and flexibility being essential to the company's success in moving quickly to maximise sales of items 'on trend'. Some suppliers have dedicated production facilities, which can be switched as and when the garment requirement dictates. The in-depth knowledge buyers gain through the close relationships with suppliers also builds their knowledge of production costs, which makes them tough negotiators and shrewd decision-makers. In order to maintain a quick response system, New Look may source fabric themselves or negotiate prices for fabric which is then delivered to suppliers, converting the cloth to styled garments at the very last moment in order to follow styling and garment detail trends.

To date, New Look has not indulged in advertising: it uses the store as its communications channel to their customers. Customers are faced with a constant flow of point of sales information about the company's promotional activity, clearly highlighting the benefits to the consumer. 'Item of the week' is an identified winner which is then promoted at an exceptionally keen price to maximise sales and customer flow, and other promotions such as 'Clothes for £1' are clearly understandable and beneficial to the bargain hunter. Multi-purchase offers are also frequently used. The average customer spend in New Look stores is £14; however, with account holders this rises to £24 per transaction. The estimated half-million New Look account holders contribute 12 per cent of the company's sales (Mintel 1998).

The lack of advertising has left customers who do not have a store nearby unaware of the New Look brand, even though in 1997 the company came second in a nationwide loyalty survey conducted in the clothing retail sector by Taylor Nelson AGB (Bickerton 1997). This lack of awareness prompted the company to launch a publicity campaign to build brand awareness through 1998–9. In a year when much press emphasis has been put on issues such as 'value for money' and 'rip-off prices', the media responded with enthusiasm, reporting the company's offer in both mass market publications and fashion press:

> Both up market and mass market publications gave us a good press. *Vogue* praised our 'clued-up clothes with spot-on detailing and just-so proportions'. The *Sun* saw New Look as 'the success story of the nineties', recognising our values offer as a huge hit with customers, and noting the incredible speed with which we translate fashion trends into latest looks at a price all can afford . . . the Press presented a New Look buy as smart, not cheap.
>
> (New Look Company Report 1999)

New Look seems to have found a formula for success in a market which is seen by many as oversubscribed, volatile, lacking in innovation and stagnant in terms of overall growth. More recent sector history points to a state of upheaval. Press reports on the decline of the sector leader Marks & Spencer have run unabated for over a year; BhS (Storehouse) is seen as a directionless takeover target; what remained of the Sears Womenswear division was taken on board by Arcadia in late 1998; and in spite of many consumer trends that point to an increased popularity in home shopping, the big catalogue houses like GUS, Littlewoods and Grattans are also struggling to meet previous year sales figures. Emerging new players, such as Matalan, Peacocks and other so-called 'value' retailers seem to be bucking the trend, whilst the whole of the retail industry waits with bated breath to see what is in store for the Wal-mart/Asda chain.

QUESTIONS

1 Make a critical analysis of New Look's stock management system.
2 Discuss the positioning of New Look's product offer. How is this supported by the company's product management operations?
3 Outline what you consider to be New Look's retail brand values. How are they communicated to the customer?
4 To what extent do you consider New Look to have a sufficiently strong retail proposition for the company to grow into a global operator?

REFERENCES

Bickerton, I. (1997), 'Customers love New Look', *Drapers Record* 11 October.
Drapers Record (1999a) 'New Look heads for lifestyle standalone', 10 July.
Drapers Record (1999b) 'New Look to roll out megastore in time for Christmas trading period', 14 November.
Hall, L. (1999) 'New Look to roll out redesigned layout', *Drapers Record* 30 October.
Mintel (1998) *Womenswear Retailing Report* (August), Mintel International Group, London.
New Look (1999) Company Report, New Look, Weymouth, Dorset.
Retail Week (1999a) 'New Look pushes into Irish Republic', 29 October.
Retail Week (1999b) 'New Look and Littlewoods on track for global cost cutting with retail.com', 10 November.
Whitehead, D. (1998) 'The DIY man gives fashion a new look', *Drapers Record* 5 September.

index